THE MASTERS AND THE PATH

The MASTERS
and
The PATH

C. W. LEADBEATER

THE THEOSOPHICAL PUBLISHING HOUSE

Adyar, Madras 600 020, India
Wheaton, Illinois, U.S.A.

© The Theosophical
Publishing House, Adyar

First Edition 1925
Second Edition, Revised and Enlarged 1927
Reprinted 1937, 1940, 1946, 1953, 1959, 1965
Third Edition, Abridged 1969
Reprinted 1973, 1975
Fourth Edition, Abridged 1983
Reprinted 1984
Third Edition, Reprinted 1992, 1995, 1997

ISBN 81-7059-198-8 (Hard Cover)
ISBN 81-7059-199-6 (Soft Cover)

Printed at the Vasanta Press
The Theosophical Society
Adyar, Madras 600 020, India

PUBLISHERS' NOTE

THIS book was first published in 1925 and was revised and enlarged in 1927. Since then it has been reprinted seven times to meet the continued demand. The material is based on talks to members of The Theosophical Society by C. W. Leadbeater, and the book is a contribution in a field about which very little is generally known.

This edition is being published in a somewhat abridged form. Like most publications of The Theosophical Publishing House, Adyar, it represents the opinions and experiences of the author, and not the collective view of The Theosophical Society.

FOREWORD TO FIRST EDITION

THERE is only one reason why I should write this Foreword to the book written by my honoured colleague. It speaks of many things which have hitherto been studied and discussed within a comparatively small circle, consisting of students well versed in Theosophical knowledge, and ready to study statements concerning regions which they could not yet enter for themselves, but hoped to enter later, and then to verify for themselves the statements made by their seniors. I desire to associate myself with the statements made in this book, for the accuracy of nearly all of which I can personally vouch ; and also to say on behalf of my colleague as well as of myself, that the book is issued as a record of observations carefully made and carefully recorded, but not claiming any authority, nor making any demand for acceptance. It makes no claim to inspiration, but is only an honest account of things seen by the writer.

ANNIE BESANT

CONTENTS

CONTENTS

ILLUSTRATIONS AND DIAGRAMS

PART I
THE MASTERS

CHAPTER I

THE EXISTENCE OF THE MASTERS

GENERAL CONSIDERATIONS

THE EXISTENCE of Perfected Men is one of the most important of the
many new facts which Theosophy puts before us. It follows logically
from the other great Theosophical teachings of karma and evolution
by reincarnation. As we look round us we see men obviously at all
stages of their evolution—some who, in one way or another, are in
advance of others. Since that is so, there may well be others who
are very much further advanced; indeed, if men are steadily
growing better and better through a long series of successive lives,
tending towards a definite goal, there should certainly be some who
have already reached that goal. Some of us in the process of that
development have already succeeded in unfolding some of those
higher senses which are latent in every man, and will be the
heritage of all in the future; and by means of those senses we are
enabled to see the ladder of evolution extending far above us as well
as far below us, and we can also see that there are men standing
upon every rung of that ladder.

There is a considerable amount of direct testimony to the
existence of these Perfected Men whom we call Masters, but I think
that the first step which each one of us should take is to make
certain that there *must* be such men; only as a later step will it
follow that those with whom we have come into contact belong
to that class.

The historical records of every nation are full of the doings of
men of genius in all different departments of human activity, men

who in their special lines of work and ability have stood far above
the rest—indeed, so far that at times (and probably more often than
we know) their ideals were utterly beyond the comprehension of the
people, so that not only the work that they may have done has been
lost to mankind, but their very names even have not been preserved.
It has been said that the history of every nation could be written in
the biography of a few individuals, and that it is always the few,
towering above the rest, who initiate the great forward steps in art,
music, literature, science, philosophy, philanthrophy, statecraft and
religion.   They stand high sometimes in love of God and their fellow-
men, as great saints and philanthropists ; sometimes in understanding
of man and Nature, as great philosophers, sages and scientists ; sometimes, in work for humanity, as great liberators and reformers.   Looking at these men, and realising how high they stand among humanity,
how far they have gone in human evolution, is it not logical to say
that we cannot see the bounds of human attainment, and that there
may well have been, and even now may be, men far further developed
even than they, men great in spirituality as well as knowledge or
artistic power, men complete as regards human perfections—men
precisely such as the Adepts or Supermen whom some of us have had
the inestimable privilege to encounter ?

This galaxy of human genius that enriches and beautifies the
pages of history is at the same time the glory and the hope of all
mankind, for we know that these Greater Ones are the forerunners
of the rest, and that they flash out as beacons, as veritable light-
bearers to show us the path which we must tread if we wish to
reach the glory which shall presently be revealed. We have long
accepted the doctrine of the evolution of the forms in which dwells
the Divine Life ; here is the complementary and far greater idea of
the evolution of that Life itself, showing that the very reason for that
wondrous development of higher and higher forms is that the ever-
swelling Life needs them in order to express itself. Forms are born
and die, forms grow, decay and break ; but the Spirit grows on eter-
nally, ensouling those forms, and developing by means of experience
gained in and through them ; and as each form has served its turn

and is outgrown, it is cast aside that another and better form may take its place.

Behind the evolving form burgeons out ever the Life Eternal, the Life Divine. That Life of God permeates the whole of Nature, which is but the many-coloured cloak which he has donned ; it is he who lives in the beauty of the flower, in the strength of the tree, in the swiftness and grace of the animal, as well as in the heart and soul of man. It is because his will is evolution that all life everywhere is pressing onward and upward ; and it is therefore that the existence of Perfected Men at the end of this long line of ever-unfolding power and wisdom and love is the most natural thing in the world. Even beyond them—beyond our sight and our comprehension—stretches a vista of still greater glory ; some hint of that we may endeavour to give later, but it is useless to speak of it now.

The logical consequence of all this is that there must be Perfected Men, and there are not wanting signs of the existence of such Men in all ages who, instead of leaving the world entirely to pursue a life of their own in the divine or superhuman kingdoms, have remained in touch with humanity, through love of it, to assist its evolution in beauty and love and truth, to help, as it were, to cultivate the Perfect Man—just as here and there we find a botanist who has special love for plants, and glories in the production of a perfect orange or a perfect rose.

THE TESTIMONY OF THE RELIGIONS

The records of every great religion show the presence of such Supermen, so full of the Divine Life that again and again they have been taken as the very representatives of God himself. In every religion, especially at its founding, has such an One appeared, and in many cases more than one. The Hindus have their great Avataras or divine incarnations, such as Shri Krishna, Shri Shankaracharya, and the Lord Gautama Buddha, whose religion has spread over the Far East, and a great galaxy of Rishis, of Saints, of Teachers ; and these Great Ones took interest not only in awakening men's spiritual natures, but also in all affairs that made for their well-being on earth. All who belong to the Christian world know, or ought to know, much about the great succession of prophets and teachers and saints in their own dispensation, and that in some way (perhaps not clearly understood) their Supreme Teacher, the Christ Himself, was and is Man as well as God. And all the earlier religions (decadent as some of them may be amid the decay of nations), down even to those of primitive tribes of men, show as outstanding features the existence of Super-men, helpers in every way of the childlike people among whom they dwelt. An enumeration of these, interesting and valuable as it is, would take us too far aside from our present purpose.

RECENT EVIDENCE

There is much direct and recent evidence for the existence of these Great Ones. In my earlier days I never needed any such evidence, because I was fully persuaded as a result of my studies that there *must* be such people. To believe that there were such glorified Men seemed perfectly natural, and my only desire was to meet them face to face. Yet there are many who, reasonably enough, want to know what evidence there is. There is a considerable amount of personal testimony. Madame Blavatsky and Colonel Olcott, the co-founders of the Theosophical Society, Dr. Annie Besant and I myself—all of us have seen some of these Great Ones, and many other members of the Society have also been privileged to see one or two of them, and there is ample testimony in what all these people have written.

It is sometimes objected that those who saw them, or fancied that they did so, may have been dreaming or perhaps deluded. The chief reason, I think, for the possibility of such a suggestion is that we have very rarely seen the Adepts at a time when both they and we were in our physical bodies. In the early days of the Society, when only Madame Blavatsky had developed higher faculties, the Masters not infrequently materialised themselves so that all could see them, and showed themselves thus physically on various occasions. You will find many records of such happenings in the earlier history of our Society, but of course the Great One so showing himself was not in his physical body, but in a materialised form.

Many of us habitually and constantly see them during our sleep. We go out in our astral bodies (or in the mental body, according to our development) and we visit them and see them in their physical bodies ; but we are not at that time in ours, and that is why on the physical plane people tend to be sceptical about such experiences. Men object : "But in these cases either you who saw them were out of the physical body, and may have been dreaming or deluded, or those who appeared to you came phenomenally and then disappeared again ; so how do you know that they were what you suppose them to be ?"

There are a few cases in which both the Adept and the person who saw him were in the physical body. It happened with Madame Blavatsky ; I have heard her testify that she lived for some time in a monastery in Nepal, where she saw three of our Masters constantly in their physical vehicles. Some of them have come down more than once from their mountain retreats into India in their physical bodies. Colonel Olcott spoke of having seen two of them on those occasions ; he had met the Master Morya and also the Master Kuthumi. Damodar K. Mavlankar, whom I knew in 1884, had encountered the Master Kuthumi in his physical body. There was the case of S Ramaswami Iyer, a gentleman whom I knew well in those days, who had the experience of meeting the Master Morya physically, and has written an account of that meeting which I shall quote later ; and there was the case of Mr. W. T. Brown of the London Lodge, who also was privileged to meet one of the Great Ones under similar conditions. There is also a vast amount of Indian testimony which has never been collected and sifted, mainly because those to whom these experiences came were so thoroughly persuaded of the existence of supermen and of the possibility of meeting them that they did not regard any individual case as worthy of record.

PERSONAL EXPERIENCE

I myself can report two occasions on which I have met a Master, both of us being in the physical vehicle. One of them was the Adept to whom the name of Jupiter was assigned in the book, *The Lives of Alcyone*,[1] who greatly assisted in the writing of portions of Madame Blavatsky's famous work *Isis Unveiled*, when that was being done in Philadelphia and New York. When I was living at Adyar, he was so kind as to request my revered teacher, Swami T. Subba Row, to bring me to call upon him. Obeying his summons we journeyed to his house, and were most graciously received by him. After a long conversation of the deepest interest, we had the honour of dining with him, Brahmin though he be, and spent the night and part of the next day under his roof. In that case it will be admitted that there could be no question of illusion. The other Adept whom I had the privilege of encountering physically was the Master the Comte de St. Germain, called sometimes the Prince Rakoczy. I met him under quite ordinary circumstances (without any previous appointment, and as though by chance) walking down the Corso in Rome, dressed just as any Italian gentleman might be. He took me up into the gardens on the Pincian Hill, and we sat for more than an hour talking about the Society and its work; or perhaps I should rather say that he spoke and I listened, although when he asked questions I answered.

Other members of the Brotherhood I have seen under varying circumstances. My first encounter with one of them was in a hotel in Cairo; I was on my way out to India with Madame Blavatsky and some others, and we stayed in that city for a time. We all used to gather in Madame Blavatsky's room for work, and I was sitting on the floor, cutting out and arranging for her a quantity of newspaper articles which she wanted. She sat at a table close by; indeed my left arm was actually touching her dress. The door of the room was in full sight, and it certainly did not open; but quite suddenly, without any preparation, there

[1] Out of print.

was a man standing almost between me and Madame Blavatsky, within touch of both of us. It gave me a great start, and I jumped up in some confusion; Madame Blavatsky was much amused and said: "If you do not know enough not to be startled at such a trifle as that, you will not get far in this occult work." I was introduced to the visitor, who was not then an Adept, but an Arhat, which is one grade below that state; he has since become the Master Djwal Kul.

Some months after that the Master Morya came to us one day, looking exactly as though in a physical body; he walked through the room where I was in order to communicate with Madame Blavatsky, who was in her bedroom inside. That was the first time I had seen him plainly and clearly, for I had not then developed my latent senses sufficiently to remember what I saw in the subtle body. I saw the Master Kuthumi under similar conditions on the roof of our Headquarters at Adyar; he was stepping over a balustrade as though he had just materialised from the empty air on the other side of it. I have also many times seen the Master Djwal Kul on that roof in the same way.

This would, I suppose, be considered less certain evidence, since the Adepts came as apparitions do; but, as I have since learned to use my higher vehicles freely, and to visit these Great Ones in that way, I can testify that those who in the early years of the Society came and materialised for us are the same Men whom I have often since seen living in their own homes. People have suggested that I and others who have the same experience may be but dreaming, since these visits take place during the sleep of the body; I can only reply that it is a remarkably consistent dream, extending in my own case over forty years, and that it has been dreamt simultaneously by a large number of people.

Those who wish to collect evidence about these matters (and it is quite reasonable that they should wish to do so) should turn to the earlier literature of the Society. They could have heard from Dr. Besant how many of the Great Ones she had seen on different occasions; and there are many of our members who will bear witness without hesitation that they have seen a Master. It may be that in meditation they have seen his face, and later have had definite proof that he is a real being. Much evidence may be found in Colonel Olcott's *Old Diary Leaves*, and there is an interesting treatise called *Do the Brothers Exist ?*[1] written by Mr. A. O. Hume, a man who stood high in the Civil Service in India, and worked much with our late Vice-President, Mr. A. P. Sinnett. It was published in a book entitled *Hints on Esoteric Theosophy*.[1] Mr. Hume, who was a sceptical Anglo-Indian with a legal mind, went into the question of the existence of the Brothers (as the Masters are also called, because they belong to a great Brotherhood, and also because they are the Elder Brothers of humanity) and even at that early date decided that he had overwhelming testimony that they did exist; and very much more evidence has accumulated since that book was published.

The possession of extended vision and other faculties resulting from the unfolding of our latent powers has also brought within our constant experience the fact that there are other orders of beings than the human, some of whom rank alongside the Adepts in a grade of existence higher than our own. We meet with some whom we call Devas or Angels, and with others whom we see to be far beyond ourselves in every respect.

THE EVOLUTION OF LIFE

Since in the course of our development we have become able to communicate with the Adepts, we have naturally asked them with all reverence how they have attained to that level. They tell us with one accord that no long time ago they stood where we stand now. They have risen out of the ranks of ordinary humanity, and they have told us that we in time to come shall be as they are now, and that the whole system is a graded evolution of Life extending up and up, further than we can follow it, even unto the Godhead itself.

We find that as there are definite stages in the earlier evolution —the vegetable above the mineral, the animal above the vegetable and

[1] Out of print.

the human above the animal—so in the same way the human kingdom has a definite end, a boundary at which it passes into a kingdom distinctly higher than itself, that beyond men there are the Supermen.

In the study of this system of evolution, we have learnt that there are in every man three great divisions—body, soul and spirit ; and each of these is capable of further subdivision. That is the definition which was given by St. Paul two thousand years ago. The Spirit or Monad is the breath of God (for the word *spirit* means breath, from the Latin *spiro*), the divine spark which is truly the Man, though it may more accurately be described as hovering over man as we know him. The scheme of its evolution is that it should descend into matter, and through its descent obtain definiteness and accuracy in material detail.

So far as we are able to see, this Monad, which is a spark of the Divine Fire, cannot descend as far as our present level, cannot directly reach this physical plane in which we are now thinking and working—probably because the rates of its vibration and those of physical matter differ too widely, so that there must be intermediate states and conditions. On what plane of Nature that divine spark originally exists we do not know, for it is far above, out of our reach. The lowest manifestation of it, which might be called a reflection of it, descends into the lowermost of the Cosmic Planes, as described in *A Textbook of Theosophy*.

We speak commonly of seven planes of existence, which are subdivisions or subplanes of the lowest Cosmic Plane, called in our books the Prakritic, meaning the physical plane of the Cosmos. The Monad can descend to the second of these subplanes (which we consequently call the Monadic plane) but it does not seem able to penetrate lower than this. In order to obtain the necessary contact with still denser matter, it puts down part of itself through two whole planes, and that fragment is what we call the ego or soul.

The Divine Spirit above us merely hovers over us ; the soul, which is a small and partial representation of it (it is as though the Monad puts down a finger of fire, and the end of that finger is the soul) cannot descend below the higher part of the mental plane (which is the fifth plane counting downwards, the physical being the seventh and lowest) ; and, in order that it may reach a still lower level, *it* must in turn put down a small portion of itself, which becomes the personality that we know. So this personality, which each person commonly thinks to be himself, is in truth but the fragment of a fragment.

All the evolution through the lower kingdoms is preparatory to the development of this human constitution. An animal during its life on the physical plane (and for some time after that in the astral world) has a soul just as individual and separate as a man's ; but when the animal comes to the end of its astral life, that soul does not reincarnate again in a single body, but returns to a kind of reservoir of soul-matter, called in our books a group-soul. It is as though the group-soul were a bucket of water, supplying the need of several animals of the same kind—say, for example, twenty horses. When a horse is to be born from that group-soul, it is as though one dipped a vessel into that bucket and brought it out full of water. During the life of that horse all kinds of experiences come to him which modify his soul, from which he learns lessons, and these may be compared to various kinds of colouring matter cast into the vessel of water. When the horse dies, the water in the vessel is emptied back into the bucket, and the colouring matter which it has acquired spreads all through the whole bucket. When another horse is born from the same group-soul, another vessel of water is filled from the bucket ; but it will be obvious that it is impossible to take out in it exactly the same drops of water which constituted the soul of the previous horse.[1]

When an animal has developed far enough to become human, that means that at the end of his life his soul is not poured back again into the group-soul, but remains as a separate entity. And now a very curious but very beautiful fate befalls him. The soul-matter, the water in the vessel, becomes itself a vehicle for something much higher, and instead of acting as a soul, it is itself ensouled. We have no exact analogy on the physical plane, unless we think of pumping air into water under high pressure, and thereby making it aerated water. If we accept that symbolism, the water which was previously

---

[1] For further details of this process see *A Textbook of Theosophy*.

the animal soul has now become the causal body of a man ; and the air pumped into it is the ego of which I have spoken—that soul of man which is but a partial manifestation of the Divine Spirit. This descent of the ego is symbolized in ancient mythology by the Greek idea of the *krater* or Cup, and by the mediæval story of the Holy Grail, for the Grail or the Cup is the perfected result of all that lower evolution, into which is poured the Wine of the Divine Life, so that the soul of man may be born. So, as we have said, this which has previously been the animal soul becomes in the case of man what is called the causal body, which exists in the higher part of the mental plane as the permanent vehicle occupied by the ego or human soul ; and all that has been learnt in its evolution is transferred to this new centre of life.

The evolution of this soul consists in its gradual return to the higher level on the plane next below the Monadic, carrying with it the result of its descent in the shape of experiences gained and qualities acquired. The physical body in all of us is fully developed, and because that is so, we are supposed to have conquered it ; but it should be fully under the control of the soul. Among more developed men at the present day it usually is so, though it may break away and run wild for a little at times. The astral body is also fully developed, but it is not yet by any means under perfect control ; even among the races to which we belong, there are many people who are the victims of their own emotions. Instead of being able to govern them perfectly, they too often allow themselves to be governed by them. They let their emotions run away with them, just as a wild horse may run away with its rider, and take him into many places whereto he does not wish to go.

We may take it, then, that in all the more evolved men at the present day the physical body is fully developed, and fairly under control ; the astral body is also fully developed, but not by any means under perfect control ; the mental body is in process of unfoldment, but its growth is yet very far from complete. When these three bodies, the physical, the astral and the mental, are entirely subordinate to the soul, the lower self will have been absorbed into the higher self, and the ego, the soul, will have dominated the man. Though the man is not yet perfect, the different vehicles are so far harmonised that they have but one aim.

Up to this time the soul has been slowly controlling the personal vehicles until they become one with it, but now the Monad in its turn begins to dominate the soul; and there will presently come a time when, just as the personality and the soul have become one, the Spirit and the soul will become one in their turn. This is the unification of the ego with the Monad; and when that is achieved the man has attained the object of his descent into matter—he has become the Superman, or Adept.

SUPERHUMAN LIFE

Now only, for the first time, does he enter upon his real life, for the whole of this stupendous process of evolution (through all the lower kingdoms and then through the human kingdom up to the attainment of Adeptship) is but a preparation for the true life of the Spirit which begins only when man becomes more than man. Humanity is the final class of the world-school; and when a man has been trained therein he passes out into the real life, the life of the glorified Spirit, the life of the Christ. What that is we know but little as yet, though we see some of those who are sharing it. It has a glory and a splendour which is beyond all comparison, beyond our comprehension; and yet it is a vivid and living fact, and the attainment of it by every one of us is an absolute certainty from which we cannot escape even if we would. It we act selfishly, if we set ourselves against the current of evolution, we can delay our progress; but we cannot finally prevent it.

Having finished with human life, the Perfected Man usually drops his various material bodies, but he retains the power to take up any of them if he should need them in the course of his work. In the majority of cases, one who gains that level no longer needs a physical body. He no longer retains an astral, a mental or even a causal body, but lives permanently at his higher level. Whenever for any purpose he needs to deal with a lower plane, he must take a temporary vehicle belonging to that plane, because only through the medium of its matter can he come into contact with those who live therein. If he wishes to talk to men physically, he must take a physical body ; he must have at least a partial materialisation, or he cannot speak. In the same way, if he wishes to impress our minds, he must draw round himself a mental body. Whenever he needs in his work to take a lower vehicle, he has the power to do so ; but he holds it only temporarily. There are seven lines of still further progress along which the Perfect Man can go, a list of which we shall give in a later chapter.

THE BROTHERHOOD OF ADEPTS

The world is guided and directed to a large extent by a Brotherhood of Adepts to which our Masters belong. Theosophical students make all sorts of mistakes about them. They often regard them as a great monastic community, all living together in some secret place. They suppose them sometimes to be Angels, and many of our students have thought that they were all Indian, or that they all resided in the Himalayas. None of these hypotheses is true. There is a great Brotherhood, and its members are in constant communication with one another ; but their communication is on higher planes and they do not necessarily live together. As part of their work, some of these great Brothers whom we call Masters of the Wisdom are willing to take pupil-apprentices and teach them ; but they form only a small section of the mighty body of Perfected Men.

As will be explained later on, there are seven types of men, for every one belongs to one of the seven Rays into which the great wave of evolving life is distinctly divided. It would seem that one Adept on each of the Rays is appointed to attend to the training of beginners, and all those who are coming along his particular Ray of evolution pass through his hands.

No one below the rank of Adept is permitted to assume full responsibility for a novice, though those who have been chelas (disciples) for a number of years are often employed as deputies, and receive the privilege of helping and advising promising young aspirants. These older pupils are gradually being trained for their future work when they in turn shall become Adepts, and they are learning to take more and more of the routine work off the hands of their Masters, so that the latter may be set free for higher labours which only hey can undertake. The preliminary selection of candidates for discipleship is now left to a large extent in the hands of these older workers, and the candidates are temporarily linked with such representatives rather than directly with the great Adepts. But the pupils and the Master are so wonderfully one that perhaps this is almost " a distinction without a difference ".

THE POWERS OF THE ADEPT

The powers of the Adept are indeed many and wonderful, but they all follow in natural sequence from faculties which we ourselves possess. It is only that they have these faculties in a very much greater degree. I think that the outstanding characteristic of the Adept, as compared with ourselves, is that he looks upon everything from an absolutely different point of view; for there is in him nothing whatever of the thought of self which is so prominent in the majority of men. The Adept has eliminated the lower self, and is living not for self but for all, and yet, in a way that only he can really understand, that *all* is truly himself also. He has reached that stage in which there is no flaw in his character, nothing of a thought or feeling for a personal, separated self, and his only motive is that of helping forward evolution, of working in harmony with the Logos who directs it.

Perhaps the next most prominent characteristic is his all-round development. We are all of us imperfect; none has attained the highest level in any line, and even the great scientist or the great saint has usually reached his excellence in one thing only, and there remain other sides of his nature not yet unfolded. All of us possess some germ of all the different characteristics, but always they are but partially awakened, and one much more than another. An Adept, however, is an all-round Man, a Man whose devotion and love and sympathy and compassion are perfect, while at the same time his intellect is something far grander than we can as yet realise, and his spirituality is wonderful and divine. He stands out above and beyond all men whom we know, because of the fact that he is fully developed.

CHAPTER II

THE PHYSICAL BODIES OF THE MASTERS

THEIR APPEARANCE

THERE has been among Theosophical students a great deal of vagueness and uncertainty about the Masters, so perhaps it may help us to realise how natural their lives are, and how there is an ordinary physical side to them, if I say a few words about the daily life and appearance of some of them. There is no one physical characteristic by which an Adept can be infallibly distinguished from other men, but he always appears impressive, noble, dignified, holy and serene, and anyone meeting him could hardly fail to recognise that he was in the presence of a remarkable man. He is the strong but silent man, speaking only when he has a definite object in view, to encourage, to help or to warn, yet he is wonderfully benevolent and full of a keen sense of humour—humour always of a kindly order, used never to wound, but always to lighten the troubles of life. The Master Morya once said that it is impossible to make progress on the occult Path without a sense of humour, and certainly all the Adepts whom I have seen have possessed that qualification.

Most of them are distinctly fine-looking men ; their physical bodies are practically perfect, for they live in complete obedience to the laws of health, and above all they never worry about anything. All their karma has long been exhausted, and thus the physical body is as perfect an expression of the Augoeides or glorified body of the ego as the limitations of the physical plane will allow, so that not only is the present body of an Adept usually splendidly handsome, but also any new body that he may take in a subsequent incarnation

A RAVINE IN TIBET

is likely to be an almost exact reproduction of the old one, allowing for racial and family differences, because there is nothing to modify it. This freedom from karma gives them, when for any reason they choose to take new bodies, entire liberty to select a birth in any country or race that may be convenient for the work that they have to do, and thus the nationality of the particular bodies which they happen to be wearing at any given time is not of primary importance.

To know that a certain man is an Adept it would be necessary to see his causal body, for in that his development would show by its greatly increased size, and by a special arrangement of its colours into concentric spheres, such as is indicated to some extent in the illustration of the causal body of an Arhat (Plate xxvi) in *Man, Visible and Invisible*.

A RAVINE IN TIBET

There is a certain valley, or rather ravine, in Tibet, where three of these Great Ones, the Master Morya, the Master Kuthumi and the Master Djwal Kul are living at the present time.

The Master Djwal Kul, at Madame Blavtsky's request, once made for her a precipitated picture of the mouth of that ravine, and the illustration given herewith is a reproduction of a photograph of that. The original, which is precipitated on silk, is preserved in the shrine-room of the Headquarters of the Theosophical Society at Adyar. On the left of the picture the Master Morya is seen on horse-back near the door of his house. The dwelling of the Master Kuthumi does not appear in the picture, being higher up the valley, round the bend on the right. Madame Blavatsky begged the Master Djwal Kul to put himself into the picture; he at first refused, but eventually added himself as a small figure standing in the water and grasping a pole, but with his back to the spectator! This original is faintly tinted, the colours being blue, green and black. It bears the signature of the artist—the nickname Gai Ben-Jamin, which he bore in his youth in the early days of the Society, long before he

3

reached Adeptship.[1] The scene is evidently taken early in the day, as the morning mists are still clinging to the hillsides.

The Masters Morya and Kuthumi occupy houses on opposite sides of this narrow ravine, the slopes of which are covered with pine trees. Paths run down the ravine past their houses, and meet at the bottom, where there is a little bridge. Close to the bridge a narrow door, which may be seen on the left at the bottom of the picture, leads to a system of vast subterranean halls containing an occult museum of which the Master Kuthumi is the Guardian on behalf of the Great White Brotherhood.

The contents of this museum are of the most varied character. They appear to be intended as a kind of illustration of the whole process of evolution. For example, there are here the most life-like images of every type of man which has existed on this planet from the commencement—from gigantic loose-jointed Lemurians to pigmy remains of even earlier and less human races. Models in *alto relievo* show all the variations of the surface of the earth—the conditions before and after the great cataclysms which have changed it so much. Huge diagrams illustrate the migrations of the different races of the world, and show exactly how far they spread from their respective sources. Other similar diagrams are devoted to the influence of the various religions of the world, showing where each was practised in its original purity, and where it became mingled with and distorted by the remains of other religions.

Amazingly life-like statues perpetuate the physical appearance of certain of the great leaders and teachers of long-forgotten races ; and various objects of interest connected with important and even unnoticed advancements in civilization are preserved for the examination of posterity. Original manuscripts of incredible antiquity and of priceless value are here to be seen—a manuscript, for example, written by the hand of the Lord Buddha himself in his final life as Prince Siddhartha, and another written by the Lord Christ during his birth in Palestine. Here is kept that marvellous original of

---

[1] This signature was upon the lower margin outside the actual picture, and consequently it does not appear in our reproduction.

the *Book of Dzyan*, which Madame Blavatsky describes in the opening of *The Secret Doctrine*. Here too are strange scripts from other worlds than ours. Animal and vegetable forms are also depicted, some few of which are known to us as fossils, though most of them are unimagined by our modern science. Actual models of some of the great cities of remote and forgotten antiquity are here for the study of the pupils.

All statues and models are vividly coloured exactly as were the originals ; and we may note that the collection here was intentionally put together at the time, in order to represent to posterity the exact stages through which the evolution or civilization of the time was passing, so that instead of mere incomplete fragments, such as our museums so often present to us, we have in all cases an intentionally educative series of presentations. There we find models of all the kinds of machinery which the different civilizations have evolved, and also there are elaborate and abundant illustrations of the types of magic in use at the various periods of history.

In the vestibule leading to these vast halls are kept the living images of those pupils of the Masters Morya and Kuthumi who happen at the time to be on probation, which I will describe later. These images are ranged round the walls like statues, and are perfect representations of the pupils concerned. It is not probable, however, that they are visible to physical eyes, for the lowest matter entering into their composition is etheric.

Near the bridge there is also a small temple with turrets of somewhat Burmese form, to which a few villagers go to make offerings of fruit and flowers, and to burn camphor and recite the Pancha Sila. A rough and uneven track leads down the valley by the side of the stream. From either of the two houses of the Masters the other house can be seen; they are both above the bridge, but both cannot be seen from it, since the ravine bends round. If we follow the path up the valley past the house of the Master Kuthumi it will lead us to a large pillar of rock, beyond which, the ravine bending round again, it passes out of sight. Some distance further on the ravine opens out into a plateau on which there is a lake, in which, tradition tells us, Madame Blavatsky used to bathe ;

and it is said that she found it very cold. The valley is sheltered and faces south, and though the surrounding country is under snow during the winter, I do not remember having seen any near the Masters' houses. These houses are of stone, very heavily and strongly built.

THE HOUSE OF THE MASTER KUTHUMI

The house of the Master Kuthumi is divided into two parts by a passage-way running straight through it. As will be seen from our diagram 1 (p. 23), which shows the ground plan of the southern half of the house, on entering the passage, the first door on the right leads into the principal room of the house, in which the Master usually sits. It is large and lofty (about fifty feet by thirty feet), in many ways more like a hall than a room, and it occupies the whole of the front of the house on that side of the passage. Behind that large room are two other nearly square rooms, one of which he uses as a library, and the other as a bedroom. That completes that side or division of the house, which is apparently reserved for the Master's personal use, and is surrounded by a broad veranda. The other side of the house, on the left of the passage as one enters, seems to be divided into smaller rooms and offices of various kinds ; we have had no opportunity of closely examining them, but we have noted that just across the passage from the bedroom is a well-appointed bathroom.

The large room is well supplied with windows, both along the front and the end—so well that on entering one gets the impression of an almost continuous outlook, and under the windows runs a long seat. There is also a somewhat unusual feature for that country, a large open fireplace in the middle of the wall opposite the front windows. This is so arranged as to heat all three rooms, and it has a curious hammered iron cover, which I am told is unique in Tibet. Over the opening of that fireplace is a mantelpiece, and nearby stands the Master's armchair of very old carved wood, hollowed to fit the sitter, so that for it no cushions are required. Dotted about the room are tables and settees or sofas, mostly without backs, and in one corner is the keyboard of the Master's organ. The ceiling is perhaps twenty feet high, and is very handsome, with its fine carved beams, which descend into ornamental points where they meet one another and divide the ceiling into oblong sections. An arched opening with a pillar in the centre, somewhat in the Gothic style, but without glass, opens into the study, and a similar window opens into the bedroom. This latter room is very simply furnished. There is an ordinary bed, swung hammock-like between two carved wooden supports fixed in the wall (one of these carved to imitate a lion's head, and the other an elephant's) and the bed when not in use folds up against the wall.

The library is a fine room, containing thousands of volumes. Running out from the wall there are tall bookshelves, filled with books in many languages, a number of them being modern European

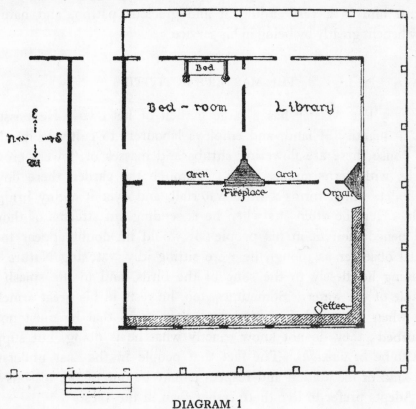

DIAGRAM 1

works and at the top there are open shelves for manuscripts. The Master is a great linguist, and besides being a fine English scholar has a thorough knowledge of French and German. The library also contains a typewriter, which was presented to the Master by one of his pupils.

Of the Master's family I know but little. There is a lady, evidently a pupil, whom he calls ' sister '. Whether she is actually his sister or not I do not know ; she might possibly be a cousin or a niece. She looks much older than he, but that would not make the relationship improbable, as he has appeared of about the same age for a long time. She resembles him to a certain extent, and once or twice when there have been gatherings she has come and joined the party, though her principal work seems to be to look after the house-keeping and manage the servants. Among the latter are an old man and his wife, who have been for a long time in the Master's service. They do not know anything of the real dignity of their employer, but regard him as a very indulgent and gracious patron, and naturally they benefit greatly by being in his service.

THE MASTER'S ACTIVITIES

The Master has a large garden of his own. He possesses too, a quantity of land, and employs labourers to cultivate it. Near the house there are flowering shrubs and masses of flowers growing freely, with ferns among them. Through the garden there flows a streamlet, which forms a little waterfall, and over it a tiny bridge is built. Here he often sits when he is sending out streams of thought and benediction upon his people ; it would no doubt appear to the casual observer as though he were sitting idly watching Nature, and listening heedlessly to the song of the birds, and to the splash and tumble of the water. Sometimes, too, he rests in his great armchair, and when his people see him thus, they know that he must not be disturbed ; they do not know exactly what he is doing, but suppose him to be in *samadhi*. The fact that people in the East understand this kind of meditation and respect it may be one of the reasons why the Adepts prefer to live there rather than in the West.

In this way, we get the effect of the Master sitting quietly for a considerable part of the day and, as we should say, meditating; but while he is apparently resting so calmly, he is in reality engaged all the time in most strenuous labour on higher planes, manipulating various natural forces and pouring forth influences of the most diverse character on thousands of souls simultaneously; for the Adepts are the busiest people in the world. The Master, however, does much physical-plane work as well; he has composed some music, and has written notes and papers for various purposes. He is also much interested in the growth of physical science, although this is especially the province of one of the other great Masters of the Wisdom.

From time to time the Master Kuthumi rides on a big bay horse, and occasionally, when their work lies together, he is accompanied by the Master Morya, who always rides a magnificent white horse. Our Master regularly visits some of the monasteries, and sometimes goes up a great pass to a lonely monastery in the hills. Riding in the course of his duties seems to be his principal exercise, but he sometimes walks with the Master Djwal Kul, who lives in a little cabin which he built with his own hands, quite near to the great crag on the way up to the plateau.

Sometimes our Master plays on the organ which is in the large room in his house. He had it made in Tibet under his direction, and it is in fact a combined piano and organ, with a keyboard like those which we have in the West, on which he can play all our western music. It is unlike any other instrument with which I am acquainted, for it is in a sense double-fronted, as it can be played either from the sitting-room or the library. The principal keyboard (or rather the three keyboards, great organ, swell and choir) is in the sitting-room, whereas the piano keyboard is in the library; and these keyboards can be used either together or separately. The full organ with its pedals can be played in the ordinary way from the sitting-room; but by turning a handle somewhat equivalent to a stop, the piano mechanism can be linked with the organ, so that it all plays simultaneously. From that point of view, in fact, the piano is treated as an additional stop on the organ.

From the keyboard in the library, however, the piano can be played alone as a separate instrument, quite dissociated from the organ ; but by some complicated mechanism the choir-organ is also linked to that keyboard, so that by it one can play the piano alone precisely as though it were an ordinary piano, or one can play the piano accompanied by the choir-organ, or at any rate by certain stops of that organ. It is also possible, as I said, to separate the two completely, and so, with a performer at each keyboard, to play a piano-organ duet. The mechanism and the pipes of this strange instrument occupy almost the whole of what might be called the upper story of this part of the Master's house. By magnetisation he has placed it in communication with the Gandharvas, or Devas of music, so that whenever it is played they co-operate, and thus he obtains combinations of sound never to be heard on the physical plane ; and there is, too, an effect produced by the organ itself as of an accompaniment of string and wind instruments.

The song of the Devas is ever being sung in the world ; it is ever sounding in men's ears, but they will not listen to its beauty. There is the deep bourdon of the sea, the sighing of the wind in the trees, the roar of the mountain torrent, the music of stream, river and waterfall, which together with many others form the mighty song of Nature as she lives. This is but the echo in the physical world of a far grander sound, that of the *Being* of the Devas. As is said in *Light on the Path* :

> Only fragments of the great song come to your ears while yet you are but man. But, if you listen to it, remember it faithfully, so that none, which has reached you, is lost, and endeavour to learn from it the meaning of the mystery which surrounds you. In time you will need no teacher. For as the individual has voice, so has that in which the individual exists. Life itself has speech, and is never silent. And its utterance is not, as you that are deaf may suppose, a cry ; it is a song. Learn from it that you are part of the harmony ; learn from it to obey the laws of the harmony.

Every morning a number of people—not exactly pupils, but followers—come to the Master's house, and sit on the veranda and outside it. Sometimes he gives them a little talk—a sort of lecturette ; but more often he goes on with his work and takes no notice of them beyond a friendly smile, with which they seem equally contented. They evidently come to sit in his aura and venerate him. Sometimes he takes his food in their presence, sitting on the veranda, with this crowd of Tibetans and others on the ground around him ; but generally he eats by himself at a table in his room. It is possible that he keeps the rule of the Buddhist monks, and takes no food after noon ; for I do not remember ever to have seen him eat in the evening ; it is even possible that he does not need food every day. Most probably when he feels inclined he orders the food that he would like, and does not take his meals at stated times. I have seen him eating little round cakes, brown and sweet ; they are made of wheat and sugar and butter, and are of the ordinary kind used in the household, cooked by his sister. He also eats curry and rice, the curry being somewhat in the form of soup, like *dhal*. He uses a curious and beautiful golden spoon, with an exquisite image of an elephant at the end of the handle, the bowl of which is set at an unusual angle to the stem. It is a family heirloom, very old and probably of great value. He generally wears white clothes, but I do not remember ever having seen him wearing a head-dress of any kind, except on the rare occasions when he assumes the yellow robe of the Gelugpa sect or clan, which includes a hood somewhat of the shape of the Roman helmet. The Master Morya, however, generally wears a turban.

OTHER HOUSES

The house of the Master Morya is on the opposite side of the valley, but much lower down—quite close, in fact, to the little temple and the entrance to the caves. It is of an entirely different style of architecture, having at least two storeys, and the front facing the road has verandas at each level which are almost entirely glassed in. The general method and arrangement of his life is much the same as that already described in the case of the Master Kuthumi.

If we walk up the road on the left bank of the stream, rising gradually along the side of the valley, we pass on the right the house and grounds of the Master Kuthumi, and further up the hill we find

on the same side of the road a small hut or cabin which he who is
now the Master Djwal Kul constructed for himself with his own
hands in the days of his pupilage, in order that he might have an
abiding-place quite near to his Master.   In that cabin hangs a sort
of plaque upon which at his request one of the English pupils of the
Master Kuthumi precipitated many years ago an interior view of the
larger room in the house of the Master Kuthumi, showing the figures
of various Masters and pupils.   This was done in commemoration of
a certain especially happy and fruitful evening at the Master's house.

THE FIRST RAY ADEPTS

Turning now to a consideration of the personal appearance of
these Great Ones: that is modified to some extent by the Ray or type
to which each of them belongs.   The First Ray has power for its
most prominent characteristic, and those who are born upon it are
the kings, the rulers, the governors of the world—of the inner and
spiritual world in the first place, but also of the physical plane.   Any
man who possesses in a very unusual degree the qualities which enable
him to dominate men and to guide them smoothly along the course
which he desires is likely to be either a First Ray man or one who is
tending towards the First Ray.

Such a kingly figure is the Lord Vaivasvata Manu, the Ruler
of the fifth root race, who is the tallest of all the Adepts, being six feet
eight inches in height, and perfectly proportioned.   He is the Representative Man of our Race, its prototype, and every member of that
race is directly descended from him.   The Manu has a very striking
face of great power, with an acquiline nose, a full and flowing brown
beard, brown eyes, and a magnificent head of leonine poise.   " Tall
is he," says Dr. Besant, " and of King-like majesty, with eyes
piercing as an eagle's, tawny and brilliant with golden lights."   He
is living at present in the Himalaya mountains, not far from the house
of his great Brother, the Lord Maitreya.

Such a figure also is the Master Morya, the lieutenant and successor of the Lord Vaivasvata Manu, and the future Manu of the sixth

root race.   He is a Rajput King by birth, and has a dark beard divided into two parts, dark, almost black, hair falling to his shoulders, and dark and piercing eyes, full of power.   He is six feet six inches in height, and bears himself like a soldier, speaking in short terse sentences as if he were accustomed to being instantly obeyed.   In his presence there is a sense of overwhelming power and strength, and he has an imperial dignity that compels the deepest reverence.

Madame Blavatsky has often told us how she met the Master Morya in Hyde Park, London, in the year 1851, when he came over with a number of other Indian Princes to attend the first great International Exhibition.   Strangely enough, I myself, then a little child of four, saw him also, all unknowing.   I can remember being taken to see a gorgeous procession, in which among many other wonders came a party of richly-dressed Indian horsemen.   Magnificent horsemen they were, riding steeds as fine, I suppose, as any in the world, and it was only natural that my childish eyes were fixed upon them in great delight, and that they were perhaps to me the finest exhibit of that marvellous and fairy-like show.   And even as I watched them pass, as I stood holding my father's hand, one of the tallest of those heroes fixed me with gleaming black eyes, which half-frightened me, and yet at the same time filled me somehow with indescribable happiness and exaltation.   He passed with the others and I saw him no more, yet often the vision of that flashing eye returned to my childish memory.

Of course, I knew nothing then of who he was, and I should never have identified him had it not been for a gracious remark which he made to me many years afterwards.   Speaking one day in his presence of the earlier days of the Society I happened to say that the first time I had had the privilege of seeing him in materialised form was on a certain occasion when he came into Madame Blavatsky's room at Adyar, for the purpose of giving her strength and issuing certain directions. He himself, who was engaged in conversation with some other Adepts, turned sharply upon me and said: "No, that was not the first time.   You had seen me before then in my physical body.   Do you not remember, as a tiny child, watching the Indian horsemen ride past in Hyde Park, and did you not see how even then I singled you out ? " I remembered instantly, of course, and said : " Oh, Master, was that you ? But I ought to have known it." I do not mention this incident among the occasions when I have met and spoken with a Master, both parties to the interview being in the physical body, because I did not at the time know that great horseman to be the Master, and because the evidence of so small a child might well be doubted or discounted.

Mr. S. Ramaswami Iyer, in his account of the experience mentioned in Chapter I, writes :

I was following the road to the town, whence, I was assured by people I met on the road, I could cross over to Tibet easily in my pilgrim's garb, when I suddenly saw a solitary horseman galloping towards me from the opposite direction. From his tall stature and skill in horsemanship, I thought he was some military officer of the Sikkhim Rajah. . . . As he approached me, he reined up. I looked at him and recognized him instantly. . . . I was in the awful presence of him, of the same Mahatma, my own revered Guru, whom I had seen before in his astral body on the balcony of the Theosophical Headquarters. It was he, the Himalayan Brother of the ever-memorable night of December last, who had so kindly dropped a letter in answer to one I had given but an hour or so before in a sealed envelope to Madame Blavatsky, whom I had never lost sight of for one moment during the interval. The very same instant saw me prostrated on the ground at his feet. I arose at his command, and, leisurely looking into his face, forgot myself entirely in the contemplation of the image I knew so well, having seen his portrait (that in Colonel Olcott's possession) times out of number. I knew not what to say; joy and reverence tied my tongue. The majesty of his countenance, which seemed to me to be the impersonation of power and thought, held me rapt in awe. I was at last face to face with the Mahatma of the Himavat, and he was no myth, no creation of the imagination of a medium, as some sceptics had suggested. It was no dream of the night; it was between nine and ten o'clock of the forenoon. There was the sun shining and silently witnessing the scene from above. I see him before me in flesh and blood, and he speaks to me in accents of kindness and gentleness. What more could I want ? My excess of happiness made me dumb. Nor was it until some time had elapsed that I was able to utter a few words, encouraged by his gentle tone and speech. His complexion is not as fair as that of Mahatma Kuthumi; but never have I seen a countenance so handsome, a stature so tall and so majestic. As in his portrait, he wears a short black beard, and long black hair hanging down to his breast; only his dress was different. Instead of a white, loose robe he wore a yellow mantle lined with fur, and on his head, instead of the turban, a yellow Tibetan felt cap, such as I have seen some Bhutanese wear in this country. When the first moments of rapture and surprise were over, and I calmly comprehended the situation, I had a long talk with him.[1]

---

[1] *Five Years of Theosophy* (2nd Edition), p. 284, out of print.

Another such regal figure is the Lord Chakshusha Manu, the Manu of the fourth root race, who is Chinese by birth, and of very high caste. He has the high Mongolian cheek-bones, and his face looks as though it were delicately carven from old ivory. He generally wears magnificent robes of flowing cloth-of-gold. As a rule we do not come into contact with him in our regular work, except when it happens that we have to deal with a pupil belonging to his root race.

THE SECOND RAY ADEPTS

In the persons of our Lord the Bodhisattva, the World-Teacher, and of the Master Kuthumi, his principal lieutenant, the influence that is especially noticeable is the radiance of their all-embracing Love. The Lord Maitreya is wearing a body of the Keltic race at the present time. His is a face of wondrous beauty, strong and yet most tender, with rich hair flowing like red gold about his shoulders. His beard is pointed, as in some of the old pictures, and his eyes, of a wonderful violet, are like twin flowers, like stars, like deep and holy pools filled with the waters of everlasting peace. His smile is dazzling beyond words, and a blinding glory of Light surrounds him, intermingled with that marvellous rose-coloured glow which ever shines from the Lord of Love.

We may think of him as seated in the great front room of his house in the Himalayas, the room with many windows, that overlooks the gardens and the terraces and, far below, the rolling Indian plains; or in flowing robes of white, edged with a deep border of gold, as walking in his garden in the cool of the evening, among the glorious flowers, whose perfume fills the surrounding air with a rich, sweet fragrance. Wondrous beyond measure is our Holy Lord the Christ, wondrous beyond any power of description, for through him flows the Love which comforts millions, and his is the Voice that speaks, as never man spake, the words of teaching that bring peace to angels and to men.

The Master Kuthumi wears the body of a Kashmiri Brahmin, and is as fair in complexion as the average Englishman. He, too, has flowing hair, and his eyes are blue and full of joy and love. His hair and beard are brown, which, as the sunlight catches it, becomes ruddy with glints of gold. His face is somewhat hard to describe, for his expression is ever changing as he smiles; the nose is finely chiselled, and the eyes are large and of a wonderful liquid blue. Like the great Lord, he, too, is a Teacher and Priest, and many centuries hence he will succeed him in his high Office, and will assume the sceptre of the World-Teacher, and become the Bodhisattva of the sixth root race.

THE OTHER RAYS

The Mahachohan is the type of the Statesman, the great Organiser, though he too has many military qualities. He wears an Indian body, and is tall and thin, with a sharp profile, very fine and clear-cut, and no hair on the face. His face is rather stern, with a strong, square chin; his eyes are deep and penetrating, and he speaks somewhat abruptly, as a soldier speaks. He generally wears Indian robes and a white turban.

The Master the Comte de St. Germain resembles him in many ways. Though he is not especially tall, he is very upright and military in his bearing, and he has the exquisite courtesy and dignity of a *grand seigneur* of the eighteenth century; we feel at once that he belongs to a very old and noble family. His eyes are large and brown, and are filled with tenderness and humour, though there is in them a glint of power; and the splendour of his Presence impels men to make obeisance. His face is olive-tanned, his close-cut brown hair is parted in the centre and brushed back from the forehead, and he has a short and pointed beard. Often he wears a dark uniform with facings of gold lace—often also a magnificent red military cloak—and these accentuate his soldier-like appearance. He usually resides in an ancient castle in Eastern Europe that has belonged to his family for many centuries.

The Master Serapis is tall, and fair in complexion. He is a Greek by birth, though all his work has been done in Egypt and in connection with the Egyptian Lodge. He is very distinguished and ascetic in face, somewhat resembling the late Cardinal Newman.

Perhaps the Venetian Chohan is the handsomest of all the Members of the Brotherhood. He is very tall—about six feet five inches, and has a flowing beard and golden hair somewhat like those of the Manu ; and his eyes are blue. Although he was born in Venice, his family undoubtedly has Gothic blood in its veins, for he is a man distinctly of that type.

The Master Hilarion is a Greek and, except that he has a slightly aquiline nose, is of the ancient Greek type. His forehead is low and broad, and resembles that of the Hermes of Praxiteles. He too is wonderfully handsome, and looks rather younger than most of the Adepts.

He who was once the disciple Jesus is now wearing a Syrian body. He has the dark skin, dark eyes and black beard of the Arab, and generally wears white robes and a turban. He is the Master of devotees, and the keynote of his Presence is an intense purity, and a fiery type of devotion that brooks no obstacles. He lives amongst the Druses of Mount Lebanon.

Two of the Great Ones with whom we have come into contact diverge slightly from what perhaps we may call, with all reverence, the usual type of the physical body of the Adept. One of these is the spiritual Regent of India, he of whom Colonel Olcott several times writes, to whom the name Jupiter was assigned in the book *Man : Whence, How and Whither*. He is shorter than most members of the Brotherhood, and is the only one of them, so far as I am aware, whose hair shows streaks of grey. He holds himself very upright and moves with alertness and military precision. He is a landed proprietor, and during the visit which I paid to him with Swami T. Subba Row, I saw him several times transacting business with men who appeared to be foremen, bringing reports to him and receiving instructions. The other is the Master Djwal Kul, who is still wearing the same body in which he attained Adeptship only a few years ago. Perhaps for that reason it has not been possible to make that body a perfect reproduction of the Augoeides. His face is distinctly Tibetan in character, with high cheek bones, and is somewhat rugged in appearance, showing signs of age.

PERFECT PHYSICAL VEHICLES

Those who, attaining the level of Adeptship, choose as their future career to remain upon this world and help directly in the evolution of their own humanity, find it convenient for their work to retain physical bodies. In order to be suitable for their purposes, these bodies must be of no ordinary kind. Not only must they be absolutely sound in health, but they must also be perfect expressions of as much of the ego as can be manifested on the physical plane.

The building up of such a body as this is no light task. When the ego of an ordinary man comes down to his new baby body, he finds it in charge of an artificial elemental, which has been created according to his karma, as I have described in *The Inner Life*. This elemental is industriously occupied in modelling the form which is soon to be born in the outer world, and it remains after birth and continues that moulding process usually until the body is six or seven years old. During this period the ego is gradually acquiring closer contact with his new vehicles, emotional and mental as well as physical, and is becoming accustomed to them; but the actual work done by himself upon these new vehicles up to the point at which the elemental withdraws is, in most cases, inconsiderable. He is certainly in connection with the body, but generally pays but little attention to it, preferring to wait until it has reached a stage where it is more responsive to his efforts.

The case of an Adept is very different from this. As there is no karma to be worked out, no artificial elemental is at work, and the ego himself is in sole charge of the development of the body from the beginning, finding himself limited only by its heredity. This enables a far more refined and delicate instrument to be produced, but it also involves more trouble for the ego, and engages for some years a considerable amount of his time and energy. In consequence of this, and no doubt for other reasons as well, an Adept does not wish to repeat the process more often than is strictly necessary, and he therefore makes his physical body last as long as possible. Our bodies grow old and die for various reasons, from inherited weakness, disease, accident and self-indulgence, worry and overwork. But in the case of an Adept none of these causes is present, though we must of course remember that his body is fit for work and capable of endurance immeasurably beyond those of ordinary men.

The bodies of the Adepts being such as we have described, they are usually able to hold possession of them much longer than an ordinary man can, and the consequence is that we find on inquiry that the age of any such body is usually much greater than from appearances we had supposed it to be. The Master Morya, for example, appears to be a man absolutely in the prime of life—possibly thirty-five or forty years of age ; yet many of the stories which his pupils tell of him assign to him an age four or five times greater than that, and Madame Blavatsky herself told us that when she first saw him in her childhood he appeared to her exactly the same as at the present time. Again, the Master Kuthumi has the appearance of being about the same age as his constant friend and companion, the Master Morya ; yet it has been said that he took a University Degree in Europe just before the middle of last century, which would certainly make him something very like a centenarian. We have at present no means of knowing what is the limit of prolongation, though there is evidence to show that it may easily extend to more than double the three-score years and ten of the Psalmist.

A body thus made suitable for higher work is inevitably a sensitive one, and for that very reason it requires careful treatment if it is to be always at its best. It would wear out as ours do if it were subjected to the innumerable petty frictions of the outer world, and its constant torrent of unsympathetic vibrations. Therefore, the Great Ones usually live in comparative seclusion, and appear but rarely in that cyclonic chaos which we call daily life. If they were to bring their bodies into the whirl of curiosity and vehement emotion, there can be no doubt that the life of these bodies would be greatly shortened, and also, because of their extreme sensitiveness, there would be much unnecessary suffering.

BORROWED VEHICLES

By temporarily occupying the body of a pupil, the Adept avoids these inconveniences, and at the same time gives an incalculable impetus to the pupil's evolution. He inhabits the vehicle only when he needs it—to deliver a lecture, perhaps, or to pour out a special flood of blessing ; and as soon as he has done what he wishes, he steps out of the body, and the pupil, who has all the while been in attendance, resumes it, as the Adept goes back to his own proper vehicle to continue his usual work for the helping of the world. In this way his regular business is but little affected, yet he has always at his disposal a body through which he can work, when required, on the physical plane.

We can readily imagine in what way this will affect the pupil who is so favoured as to have the opportunity of thus lending his body to a Great One, though the extent of its action may well be beyond our calculation. A vehicle tuned by such an influence will be to him verily an assistance, not a limitation ; and while his body is in use he will always have the privilege of bathing in the Adept's marvellous magnetism, for he must be at hand to resume charge as soon as the Master has finished with it.

This plan of borrowing a suitable body is always adopted by the Great Ones when they think it well to descend among men, under conditions such as those which now obtain in the world. The Lord Gautama employed it when he came to attain the Buddhahood, and the Lord Maitreya took the same course when he visited Palestine two thousand years ago. The only exception known to me is that when a new Bodhisattva assumes the office of World-Teacher after his predecessor has become the Buddha, on his first appearance in the world in that capacity he takes birth as a little child in the ordinary way. Thus did our Lord, the present Bodhisattva, when he took birth as Shri Krishna on the glowing plains of India, to be reverenced and loved with a passion of devotion that has scarcely ever been equalled.

This temporary occupation of a pupil's body should not be confused with the permanent use by an advanced person of a vehicle prepared for him by some one else. Our great Founder, Madame Blavatsky, when she left the body in which we knew her, entered another which had just been abandoned by its original tenant. As to whether that body had been specially prepared for her use, I have no information; but other instances are known in which that was done. There is always in such cases a certain difficulty in adapting the vehicle to the needs and idiosyncrasies of the new occupant; and it is probable that it never becomes a perfectly fitting garment. There is for the incoming ego a choice between devoting a considerable amount of time and trouble to superintending the growth of a new vehicle, which would be a perfect expression of him, as far as that is possible on the physical plane; or of avoiding all that difficulty by entering the body of another—a process which will provide a reasonably good instrument for all ordinary purposes; but it will never fulfil in every respect all that its owner desires. In all cases, a pupil is naturally eager to have the honour of giving up his body to his Master; but few indeed are the vehicles pure enough to be so used.

The question is often raised as to why an Adept, whose work seems to lie almost entirely on higher planes, needs a physical body at all. It is really no concern of ours, but if speculation on such a matter be not irreverent, various reasons suggest themselves. The Adept spends much of his time in projecting streams of influence, and while, so as far as has been observed, these are most often on the higher mental level, or on the plane above that, it is probable that they may sometimes at least be etheric currents, and for the manipulation of these the possession of a physical body is undoubtedly an advantage. Again, most of the Masters whom I have seen have a few pupils or assistants who live with or near them on the physical plane, and a physical body may be necessary for their sake. Of this we may be certain, that if an Adept chooses to take the trouble to maintain such a body, he has a good reason for it; for we know enough of their methods of working to be fully aware that they always do everything in the best way, and by the means which involve the least expenditure of energy.

PART II
THE PUPILS

CHAPTER III

THE WAY TO THE MASTER

THE ENTRANCE TO THE PATH

THERE has always been a Brotherhood of Adepts; there have always been those who knew, those who possessed this inner wisdom, and our Masters are among the present representatives of that mighty line of Seers and Sages. Part of the knowledge which they have garnered during countless æons is available to every one on the physical plane under the name of Theosophy. But there is far more behind. The Master Kuthumi himself once said smilingly, when someone spoke of the enormous change that Theosophical knowledge had made in our lives, and of the wonderful comprehensiveness of the doctrine of reincarnation: " Yes, but we have lifted only a very small corner of the veil as yet." When we have thoroughly assimilated the knowledge given us, and are all living up to its teaching, the Brotherhood will be ready to lift the veil further; but only when we have complied with those conditions.

For those who wish to know more and to draw nearer, the Path is open. But the man who aspires to approach the Masters can reach them only by making himself unselfish as they are unselfish, by learning to forget the personal self, and by devoting himself wholly to the service of humanity as they do. In her article on *Occultism versus the Occult Arts* Madame Blavatsky has expressed this necessity in characteristically vigorous language :

True Occultism or Theosophy is the great renunciation of self unconditionally and absolutely, in thought as in action. It is altruism, and it throws him who practises it out of the calculation of the ranks of the living altogether. Not for himself but for the world he lives, as soon as he has pledged himself to the work. Much is forgiven during the first years of probation. But no sooner is he accepted than his personality must disappear, and he has to become a mere beneficent force in Nature. . . . It is only when the power of the passions is dead altogether, and when they have been crushed and annihilated in the retort of an unflinching will; when not only all the lusts and longings of the flesh are dead but also the recognition of the personal self is killed out and the astral has been reduced in consequence to a cipher, that the union with the Higher Self can take place. Then, when the astral reflects only the conquered man—the still living, but no more the longing, selfish personality—then the brilliant Augoeides, the divine Self, can vibrate in conscious harmony with both the poles of the human entity—the man of matter purified, and the ever pure Spiritual Soul—and stand in the presence of the Master-Self, the Christos of the mystic Gnostic, blended, merged into and one with It for ever. . . . The aspirant has to choose absolutely between the life of the world and the life of Occultism. It is useless and vain to endeavour to unite the two, for no man can serve two masters and satisfy both.

The point of view of the Masters is so radically different from ours that it is difficult at first for us to grasp it. They have their private affections just as we have, and assuredly they love some men more than others; but they will never allow such feelings as those to influence their attitude in the very slightest degree when the work is in question. They will take much trouble over a man if they see in him the seeds of future greatness, if they think that he will prove a good investment for the amount of time and force spent upon him. There is no such possibility as the faintest thought of favouritism in the minds of these Great Ones. They consider simply and solely the work which has to be done, the work of evolution, and the value of the man in relation to it; and if we will fit ourselves to take part in that, our progress will be rapid.

THE MAGNITUDE OF THE TASK

Few people realize the magnitude of this undertaking, and therefore the seriousness of what they are asking when they want to be taken as pupils. The Adepts are dealing with the entire world in enormous comprehensive sweeps of power; they are influencing millions in their causal bodies or on the buddhic plane, and all the time steadily, though by almost imperceptible degrees, raising the higher bodies of the people on a wholesale scale. And yet the same Master who spends his life in doing that work will sometime turn aside and pay personal attention to little details connected with one pupil.

All who dare to ask to become pupils should try to realize the stupendous character of the forces and the work, and the magnitude of the Beings with whom they propose to come into contact. The least understanding of the greatness of all these things will make it clear why the Adepts will not spend some of their energy on a pupil unless they have evidence that in a reasonable time he will add to the support of the world a strong current of strength and power in the right direction. They live to do the work of the Logos of the System, and those of us who wish to draw near to them must learn to do likewise, and live only for the work. Those who do that will certainly attract the attention of the Holy Ones, and be trained by them to help and bless the world.

Human progress is slow, but it is constant; therefore the number of the Perfected Men is increasing, and the possibility of attaining to their level is within the reach of all who are willing to make the stupendous effort required. In normal times we should need many births before we could gain Adeptship, but it is possible for us to hasten our progress on that Path, to compress into a few lives the evolution which otherwise would take many thousands of years. That preparation needs great self-control, determined effort carried on year after year, and often with but little to show outwardly in the way of definite progress; for it involves the training of the higher bodies far more than the physical body, and the training of the higher does not always manifest itself very obviously on the physical plane.

THE IMPORTANCE OF WORK

Anyone who hears about the Masters and their teaching, if he has any grasp at all of what it means and involves, must instantly be seized with a most intense desire to understand them and enter their service; the more he learns the more does he become filled with the wonder and beauty and glory of God's plan, and the more anxious does he become to take part in the work. Once he has realized that God has a plan of evolution, he wants to be a fellow-labourer with God, and nothing else can possibly bring satisfaction.

Then he begins to ask himself the question : " What must I do next ? " and the answer is : " Work. Do what you can to help the progress of humanity in the Master's way. Begin with what you have the opportunity to do and what you can do, which may be any little external thing at first, and presently, as you acquire the necessary qualities of character, you will be drawn into the higher side of it all, until, through striving to be and do your best, you will find youself possessed of the qualifications which admit to Initiation and member-ship in the Great White Brotherhood itself." When first I had the privilege of coming into somewhat closer touch with the Master, I asked him in a letter what I should do. He answered to the following effect : " You must find work for yourself ; you know what we are doing. Throw yourself into our work in any way you can. If I gave you a definite piece of work to do you would do it, but in that case the karma of what was done would be mine, because I told you to do it. You would have only the karma of willing obedience, which of course is very good, but it is not the karma of initiating a fruitful line of action. I want you to initiate work for yourself, because then the karma of the good deed will come to you ."

I think we might all take that unto ourselves. We might realize that it is our business not to wait until we are asked to do something, but to set to work. There is a good deal of quite humble work to be done in connection with Theosophy. Often perhaps some of us would prefer the more spectacular part ; we should like to stand up and deliver lectures in public to large audiences. We can generally find people who are willing to offer themselves for that ; but there is a great deal of humdrum office work to be done in connection with our Society, and we do not always find so many volunteers for that. Reverence and love for our Masters will lead us to be willing to do anything whatever in their service, however humble ; and we may be sure that we are working in their service when we are helping the Society which two of them founded.

THE ANCIENT RULES

The qualifications for admission to the Great White Brotherhood, which have to be acquired in the course of the work in the earlier part of the Path, are of a very definite character, and are always essentially the same, although they have been described in many different terms during the last twenty-five centuries. In the early days of the Theosophical Society, when all its wonderful teaching was new to us, this question of qualifications was naturally one of those about which some of us were most eager to learn ; and before Madame Blavatsky wrote down for us that most marvellous manual *The Voice of the Silence* she had already given us two lists of the requirements for chelaship. I cannot do better than quote them here for comparison with the later directions. She writes :

A Chela is a person who has offered himself to a master as a pupil to learn practically the hidden mysteries of nature and the psychical powers latent in man. The master who accepts him is called in India a Guru ; and the real Guru is always an Adept in the Occult Science. A man of profound knowledge, exoteric and esoteric, especially the latter, and one who has brought his carnal nature under the subjection of the will ; who has developed in himself both the power (Siddhi) to control the forces of Nature, and the capacity to probe her secrets by the help of the formerly latent but now active powers of his being—this is the real Guru. To offer oneself as candidate for Chelaship is easy enough ; to develop into an Adept is the most difficult task any man could possibly undertake. There are scores of natural-born poets, mathematicians, mechanics, statesmen, etc. but a natural-born Adept is something practically impossible. For, though we do hear at very rare intervals of one who has an extraordinary innate capacity for the acquisition of Occult knowledge and power, yet even he has to pass the self-same tests and probations, go through the self-same training as any less endowed fellow-aspirant. In this matter it is most true that there is no royal road by which favourites may travel.

For centuries the selection of Chelas—outside the hereditary group within the Gon-pa (temple)—has been made by the Himalayan Mahatmas themselves from among the class—in Tibet a considerable one as to number—of natural mystics. The only exceptions have been in the cases of Western men like Fludd, Thomas Vaughan, Paracelsus, Pico de Mirandolo, Count St. Germain, etc. whose temperamental affinity to this celestial science more or less forced the distant Adepts to come into personal relations with them, and enabled them to get such small (or large) proportion of the whole truth as was possible under their social surroundings. From Book IV of *Kiu-te*, Chapter on "The Laws of Upasanas", we learn that the qualifications expected in a Chela were :

1. Perfect physical health ;

2. Absolute mental and physical purity ;

3. Unselfishness of purpose; universal charity; pity for all animate beings;

4. Truthfulness and unswerving faith in the law of Karma, independent of the intervention of any power in Nature—a law whose course is not to be obstructed by any agency, not to be caused to deviate by prayer or propitiatory exoteric ceremonies;

5. A courage undaunted in every emergency, even by peril of life;

6. An intuitional perception of one's being the vehicle of the manifested Avalokiteshvara or Divine Atma (Spirit);

7. Calm indifference for, but a just appreciation of, everything that constitutes the objective and transitory world, in its relation with, and to, the invisible regions.

Such, at the least, must have been the recommendations of one aspiring to perfect Chelaship. With the sole exception of the first, which in rare and exceptional cases might have been modified, each one of these points has been invariably insisted upon, and all must have been more or less developed in the inner nature by the Chela's unhelped exertions, before he could be actually put to the test.

When the self-evolving ascetic—whether in, or outside the active world—has placed himself according to his natural capacity, above (and hence made himself master of) his (1) Sharira, body; (2) Indriya, senses; (3) Dosha, faults; (4) Dukkha, pain; and is ready to become one with his Manas, mind, Buddhi, intellection or spirit intelligence, and Atma, highest soul, i.e. spirit; when he is ready for this, and, further, to recognise in Atma the highest ruler in the world of perceptions, and in the will the highest executive energy (power)—then may he, under the time-honoured rules, be taken in hand by one of the Initiates. He may then be shown the mysterious path at whose farther end is obtained the unerring discernment of Phala, or the fruits of causes produced, and given the means of reaching Apavarga—emancipation from the misery of repeated births, Pretyabhava, in whose determination the ignorant has no hand.[1]

The second set of rules which she gives us occurs in her book *Practical Occultism*. They are twelve in number, but she tells us that they are taken from a list of seventy-three, to enumerate which would be useless, as they would be meaningless in Europe, though she says that every instructor in the East is furnished with them. The explanations in brackets are by Madame Blavatsky herself. They are as follows:

1. The place selected for receiving instruction must be a spot calculated not to distract the mind, and filled with influence-evolving (magnetic) objects. The five sacred colours gathered in a circle must be there among other things. The place must be free from any malignant influences hanging about in the air.

---

[1] *Five Years of Theosophy*, second edition, pp. 31-2.

(The place must be set apart, and used for no other purpose. The five sacred colours are the prismatic hues arranged in a certain way, as these colours are very magnetic. By malignant influences are meant any disturbances through strifes, quarrels, bad feelings, etc. as these are said to impress themselves immediately on the astral light, i.e. in the atmosphere of the place, and to hang about in the air. The first condition seems easy enough to accomplish, yet—on further consideration, it is one of the most difficult to obtain.)

2. Before the disciple shall be permitted to study face to face, he has to acquire preliminary understanding in a select company of other lay *upasaka* (disciples), the number of whom must be odd.

(" Face to face " means in this instance a study independent or apart from others, when the disciple gets his instruction *face to face* either with himself (his higher, Divine Self) or—his guru. It is then only that each receives *his due* of information, according to the use he has made of his knowledge. This can happen only towards the end of the cycle of instruction.)

3. Before thou (the teacher) shalt impart to thy *Lanoo* (disciple) the good (holy) words of Lamrin, or shalt permit him to make ready for *Dubjed*, thou shalt take care that his mind is thoroughly purified and at peace with all, especially *with his other Selves*. Otherwise the words of Wisdom and of the good Law shall scatter and be picked up by the winds.

(Lamrin is a work of practical instructions, by Tson-kha-pa, in two portions, one for ecclesiastical and exoteric purposes, the other for esoteric use. To make ready for *Dubjed* is to prepare the vessels used for seership, such as mirrors and crystals. The " other selves " refers to the fellow-students. Unless the greatest harmony reigns among the learners, no success is possible. It is the teacher who makes the selections according to the magnetic and electric natures of the students, bringing together and adjusting most carefully the positive and the negative elements.

4. The *upasaka* while studying must take care to be united as the fingers on one hand. Thou shalt impress upon their minds that whatever hurts one should hurt the others, and if the rejoicing of one finds no echo in the breasts of the others, then the required conditions are absent, and it is useless to proceed.

(This can hardly happen if the preliminary choice made was consistent with the magnetic requirements. It is known that chelas otherwise promising and fit for the reception of truth had to wait for years on account of their temper and the impossibility they felt to put themselves *in tune* with their companions. For—)

5. The co-disciples must be tuned by the guru as the strings of a lute (*vina*), each different from the others, yet each emitting sounds in harmony with all. Collectively they must form a key-board answering in all its parts to thy lightest touch (the touch of the Master). Thus their mind shall open for the harmonies of Wisdom, to vibrate as knowledge through each and all, resulting in effects pleasing to the presiding gods (tutelary or patron-angels) and useful to the Lanoo. So shall Wisdom be impressed for ever on their hearts and the harmony of the law shall never be broken.

6. Those who desire to acquire the knowledge leading to the *Siddhis* (occult powers) have to renounce all the vanities of life and of the world (here follows enumeration of the Siddhis).

7. None can feel the difference between himself and his fellow-students, such as " I am the wisest ", " I am more holy and pleasing to the teacher, or in my community, than my brother ", etc.—and remain an *upasaka*. His thoughts must be predominantly fixed upon his heart, chasing therefrom every hostile thought to any living being. It (the heart) must be full of the feeling of its non-separateness from the rest of beings as from all in Nature ; otherwise no success can follow.

8. A *Lanoo* (disciple) has to dread external living influence alone (magnetic emanations from living creatures). For this reason while at one with all in his *inner nature*, he must take care to separate his outer (external) body from every foreign influence : none must drink out of, (or eat in) his cup but himself. He must avoid bodily contact (i.e. being touched or touch) with human, as with animal being.

(No pet animals are permitted and it is forbidden even to touch certain trees and plants. A disciple has to live, so to say, in his own atmosphere in order to individualize it for occult purposes.)

9. The mind must remain blunt to all but the universal truths in nature, lest the Doctrine of the Heart should become only the Doctrine of the Eye (i.e. empty exoteric ritualism).

10. No animal food of whatever kind, nothing that has life in it, should be taken by the disciple. No wine, no spirits, or opium should be used; for these are like the *Lhamayin* (evil spirits), who fasten upon the unwary ; they devour the understanding.

(Wine and spirits are supposed to contain and preserve the bad magnetism of all the men who helped in their fabrication ; the meat of each animal, to preserve the psychic characteristics of its kind.)

11. Meditation, abstinence in all, the observation of moral duties, gentle thoughts, good deeds and kind words, goodwill to all and entire oblivion of Self, are most efficacious means of obtaining knowledge and preparing for the reception of higher wisdom.

12. It is only by virtue of a strict observance of the foregoing rules that a Lanoo can hope to acquire in good time the Siddhis of the Arhats, the growth which makes him become gradually One with the Universal All.

The first set of rules calls for no comments, as they are evidently of universal application, and differ only in the form of their expression from those which have been given in later books.

The second set is obviously on a very different footing. It is clearly formulated for Eastern students, and even among them chiefly for those who are able to devote their whole lives to their study, and to live secluded from the world in a monastery or occult community. The mere fact that there are sixty-one other rules which would be meaningless to European pupils show that they are neither intended

for all nor necessary for progress upon the Path, since many have
trodden that Path without knowing them. They are nevertheless of
great interest and value as recommendations. The moral and ethical
regulations are familiar to us, and so is the insistence upon the
necessity of perfect harmony and mutual understanding among those
disciples who have to learn and work together. It is to this latter
object that most of the rules here quoted are directed, and in the
case of a group of students its importance can scarcely be exaggerated.
In Western life we have insisted so strongly upon individualism, and
upon the undoubted right of each person to live his own life so long
as he does not incommode others, that we have to a large extent
forgotten the possibility of a really intimate union. Instead of being
united as the fingers of one hand, we live together as a number of
marbles in a bag, which is far from ideal from the inner point of view.

It might be supposed that these earnest exhortations to close
comradeship are inconsistent with rule 8, in which the chela is
instructed to avoid contact with others. This is not so, for the
directions refer to entirely different matters. The suggestion that
each should have his own cup (yes, and his own plate, knife, fork
and spoon also) is most excellent, for our present scheme of the
promiscuous use of half-washed cutlery and crockery is revolting
to persons of taste. The avoidance of unnecessary contact with
others has its advantage, for the indiscriminate mingling of auras is
highly undesirable. In the leisurely Indian life of the old days it was
so easy to escape uncomfortable proximity ; now that trains and
tramways have been introduced, and that the hurry of modern
business compels people to use them, even in the immemorial East
it is somewhat more difficult, and in Europe it would be practically
impossible. That is why a different method of dealing with this
problem of propinquity is now offered to us.

We can readily and effectively protect ourselves against
undesirable magnetism by forming round our bodies a shell which
will exclude it. Such a shell may be of etheric, astral or mental
matter, according to the purpose for which it is required. A description of the various kinds and the way to make them will be found in

my book on *The Hidden Side of Things*, which also includes the beautiful story of the Alexandrian monks, showing that there is another way of protecting oneself from evil influence which is even better than the formation of a shell; and that is by so filling one's heart with Divine Love that it radiates perpetually in all directions in the shape of torrents of love for one's fellow-men, so that that mighty stream acts as the most perfect of shields against the entrance of any current from without.

The regulation against keeping pet animals leaves out of account the fact that it is only through association with man that these creatures can be individualized. It appears to consider only the possibility that the man may allow himself to be adversely affected by the animal, and to forget altogether the beneficent influence which the man may intentionally bring to bear upon his younger brother. But quite possibly in the remote ages in which these rules were formulated there were no animals sufficiently developed to be approaching individualization.

In writing of the progress of the pupil, Madame Blavatsky advises strongly against marriage, maintaining that he cannot devote himself both to occultism and to a wife. It occurs to one that if the wife shared his devotion to occultism, this rather severe stricture would no longer be applicable. While it is true that the bachelor is in certain ways freer—as, for example, to throw up his business and start off to take up work in some foreign country, which he could hardly do if he had the responsibility of a wife and family—it must never be forgotten that the married man has the opportunity of serving the Cause in quite another way, by providing suitable vehicles and favourable surroundings for the many advanced egos who are waiting to descend into incarnation. Both types of work are needed, and there is room among the ranks of the disciples for both married and single. We find no condemnation of the married state in any of the three great guide-books which are given to us to light us on our way. The latest and simplest of these is Mr. J. Krishnamurti's wonderful little book, *At the Feet of the Master*.

AT THE FEET OF THE MASTER

Although Mr. Krishnamurti puts this book before the world, the words which it contains are almost entirely those of the Master Kuthumi. "These are not my words," the author says in his Foreword; "they are the words of the Master who taught me." When the book was written, Mr. Krishnamurti's body was thirteen years old, and it was necessary for the Master's plans that the knowledge requisite for Initiation should be conveyed to him as quickly as possible. The words contained in the book are those in which the Master tried to convey the whole essence of the necessary teaching in the simplest and briefest form. But for the requirements of this particular case, we might never have had a statement so concise and yet so complete, so simple and yet so all-inclusive. Many books have been written expounding the details of the stages of this preparatory path, and there has been much argument over the exact shades of meaning of Sanskrit and Pali words; but in this little manual the master boldly brushes all that aside and gives nothing but the essence of the teaching, expressed as far as may be in modern terms and illustrated from modern life.

For example, he translates the four qualifications *Viveka, Vairāgya, Shatsampatti* and *Mumukshutva* as Discrimination, Desirelessness, Good Conduct and Love. By no possible licence can the English word love be taken as a literal translation of the Sanskrit word *Mumukshutva*, for that unquestionably means simply the desire for liberation. The Master apparently argues thus: that the intense desire for freedom is desire for escape from all worldly limitations, so that even when among them, one may be absolutely free from the slightest feeling of bondage to them. Such freedom can be attained only by union with the Supreme, with the One who is behind all, that is to say, by union with God—and God is Love. Therefore only by our becoming thoroughly permeated with the Divine Love can freedom become possible for us.

There is no more beautiful or satisfactory description of the qualifications than that given in this book, and one may say with confidence that anyone who will thoroughly carry out its teaching will certainly pass immediately through the portal of Initiation. It was a very exceptional case for the Master to spend so much of his time in the direct teaching of one individual, but through Mr. Krishnamurti it has reached tens of thousands of others, and helped them to an immeasurable extent.

The story of how this little book came to be written is comparatively simple. Every night I had to take this boy in his astral body to the house of the Master, that instruction might be given him. The Master devoted perhaps fifteen minutes each night to talking to him, but at the end of each talk he always gathered up the main points of what he had said into a single sentence, or a few sentences, thus making an easy little summary which was repeated to the boy, so that he learnt it by heart. He remembered that summary in the morning and wrote it down. The book consists of these sentences, of the epitome of the Master's teaching, made by himself, and in his words. The boy wrote them down somewhat laboriously, because his English was not then very good. He knew all these things by heart and did not trouble particularly about the notes that he had made. A little later he went up to Benares with Dr. Annie Besant. While there he wrote to me, I being down at Adyar, and asked me to collect and send to him all the notes that he had made of what the Master had said. I arranged his notes as well as I could, and typed them all out. . . . and in due course the book was published.

Numbers of people, literally thousands, have written to say how their whole lives have been changed by the book, how everything has become different to them because they have read it. It has been translated into twenty-seven languages. There have been some forty editions of it, or more, and over a hundred thousand copies have been printed.[1] A wonderful work has been done by it. Other books also there are which the pupil will find of the utmost use to him in his endeavour to enter upon this

---

[1] Since this was written in 1925 many more editions and many tens of thousands of copies have been printed of *At the Feet of the Master*.

Path : *The Voice of the Silence* and *Light on the Path* were given to us for this purpose, and Dr. Annie Besant's wonderful books *In the Outer Court* and *The Path of Discipleship* will also be found of inestimable value. Since the first edition of this book was published Dr. Besant and I have jointly issued three volumes entitled *Talks on the Path of Occultism*, which form a commentary on the three classics above-mentioned.

THE DISCIPLE'S ATTITUDE

Having these books before him the pupil is left in no doubt as to what he should do. He should obviously make efforts along two particular lines—the development of his own character, and the undertaking of definite work for others. Clearly what is set before him in this teaching implies an altogether different attitude towards life in general ; that has been expressed by one of the Masters in the phrase : " He who wishes to work with us and for us must leave his own world and come into ours." That does not mean, as might usually be supposed by students of Oriental Literature, that the pupil must abandon the ordinary world of physical life and business, and retire to the jungle, the cave or the mountain ; but it does mean that he must abandon altogether the worldly attitude of mind and adopt instead of it the attitude of the Master.

The man of the world thinks of the events of life chiefly as they affect himself and his personal interest ; the Master thinks of them *only* as they affect the evolution of the world. Whatsoever on the whole tends to progress, and helps humanity along its path—that is good and to be supported ; whatsoever in any way hinders these things—that is undesirable and should be opposed or set aside. That is good which helps evolution ; that is evil which retards it. Here we have a criterion very different from that of the outer world ; a touch-stone by means of which we can quickly decide what we must support and what we must resist ; and we can apply it to qualities in our own character as well as to outer events. We shall be of use to the Master just in so far as we can work along with him, in however humble a fashion; we can best work along with him by making ourselves like to him, so that we shall regard the world as he regards it.

THE THREE DOORS

There is a poem which says:

> Three doors there are to the Temple
> To know, to work, to pray;
> And they who wait at the outer gate
> May enter by either way.

There are always the three ways: a man may bring himself to the Master's feet by deep study, because in that way he comes to know and to feel; and certainly he may be reached by deep devotion long continued, by the constant uplifting of the soul towards him. And there is also the method of throwing oneself into some definite activity for him. But it must be something definitely done for him with that thought in mind: " If there be credit or glory in this work I do not want it; I do it in my Master's name; to him be the glory and praise." The poem quoted above also says: " There be who nor pray nor study, but yet can work right well." And that is true. There are some who cannot make anything much of meditation, and when they try to study they find it very hard. They ought to continue to try both these things, because we must develop all sides of our nature, but most of all they should throw themselves into the work, and do something for their fellow-men.

That is the surest of all appeals—to do a thing in his name, to do a good act thinking of him, remembering that he is much more sensitive to thought than ordinary people. If a man thinks of a friend at a distance, his thought goes to that friend and influences him, so that the friend thinks of the sender of the thought unless his mind is much engaged at the moment with something else. But however much occupied a Master may be, thought directed to him makes a certain impression, and although perhaps at the moment he may not take any notice, yet the touch is there, and he will know of that and will send out his love and his energy in response to it.

THE MASTER'S WORK

The question is sometimes asked as to what particular labour should be undertaken. The answer is that all good work is the Master's work. Every one can find some good that he is able to do. In addition, some of the pupil's activity must consist in preparing himself for greater responsibility in the future. The duties of common life often combine something of both these things, for they provide a splendid training and education for those who do them well, and also offer many occasions for helping other people to progress in character and ideals, which is most emphatically the Master's business. All the varied activities of daily life come within our endeavour to serve the Master, when we learn to do all in his name and for him.

> The common course of life,
> The daily round we plod,
> The tasks that seem so wearisome
> May all be done for God.
>
> All may of Him partake;
> Nothing can be so mean
> Which, with this tincture, for His sake,
> Will not grow bright and clean.
>
> A servant with this clause
> Makes drudgery divine.
> Who sweeps a room, as for His laws
> Makes that small action fine.[1]

The Master's work is not something peculiar and apart from our fellows. To raise a good family who will serve him in turn, to make money to use in his service, to win power in order to help him with it—all these may be part of it; yet in doing these things the disciple must be ever on guard against self-deception, must see that he is not cloaking with the holiness of the Master's name what is, underneath, a selfish desire to wield power or handle money. The disciple of the Master has to look round and see what there is to do which is within his power. He must not look with disfavour upon the humblest task, thinking: "I am too good for this." In the

---

[1] Rev. George Herbert (A.D. 1593).

Master's business no part is more important than any other, though some portions are more difficult than others, and therefore require special training or unusual faculties or abilities.

At the same time certain organized efforts are being made in which the Masters take special interest. Foremost among these is the Theosophical Society, which was founded at their bidding and for their purposes. So unquestionably anything that one can do for his Theosophical Lodge is the very best thing to do. It may easily happen in many cases that one has no opportunity to do that ; he must then find some other way of service.

In quite unorganized ways also a great deal can be done. For example, the influence of beauty in human life is immeasurably uplifting, for beauty is God's manifestation in Nature, so—to give one instance—the roadside gardens of all who are striving along these lines should be notable for their neatness and beauty. Many people are careless in these small matters ; they are untidy ; they leave rubbish in their wake ; but all that indicates a character very far removed from the spirit of the Master.

If we work along the same lines as the Master works we shall come more and more into sympathy with him, and our thoughts will become more and more like his. This will bring us nearer and nearer to him both in thought and activity, and in so doing presently we shall attract his attention, for he is all the time watching the world in order to find those who will be of use in his work. Noticing us, he will presently draw us nearer to him for still closer and more detailed observation. That is usually done by bringing us into contact with one who is already his pupil. It is thus quite unnecessry for anyone to make any direct effort to attract his attention.

NONE IS OVERLOOKED

Madame Blavatsky told us that whenever a person joined the outer Theosophical Society the Master looked at him, and furthermore she said that in many cases the Great Ones guided people to join the Society because of their previous lives. So it would seem that they usually know a great deal about us before we know anything about them. The Adept never forgets anything. He appears to be always in full possession of all that has happened to him, and so if he does cast even a most casual glance at a person he will never thereafter overlook that person.

When a student understands this he will no longer ask: "What can I do that will attract the Master's attention?" He will know that it is quite unnecessary that we should try to do so, and that there is not the slightest fear that anyone will be overlooked.

I remember very well an incident of the early days of my own connection with the Great Ones, which bears on this point. I knew on the physical plane a man of vast erudition and of the most saintly character, who believed thoroughly in the existence of the Masters, and devoted his life to one object of qualifying himself for their service. He seemed to me a man in every way so entirely suitable for discipleship, so obviously better than myself in many ways, that I could not understand how it was that he was not already recognized; and so, being young in the work and ignorant, one day, when a good opportunity offered itself, very humbly and as it were apologetically, I mentioned his name to the Master, with the suggestion that he might perhaps prove a good instrument. A smile of kindly amusement broke out upon the Master's face as he said:

"Ah, you need not fear that your friend is being overlooked; no one can ever be overlooked; but in this case there still remains a certain karma to be worked out, which makes it impossible at the moment to accept your suggestion. Soon your friend will pass away from the physical plane, and soon he will return to it again, and then the expiation will be complete, and what you desire for him will have become possible."

And then, with the gentle kindness which is always so prominent a characteristic in him, he blended my consciousness with his in an even more intimate manner, and raised it to a plane far higher than I could then reach, and from that elevation he showed me how the Great Ones look out upon the world. The whole earth lay before us with all its millions of souls, undeveloped, most of them, and therefore inconspicuous ; but wherever amidst all that mighty multitude there was one who was approaching even at a great distance the point at which definite use could be made of him, he stood out among the rest just as the flame of a lighthouse stands out in the darkness of the night.

" Now you see," said the Master, " how utterly impossible it would be that anyone should be overlooked who is even within measurable distance of the possibility of acceptance as a probationer."

We can do nothing on our side but steadily work at the improvement of our character, and endeavour in every possible way, by the study of Theosophical works, by self-development, and by the unselfishness of our devotion to the interests of others, to fit ourselves for the honour which we desire, having within our minds the utter certainty that as soon as we are ready the recognition will assuredly come. But until we can be utilized economically—until, that is to say, the force spent upon us will bring forth, through our actions, at least as much result as it would if spent in any other way, it would be a violation of duty on the part of the Master to draw us into close relations with him.

We may be quite sure that there are in reality no exceptions to this rule, even though we may sometimes think that we have seen some. A man may be put upon probation by an Adept while he has still some obvious faults, but we may be sure that in such a case there are good qualities under the surface which far more than counterbalance the superficial defects. It is only the Master who can judge how far our faults affect our usefulness to Him. We cannot tell exactly to what extent any failings of ours would react upon his work ; but he, looking at the problem from above, can see quite clearly all the factors in the case, so that his decision is always just, and in the best interests of all. Sentimental considerations have no place in occultism, which has been defined as the apotheosis of common sense, working always for the greatest good of the greatest number. In it we learn of many new facts and forces, and we remodel our lives in accordance with this additional knowledge.

This after all differs in no way from our practice (or what *ought* to be our practice) on the physical plane. New discoveries along scientific lines are constantly being made, and we use them and adapt our lives to them. Why should we not do the same when the discoveries are on higher planes and connected with the inner life ? To understand the laws of nature and to live in harmony with them is the way to comfort, health and progress, both spiritual and physical.

Another consideration which sometimes comes into play is the working of the law of karma. Like the rest of us, the Great Masters of Wisdom have a long line of lives behind them, and in those lives they, like others, have made certain karmic ties and so sometimes it happens that a particular individual has a claim on them for some service rendered long ago. In the lines of past lives which we have examined we have sometimes come across instances of such a karmic link.

THE RESPONSIBILITY OF THE TEACHER

It is obviously necessary that a Master should be cautious in selecting candidates for discipleship, not only because his own work might be prejudicially affected by an unworthy pupil, but because the Teacher has a certain definite responsibility for the mistakes of the chela. Madame Blavatsky writes on this subject as follows :

There is one important fact with which the student should be made acquainted, namely, the enormous, almost limitless, responsibility assumed by the Teacher for the sake of the pupil. From the Gurus of the East who teach openly or secretly, down to the few Kabalists in Western lands who undertake to teach the rudiments of the Sacred Science to their disciples—those western Hierophants being often themselves ignorant of the danger they incur—one and all of these Teachers are subject to the same inviolable law. From the moment they begin *really* to teach, from the instant they confer *any* power—whether psychic, mental or physical—on their pupils, they take upon themselves all the sins of that pupil, in connection with the Occult Sciences, whether of omission or commission until the moment when initiation makes the pupil a Master and responsible in his turn. . . . Thus it is clear why the Teachers are so reticent, and why chelas are required to serve a seven years' probation to prove their fitness, and develop the qualities necessary to the security of both Master and pupil. [1]

[1] *Practical Occultism*, p. 4 *et seq.*

The Spiritual Guru, taking the student by the hand, leads him into and introduces him to a world entirely unknown to him. . . . . Even in common daily life, parents, nurses, tutors and instructors are generally held responsible for the habits and future ethics of a child. . . . So long as the pupil is too ignorant to be sure of his vision and powers of discrimination, is it not natural that it is the guide who should be responsible for the sins of him whom he has led into those dangerous regions ? [1]

As we shall see in subsequent chapters, when a man comes into close relation with the Master he has much more power than he had before. One who becomes a pupil of a Master can therefore do much more good, but he could also do much more harm if he happened to let his force go in the wrong direction. Very often the young disciple does not realize the power of his own thought. The man in the street may think something foolish or untrue without producing any serious effect, because he does not know how to think strongly; he may think ill of someone else without making any very great impression upon that person ; but if a disciple, who has the power of the Master within him, and has trained himself by long practice and meditation to use it, should misunderstand another person and think evil of him, his strong thought-current would act prejudicially upon that person, and might even seriously affect the whole of his future career.

If the victim really had the undesirable quality attributed to him, the pupil's potent thought would intensify it ; if no such quality existed, the same thought-form would suggest it, and might easily awaken it if it were latent—might even plant its seeds if there were as yet no signs of it. Sometimes the mind of a human being is in a condition of balance between a good course and an evil one ; and when that is the case the impact of a vivid thought-form from without may be sufficient to turn the scale, and may cause the weaker brother to embark upon a line of action the result of which, for good or evil, may extend through many incarnations. How careful then must the pupil be to see that the enhanced thought-power, with which his connection with his Master has endowed him, shall be used always to strengthen and never to weaken those towards whom it is directed !

[1] *Lucifer*, vol. II, 257.

Everything depends upon the form in which the thought is cast. We are of course assuming that the intention of the disciple is always of the noblest, but his execution may be defective. Suppose, for example, a weaker brother is addicted to the vice of intemperance. If the thought of the pupil should happen to turn in the direction of that man, his musings might obviously take several different lines. Let us hope that there would be no danger of his despising the man for his weakness, or shrinking from him with aversion or disgust. But it is quite possible that he might think : " What a frightful crime is that man's drunkenness ; how terrible is its effect upon his wife and children ! How can he be so inconsiderate, so selfish, so cruel ? " Every word of it true, quite a reasonable thought, fully justified by the circumstances, and in no way unkind ; but *not helpful to the victim*. However correct and unimpeachable is the sentiment, the prominent idea is that of blame to the sinner, and the effect of the thought-form is to crush him still further into the mire. Why not take the far stronger line of definite mental action : " I invoke the God within that man ; I call upon the ego to assert himself, to conquer the weakness of the lower self, to say ' I can and I will ' " ? If that be done, the dominant idea is not blame but encouragement, and the effect is not to depress the sufferer, but to help him to raise himself from the slime of his hopelessness to the firm ground of virility and freedom.

WRONG IDEAS

Another quality most essential for the aspirant is open-mindedness and freedom from bigotry of any sort. Madame Blavatsky once told us that her Master had remarked that erroneous beliefs were sometimes a great obstacle. As an example he said that there were a hundred thousand of the Indian *sannyasis* who were leading the purest lives and were quite ready for discipleship, except for the fact that their ingrained wrong thought on certain subjects made it impossible for even the Masters to penetrate their auras. Such thoughts, he said, drew round them undesirable elementals, most unpleasant influences, which reacted upon them and intensified their misconceptions, so that until they developed enough reason and intuition to shake themselves free from these they were practically impervious to suggestions.

It has been said that an honest man is the noblest work of God ; and Colonel Ingersoll once parodied that proverb by reversing it, and saying that an honest God was the noblest work of man—by which he meant that each man arrives at his conception of God by personifying those qualities in himself which he thinks most worthy of admiration, and then raising them to the nth power. So if a man has a noble conception of God, it shows that there is much nobility in his own nature even though he may not always live up to his ideal.

But a wrong conception of God is one of the most serious hindrances under which a man can suffer. The idea of the Jehovah of the Old Testament, bloodthirsty, jealous, mean and cruel, has been responsible for an amount of harm in the world that cannot easily be estimated. Any thought of God which induces *fear* of him is absolutely disastrous, and precludes all hope of real progress ; it shuts a man up in the darkest of dungeons instead of leading him onward and upward into the glory of the sunlight. It draws round him a host of the type of elemental which revels in fear, gloats over it and intensifies it by every means within his power. When a man is in that parlous condition it is all but impossible to help him ; wherefore to teach a man (still more, a child) such a blasphemous doctrine is one of the worst crimes that anyone can commit. The disciple must be utterly free from all cramping superstitions of this kind.

THE EFFECT OF MEDITATION

Remember also that every one who meditates upon the Master makes a definite connection with him, which shows itself to clairvoyant vision as a kind of line of light. The Master always subconsciously feels the impinging of such a line, and sends out in response a steady stream of magnetism which continues to play long

after the meditation is over. The methodical practice of such meditation and concentration is thus of the utmost help to the aspirant,
and regularity is one of the most important factors in producing the
result. It should be undertaken daily at the same hour, and we
should steadily persevere with it, even though no obvious effect may
be produced. When no result appears we must be especially careful
to avoid depression, because that makes it more difficult for a
Master's influence to act upon us, and it also shows that we are
thinking of ourselves more than of him.

In beginning this practice of meditation it is desirable to
watch closely its physical effects. Methods prescribed by those who
understand the matter ought never to cause headache or any other
pain, yet such results do sometimes occur in particular cases. It is
true that meditation strains the thought and attention a little further
than its customary point in any individual, but that should be so
carefully done, so free from any kind of excess, as not to cause any
physical ill-effects. Sometimes a person takes it up too strenuously
and for too long at a time, or when the body is not in a fit state of
health, and the consequence is a certain amount of suffering. It is
fatally easy to press one's physical brain just a little too far, and when
that happens it is often difficult to recover equilibrium. Sometimes
a condition may be produced in a few days which it will take years
to set right; so anyone who begins to feel any unpleasant effects
should at once stop the practice for a while and attend to his physical
health, and if possible consult someone who knows more than he
does about the subject.

COMMON HINDRANCES

People very often come or write to Dr. Besant or to myself
and say: "Why does not the Master use *me*? I am so earnest and
devoted to him. I do so want to be used. I want him to take me
and teach me. Why does he not do so?"

There may be many reasons why he does not. Sometimes a
person, asking that, has some prominent fault which is in itself quite

a sufficient reason. Not infrequently, I regret to say, it is pride. A person may have so good a conceit of himself that he is not amenable to teaching, although he thinks that he is. Very often in this civilization of ours the fault is irritability. A good and worthy person may have his nerves all ajangle, so that it would be impossible for him to be drawn into very close and constant touch with the Master. Sometimes the impediment is curiosity. Some are surprised to hear that that is a serious failing, but certainly it is—curiosity about the affairs of other people, and especially about their occult standing or development. It would be quite impossible that a Master should draw near to himself one who had that failing.

Another common hindrance is readiness to be offended. Many a good and earnest aspirant is so easily offended as to be of practically no use in the work, because he cannot get on with other people. He will have to wait until he has learnt to adapt himself, and to co-operate with any person whatever.

Many people who make the inquiry have failings of this kind, and they do not like it if their fault is pointed out to them. They do not generally believe that they have it, and imagine that we are in error ; but in rare cases they are willing to profit by the suggestion. I remember very well a lady coming to me in an American city, and asking the question : " What is the matter with me ? Why may I not draw near to the Master ? " " Do you really want to know ? " I asked. Yes, certainly, she really wished to know. She adjured me to look at her occultly, or clairvoyantly or in any way I wished, at all her vehicles and her past lives, and to decide thereby. I took her at her word and said : " Well, if you really want to know, there is too much ego in your cosmos. You are thinking all about yourself and not enough about the work."

Of course she was terribly offended ; she flounced out of the room, and said she did not think much of my clairvoyance ; but that lady had the courage to come back two years later and say : " What you told me was quite true, and I am going to put it right and to work hard at it." That story has repeated itself many times, except that this is the only case in which the person came back and acknowledged the fault. Unquestionably the disciple who is willing to see himself as others see him may learn much that will help him to progress. I recollect that one of the Masters once remarked that the first duty of a chela is to hear without anger anything the guru may say. He should be eager to change himself, to get rid of his faults. Madame Blavatsky said : " Chelaship has been defined by a Master as a psychic resolvent, which eats away all dross and leaves only the pure gold behind."[1]

Self-centredness is only another form of pride, but it is very prominent at the present day. The personality which we have been building up for many thousands of years has grown strong and often self-assertive, and it is one of the hardest tasks to reverse its attitude and compel it to acquire the habit of looking at things from the standpoint of others. One must certainly step out of the centre of his own circle, as I explained in *The Inner Life*, if he wishes to come to the Master.

It sometimes happens, however, that those who ask the question have not any particular outstanding defect, and when one looks them over, one can only say : " I do not see any definite reason, any one fault which is holding you back, but you will have to grow a little all round." That is an unpalatable thing to have to tell a person, but it is the fact ; they are not yet big enough, and must grow before they will be worthy.

One thing which often prevents people from coming into touch with the Masters is lack of faith and will; unless a person tries earnestly with the full belief that he can, and with the determination that he will, succeed one day, and that that day shall come as soon as possible, it is fairly certain that he will not prevail. While we know that in some of us there are failings, yet I do think there are at least some cases among us in which it is just the lack of that intense determination which holds us back.

It requires some strength and bigness to put oneself in the attitude towards the work which the Master himself adopts, because, in addition to any defect of our own, we have the whole pressure of

---

[1] *Five Years of Theosophy*, second edition, p. 36.

the thought of the world against us.   Madame Blavatsky gave us the fullest warning in the beginning about both these difficulties.   She writes :

> As soon as anyone pledges himself as Probationer, certain occult effects ensue.   The first is the throwing outward of everything latent in the nature of the man—his faults, habits, qualities or subdued desires, whether good, bad or indifferent.   For instance, if a man be vain or a sensualist, or ambitious . . . these vices are sure to break out, even if he has hitherto successfully concealed or repressed them.   They will come to the front irrepressibly, and he will have to fight a hundred times harder than before, until he kills all such tendencies in himself.

> On the other hand, if he be good, generous, chaste and abstemious, or has any virtue latent and concealed in him, it will work its way out as irrepressibly as the rest. . . . This is an immutable law in the domain of the occult.[1]

> Does the reader recall the older proverb :   " Let sleeping dogs lie " ?   There is a world of occult meaning in it.   No man or woman knows his or her moral strength until it is tried.   Thousands go through life very respectably because they have never been put to the test. . . . One who undertakes to try for chelaship by that very act rouses . . . every sleeping passion of his animal nature. . . . The chela is called to face not only all the latent evil propensities of his nature, but in addition the momentum of maleficent forces accumulated by the community and nation to which he belongs. . . . If he is content to go along with his neighbours and be almost as they are—perhaps a little better or somewhat worse than the average—no one may give him a thought.   But let it be known that he has been able to detect the hollow mockery of social life, its hypocrisy, selfishness, sensuality, cupidity and other bad features, and has determined to lift himself up to a higher level, at once he is hated, and every bad, bigoted or malicious nature sends at him a current of opposing will-power '.[2]

Those who drift along with the current of evolution, and will reach this stage in the very far distant future, will find it much easier, for popular opinion at that period will be in harmony with these ideals.   We have now, however, to resist what the Christian world call temptation, the steady pressure of opinion from without, for millions of people round us are thinking personal thoughts.   To make a stand against these needs real effort, true courage and perseverance.   We must doggedly keep to the task, and though we may fail again and again we must not lose heart, but get up and go on.

The astral and mental bodies of an aspirant ought to be continually exhibiting four or five big and glowing emotions—love,

[1] *The Secret Doctrine*, vol. 5, p. 417.
[2] *Five Years of Theosophy*, second edition, p. 35

devotion, sympathy and intellectual aspiration among them. But instead of a few great feelings vibrating splendidly and clearly with fine colour, one generally sees the astral body spotted over with red and brown and grey and black vortices, often a hundred or more. They are somewhat like a mass of warts on a physical body, preventing the skin from being sensitive as it should be. The candidate must see to it that these are removed, and that the usual tangle of petty emotions is entirely combed away.

DEVOTION MUST BE COMPLETE

There can be no half measures on this Path. Many people are in the position of those much-maligned individuals Ananias and Sapphira. It will be remembered how they (not at all unnaturally nor in a blameworthy manner) wanted to keep something to fall back upon, as they were not quite sure that the new Christian movement was going to be a success. They were very enthusiastic, and wanted to give all that they could ; but they did feel that it was the path of wisdom to keep a little back in case the movement failed. For that they were not in the least to be blamed ; but what they *did* do which was most damaging and improper was that, though keeping something back, they did not admit the fact, but pretended that they had given all. There are many today who follow their example ; I hope the story is not true, because the Apostle was certainly somewhat severe upon them.

We do not give everything, but keep back a little bit of ourselves—I do not mean of our money, but of personal feeling deep down, which holds us back from the Master's feet. In occultism that will not do. We must follow the Master without reserve, not saying within : " I will follow the Master so long as he does not want me to work with such-and-such a person ; I will follow the Master so long as all that I do is recognized and mentioned in the papers ! " We must not make conditions. I do not mean that we should give up our ordinary physical plane duties, but simply that our whole self should be at the Master's disposal. We must be prepared to yield anything, to go anywhere—not as a test, but because the love of the work is the biggest thing in our lives.

Sometimes people ask: " If I do all these things how long will it be before the Master takes me on probation ? " There will be no delay, but there is much virtue in the word " if " in this question. It is not so easy to do them perfectly, and were that required it would no doubt be a long time before we could hope for discipleship. But one of the Masters has said : " He who does his best does enough for us." If one has not delight in service for its own sake, but is only looking for the reward of occult recognition, he has not really the right spirit. If he has the right attitude he will go on tirelessly with the good work, leaving the Master to announce his pleasure when and how he may choose.

Our Hindu brethren have a very sound tradition in this matter. They would say : " Twenty or thirty years of service is as nothing ; there are many in India who have served for the whole of their lives, and have never had any outward recognition, though inwardly they are being guided by a Master." I met with an instance of this a few years ago ; I had to make some inquiry with regard to some of our Indian brethren about these things, and the answer of the Master was : " For forty years I have had those men under observation. Let them be content with that." And they were more than content. Since then, I may mention, they have received further recognition and have become Initiates. Our Indian brother knows within himself that the Master is aware of his service ; but the pupil does not mind whether he chooses to take any outward notice of it or not. He would, of course, be exceedingly happy if the Master did notice him, but if that does not happen he goes on just the same.

CHAPTER IV

PROBATION

THE LIVING IMAGE

OUT of the ranks of earnest students and workers of the kind I have already described, the Master has on many occasions selected his pupils. But before he definitely accepts them he takes special precautions to assure himself that they are really the kind of people whom he can draw into intimate contact with himself; and that is the object of the stage called Probation. When he thinks of a man as a possible pupil, he usually asks one who is already closely linked with him to bring the candidate to him astrally. There is not generally much ceremony connected with this step; the Master gives a few words of advice, tells the new pupil what will be expected of him, and often, in his gracious way, he may find some reason to congratulate him on the work that he has already accomplished.

He then makes a living image of the pupil—that is to say, he moulds out of mental, astral and etheric matter an exact counterpart of the causal, mental, astral and etheric bodies of the neophyte, and keeps that image at hand, so that he may look at it periodically. Each image is magnetically attached to the person whom it represents, so that every variation of thought and feeling in him is accurately reproduced in it by a sympathetic vibration, and thus by a single glance at the image the Master can see at once whether during the period since he last looked at it there has been any sort of disturbance in the bodies which it represents—whether the man has been losing his temper, or allowing himself to be a prey to impure feelings, worry, depression, or anything of the kind. It is only after he has seen that for a considerable time no serious excitement has taken place in the vehicles represented by the image, that he will admit the pupil into near relation with himself.

When the pupil is accepted he must be drawn into a unity with his Master closer than anything we can imagine or understand ; the Master wants to blend his aura with his own, so that through it his forces may be constantly acting without special attention on his part. But a relation so intimate as this cannot act in one direction only ; if among the vibrations of the pupil there are some which would cause disturbance in the astral and mental bodies of the Adept as they react upon him, such union would be impossible. The prospective pupil would have to wait until he had rid himself of those vibrations. A probationary pupil is not necessarily better than other people who are not on probation ; he is only more suitable in certain ways for the Master's work, and it is advisable to subject him to the test of time, for many people, swept upwards by enthusiasm, appear at first to be most promising and eager to serve, but unfortunately become tired after a while and slip back. The candidate must conquer any emotional failings that he may have, and go on steadily working until he becomes sufficiently calm and pure. When for quite a long time there has been no serious upheaval in the living image, the Master may feel that the time has come when he can usefully draw the pupil nearer to him.

We must not think of the living image as recording only defects or disturbances. It mirrors the whole condition of the pupil's astral and mental consciousness, so it should record much of benevolence and joyousness, and should radiate forth peace on earth and good-will to men. Never forget that not only a passive but also an active goodness is always a prerequisite for advancement. To do no harm is already much ; but remember that it is written of our Great Exemplar that he went about doing good. And when the Lord Buddha was asked to epitomize the whole of his teaching in one verse, he began : " Cease to do evil," but immediately he continued : " Learn to do good."

If a pupil on probation does something usually good, for the moment the Master flashes a little more attention on him, and if he sees fit he may send a wave of encouragement of some sort, or he may put some work in the pupil's way and see how he does it. Generally, however, he delegates that task to some of his senior pupils. We are supposed to offer opportuities to the candidate, but to do so is a serious responsibility. If the person takes the opportunity, all is well ; but if he does not, it counts as a bad mark against him. We should often like to give opportunities to people, but we hesitate, because although if they take them it will do them much good, if they do not take them it will be a little harder to do so next time.

It will be seen, then, that the link of the pupil on probation with his Master is chiefly one of observation and perhaps occasional use of the pupil. It is not the custom of the Adepts to employ special or sensational tests, and in general, when an adult is put on probation, he is left to follow the ordinary course of his like, and the way in which the living image reproduces his response to the trials and problems of the day gives quite sufficient indication of his character and progress. When from this the Master concludes that the person will make a satisfactory disciple, he will draw him nearer and accept him. Sometimes a few weeks is sufficient to determine this ; sometimes the period stretches into years.

EFFECT OF CRUELTY TO CHILDREN

In the Chapter on " Our Relation to Children " in *The Hidden Side of Things* I have dealt at considerable length with what is necessary for the training of children, that they may preserve all that is best in what they bring from the past and may develop into full flower the many beautiful characteristics of their nature, which are so generally, alas, ruthlessly destroyed by uncomprehending elders. There I have spoken among other things of the devastating effects of fear induced in children by roughness and cruelty ; but on that subject I should like to add here some mention of an experience which illustrated the unspeakably terrible results which sometimes follow in its wake. Parents who have children of an age to be sent to school cannot be too careful and searching in their inquiries before they entrust those children to an instructor, lest ineradicable harm be done to the little ones for whom they are responsible.

Some time ago a very striking instance of the calamity which may in certain cases be brought about by such brutality came prominently before my notice. I had the very great honour of being present at the Initiation of one of our younger members, the Initiator on that occasion being the Lord Maitreya himself. In the course of the ceremonial the candidate, as usual, had to reply to many questions dealing largely with the manner in which help can best be given in certain difficult or unusual cases, and a special interrogation was added as to whether he forgave and could help a certain man who had treated him with terrible harshness and cruelty in early childhood.

The Initiator made an image of an aura with the most wonderfully delicate little puffs or touches or shoots of lovely colour, of light playing over its surface, as it were peeping out of it, and then drawing in again, and said : " Those are the seeds of the highest and noblest qualities of mankind—fragile, delicate as gossamer, to be developed only in an atmosphere of deepest, purest love, without one touch of fear or shrinking. He who, being otherwise ready, can unfold and strengthen them fully may reach Adeptship in that same life. That was the fate we had hoped for you, but those to whom I entrusted you (because they offered you to my service even before birth) allowed you to fall into the hands of this person, who was so utterly unworthy of such a trust. This was your aura before the blight of his wickedness fell upon you. Now see what his cruelty made of you."

Then the aura changed and twisted about horribly, and when it was still again all the beautiful little shoots had disappeared, and in their place were innumerable little scars, and the Lord explained that the harm done could not be cancelled in the present life, and said : " I hope that in this life you will attain Arhatship ; but for the final consummation we must wait awhile. In our eyes there is no greater crime than thus to check the progress of a soul."

As the candidate saw this aura writhe and harden, saw all its fair promise ruthlessly destroyed by the brutality of this man, he felt again for a moment what he had to a great extent forgotten—the agony of the small boy sent away from home, the ever-hovering fear and shrinking, the incredulous horror, the feeling of flaming outrage from which there is no escape or redress, the sickening sense of utter helplessness in the grasp of a cruel tyrant, the passionate resentment at his wicked injustice, with no hope, no foothold anywhere in the abyss, no God to whom to appeal; and seeing this in his mind, I who watched understood something of the terrible tragedy of childhood, and why its effects are so far-reaching.

It is not only when approaching Adeptship that this most loathsome sin of cruelty to children checks progress. All the new and higher qualities which should now be unfolding show themselves in light and delicate buds of a similar nature, though at a lower level than those described above. In thousands of cases these are ruthlessly crushed out by the insensate ferocity of parent or teacher, or repressed by the brutal bullying of bigger boys at the boarding-school; and thus many good people remain at the same level through several incarnations, while their tormentors fall back in evolution. There are certainly many egos coming into incarnation who, although they fall far short of the great heights of Initiation, are nevertheless unfolding rapidly, and need now to add to their characters some of these further and more delicate developments; and for the advancement intended for them also brutality would be fatal.

I had not heard, until the occasion mentioned above, that the last life in which Adeptship is attained must have absolutely perfect surroundings in childhood; but the appropriateness of the idea is obvious when once it is put before us. That is probably one reason why so few students gain Adeptship in European bodies, for we are much behind the rest of the world in that particular. It is at any rate abundantly clear that nothing but evil can ever follow from this ghastly custom of cruelty. We should certainly work wherever possible for its suppression, and should be, as I said in the beginning, most especially careful to make certain that no children for whom they are in any way responsible shall be in any danger from this particular form of crime.

THE MASTER OF CHILDREN

The Lord Maitreya has frequently been called the Teacher of Gods and Men, and that fact is sometimes expressed in a different way by saying that in the great kingdom of the spiritual work he is the Minister for Religion and Education. It is not only that at certain intervals, when he sees it to be desirable, he either incarnates himself, or sends a pupil, to state the eternal truth in some new way —as we may put it, to found a new religion. Quite apart from that, he is constantly in-charge of *all* religions, and whatever new and beautiful teaching is sent out through any of them, new or old, it is always inspired by him. We know little of the methods of world-wide instruction which he adopts ; there are many ways of teaching apart from the spoken word ; and it is certain that it is his constant and daily endeavour to raise the intellectual conceptions of millions of angels and of men.

His right-hand man in all this marvellous work is his assistant and destined successor, the Master Kuthumi, just as the assistant and destined successor of the Lord Vaivasvata Manu is the Master Morya. Just because, then, the Master Kuthumi is the ideal Teacher, it is to him that we have to bring those who are to be put on probation or accepted at an early age. It may be that later on in life they will be used by other Masters for other portions of the work ; but at any rate they all (or almost all) begin under the tutelage of the Master Kuthumi. It has been part of my task for many years to endeavour to train along the right lines any young person whom the Master regards as hopeful ; he brings them in contact with me on the physical plane and usually gives brief directions as to what qualities he wants developing in them, and what instruction should be given to them. Naturally he, in his infinite wisdom, does not deal with these younger brains and bodies exactly as with those of older people.

In the case of elder people put upon probation, they are left to a large extent to find the most suitable work for themselves ; but with the younger people he sometimes quite definitely puts a piece of work in the way of one of them and watches to see how he does it. He condescends sometimes to give special messages of encouragement and instruction to individuals among these young people, and even to give advice as to their training. Extracts from some of those messages are given here :

ADVICE FROM THE MASTER

" I know that your one object in life is to serve the Brotherhood ; yet do not forget that there are higher steps before you, and that progress on the Path means sleepless vigilance. You must not only be always *ready* to serve ; you must be ever watching for opportunities—nay, *making* opportunities to be helpful in small things, in order that when the greater work comes you may not fail to see it.

" Never for a moment forget your occult relationship ; it should be an ever-present inspiration to you—not only a shield from the fatuous thoughts which float around us, but a constant stimulus to spiritual activity. The vacuity and pettiness of ordinary life should be impossible for us, though not beyond our comprehension and compassion. The ineffable bliss of Adeptship is not yet yours, but remember that you are already one with those who live that higher life ; you are dispensers of their sunlight in this lower world, so you, too, at your level, must be radiant suns of love and joy. The world may be unappreciative, uncomprehending ; but your duty is to shine.

" Do not rest on your oars. There are still higher peaks to conquer. The need of intellectual development must not be forgotten ; and we must unfold within ourselves sympathy, affection, tolerance. Each must realize that there are other points of view than his own, and that they may be just as worthy of attention. All coarseness or roughness of speech, all tendency to argumentativeness, must absolutely disappear ; one who is prone to it should check himself when the impulse towards it arises ; he should say little, and that always with delicacy and courtesy. Never speak without first thinking whether what you are going to say is both kind and sensible. He who tries to develop love within himself will be saved from many mistakes. Love is the supreme virtue of all, without which all other qualifications water but the sand.

"Thoughts and feelings of an undesirable kind must be rigorously excluded ; you must work at them until they are impossible to you. Touches of irritability ruffle the calm sea of the consciousness of the Brotherhood. Pride must be eliminated, for it is a serious bar to progress. Exquisite delicacy of thought and speech is needed —the rare aroma of perfect tact which can never jar or offend. That is hard to win, yet you may reach it if you will.

"Definite service, and not mere amusement, should be your aim ; think, not what you want to do, but what you can do that will help someone else ; forget about yourself, and consider others. A pupil must be constantly kind, obliging, helpful—not now and then, but all the time. Remember, all time which is not spent in service (or fitting yourself for service) is for us *lost* time.

"When you see certain evils in yourself, take them in hand manfully and effectively. Persevere, and you will succeed. It is a question of will-power. Watch for opportunities and hints ; be efficient. I am always ready to help you, but I cannot do the work *for* you ; the effort must come from *your* side. Try to deepen yourself all round and to live a life of utter devotion to service."

———

"You have done well, but I want you to do better yet. I have tested you by giving you opportunities to help, and so far you have taken them nobly. I shall therefore give you more and greater opportunities, and your progress will depend upon your recognizing them and availing yourself of them. Remember that the reward of successful work is always the opening out before you of more work, and that faithfulness in what seem to you small things leads to employment in matters of greater importance. I hope that you will soon draw closer to me, and in so doing will help your brothers along the Path which leads to the feet of the King. Be thankful that you have a great power of love, that you know how to flood your world with sunlight, to pour yourself out with royal prodigality, to scatter largess like a king ; that indeed is well, but take care lest in the heart of this great flower of love there should be a tiny touch of pride, which might spread as does an almost invisible spot of decay, until it has tainted and corrupted the whole blossom. Remember what our great Brother has written : ' Be humble if thou wouldst attain to wisdom ; be humbler still when wisdom thou has mastered.' Cultivate the modest fragrant plant humility, until its sweet aroma permeates every fibre of your being.

"When you try for unity, it is not enough to draw the others into yourself, to enfold them with your aura, to make *them* one with *you*. To do that is already a long step, but you must go yet further, and make *yourself* one with each of *them* ; you must enter into the very hearts of your brothers, and understand them ; never from curiosity, for a brother's heart is both a secret and a sacred place ; one must not seek to pry into it or discuss it, but rather endeavour reverently to comprehend, to sympathize, to help. It is easy to criticize others from one's own point of view ; it is more difficult to get to know them and love them ; but that is the only way to bring them along with you. I want you to grow quickly that I may use you in the Great Work ; to help you in that I give you my blessing."

"Daughter, you have done well in exercising your influence to civilize as far as may be the rougher elements around you, and to help another pure soul upon her way to me. That will be ever a bright star in your crown of glory ; continue your help to her, and see whether there be not other stars which you can presently add to that crown. This good work of yours has enabled me to draw you closer to me far earlier than would otherwise have been the case. There is no more certain method of rapid progress than to devote oneself to helping others upon the upward Path. You have been fortunate, too, in meeting a comrade from of old, for two who can really work together are more efficient than if they were putting forth the same amount of strength separately. You have begun well; continue to move along the same line with swiftness and certainty."

———

" I welcome you, the latest recruit to our glorious band. It is not easy for you to forget yourself entirely, to yield yourself without reservation to the service of the world; yet that is what is required of us—that we should live only to be a blessing to others, and to do the work which is given us to do. You have made a good beginning in the process of self-development, but much yet remains to be done. Repress even the slightest shade of irritability, and be ready always to receive advice and instruction; cultivate humility and self-sacrifice, and fill yourself with a fervid enthusiasm for service. So shall you be a fitting instrument in the hand of the Great Master, a soldier in the army of those who save the world. To help you in that I now take you as a probationary pupil."

———

" I am pleased with you, but I want you to do more yet. For you, my child, you have the capacity of making rapid progress, and I want you to set this before yourself as an object which you are determined at all costs to achieve. Some of the obstacles which you are instructed to overcome may seem to you unimportant, but in reality they are not so, because they are the surface indications of an interior condition which must be altered. That means a radical change which it will not be easy for you to make, but the effort is well worth your while. The rules which I wish you to make for yourself are these :

" (1) Forget yourself and the desires of your personality, and remember only the service of others, devoting your strength, your thought, your enthusiasm wholly to that.

" (2) Do not offer an opinion on any matter unless directly asked for it.

" (3) Before speaking, always consider how what you say will affect others.

"'(4) Never betray, or comment upon, a brother's weakness.

" (5) Remember that you have yet much to learn, and therefore may often be in error; so speak with becoming modesty.

" (6) When called, move *at once*, not waiting to finish what you happen to be reading or doing; if you are performing a duty of importance, explain very gently what it is.

" I wish to draw you closer to me, and if you will keep these rules I shall soon be able to do so. Meantime, my blessing rests upon you."

BECOME AS LITTLE CHILDREN

Many who read these instructions may be surprised by their extreme simplicity. They may even despise them as being little suited to guide and help people in the immense complexity of our modern civilization. But he who thinks thus forgets that it is of the essence of the life of the pupil that he shall lay aside all this complexity, that he shall, as the Master put it, " come out of your world into ours ", come into a world of thought in which life is simple and one-pointed, in which right and wrong are once more clearly defined, in which the issues before us are straight and intelligible. It is the simple life that the disciple should be living; it is the very simplicity which he attains which makes the higher progress possible to him. We have made our life an entanglement and an uncertainty, a mass of

confusion, a storm of cross-currents, in which the weak fail and sink ;
but the pupil of the Master must be strong and sane, he must take
his life in his own hands, and make it simple with a divine simplicity. His mind must brush aside all these man-made confusions
and delusions and go straight as an arrow to its mark. "Except ye be converted, and become as little children, ye shall in
no wise enter into the kingdom of heaven." And the kingdom of heaven, remember, is the Great Brotherhood of the
Adepts.[1]

    We see from the extracts how high is the ideal which the
Master sets before his pupils, and perhaps it may seem to some of
them to be what in theology we call a counsel of perfection—that is
to say, a goal or condition impossible to reach perfectly as yet, but
still one at which we must constantly aim. But all aspirants are
aiming high, and no one yet can fully reach that at which he aims ;
otherwise he would not need to be in physical incarnation at all.
We are very far from being perfect, but the young people who can
be brought close to the Great Ones have a most wonderful opportunity, just because of their youth and plasticity. It is so much easier
for them to eliminate those things which are not quite what they
should be than it is for older people. If they can cultivate the habit
of taking the right point of view, of acting for the right reasons, and
of being in the right attitude, the whole of their lives, they will
steadily draw nearer and nearer to the ideal of the Masters. If the
pupil who has been put on probation could see while awake in his
physical body the living images that the Master makes, he would
understand much more fully the importance of what may seem to
be but minor details.

EFFECTS OF IRRITABILITY

    Irritability is a common difficulty ; as I have already explained,
to be irritable is a thing which is likely enough to happen to anyone
living in his present civilization, where people are always very highly

---

[1] See *The Hidden Side of Christian Festivals*, pp. 12, 446.

strung. We live to a large extent in a civilization of torturing noises ; and above all things noise jars the nerves and causes irritation. The experience of going down into the city and returning home feeling quite shattered and tired is a common one for sensitive people. Many other things are contributory, but principally the weariness is due to the constant noise, and the pressure of so many astral bodies vibrating at different rates, and all excited and disturbed by trifles. It makes it very difficult to avoid irascibility—especially for the pupil, whose bodies are more highly strung and sensitive than those of the ordinary man.

Of course, this petulance is somewhat superficial ; it does not penetrate deeply ; but it is better to avoid even a superficial peevishness as far as possible, because its effects last so much longer than we usually realize. If there is a heavy storm, it is the wind that first stirs the waves ; but the waves will continue to swell long after the wind has died down. That is the effect produced on water, which is comparatively heavy ; but the matter of the astral body is far finer than water, and the vibrations set going penetrate much more deeply, and therefore produce a more lasting effect. Some slight, unpleasant, temporary feeling, which passes out of mind in ten minutes, perhaps, may yet produce an effect on the astral body lasting for forty-eight hours. The vibrations do not settle down again for a considerable period of time.

When such a fault as this is known, it can most effectually be removed not by focussing attention upon it, but by endeavouring to develop the opposite virtue. One way of dealing with it is to set one's thought steadfastly against it, but there is no doubt that this course of action arouses opposition in the mental or astral elemental, so that often a better method is to try to develop consideration for others, based of course fundamentally on one's love towards them. A man who is full of love and consideration will not allow himself to speak or even to think irritably towards them. If the man can be filled with that idea the same result will be attained without exciting opposition from the elementals.

SELFISHNESS

There are many other forms of selfishness that can delay the pupil's progress very seriously. Laziness is one of these. I have seen a person enjoying himself very much with a book, who did not like to leave it in order to be punctual; another perhaps writes very badly, careless of the inconvenience and the damage to eyes and temper of those who have to read his calligraphy. Little negligences tend to make one less sensitive to high influences, to make life untidy and ugly for other persons, and to destroy self-control and efficiency. Efficiency and punctuality are essential, if satisfactory work is to be done. Many people are inefficient; when a piece of work is given to them, they do not finish it thoroughly, but make all kinds of excuses; or when they are asked for some information, they do not know how to find it. People differ much in this respect. We may ask a question of someone, and he will answer: "I don't know"; but another will say: "Well, I don't know, but I will go and find out", and he returns with the required information. In the same way one person goes to do a thing, and comes back and says he could not do it; but another holds on until it is done.

Yet in all good work the pupil must always think of the benefit that will result to others and of the opportunity to serve the Master in these matters—which even when they are small materially are great in spiritual value—not of the good karma resulting to himself, which would be only another and very subtle form of self-centredness. Remember how the Christ put it: "Inasmuch as ye have done it unto the least of these my brethren, ye have done it unto me."

Other subtle effects of the same kind are to be seen in depression and jealousy, and aggressive assertion of one's rights. An Adept has said: "Think less about your rights and more about your duties." There are some occasions in dealing with the outside world when the pupil might find it necessary gently to state what he needs, but amongst his fellow-pupils there are no such things as rights, but only opportunities. If a man feels annoyed, he begins to project from himself aggressive feelings ; he may not go so far as actual hatred, but he is creating a dull glow in his astral body and affecting the mental body as well.

WORRY

Similar disturbances are frequently produced in the mental body, and are equally disastrous in their effects. If a man allows himself to be greatly worried over some problem, and turns it over and over again in his mind without reaching any conclusion, he has thereby caused something like a storm in his mental body. Owing to the exceeding fineness of the vibrations at this level, the word storm only partially expresses the reality ; we should in some ways come nearer to the effect produced if we thought of it as a sore place in the mental body, as an irritation produced by friction. We sometimes encounter argumentative people, people who must argue about everything, and apparently love the exercise so much that they scarcely care on which side of the problem they are engaged. A person of that sort has his mental body in a condition of perpetual inflammation, and the inflammation is liable on very slight provocation to break out at any moment into an actual open sore For such a one there is no hope of any kind of occult progress until he has brought balance and common sense to bear on his diseased condition.

Fortunately for us, the good emotions persist even longer than the evil, because they work in the finer part of the astral body ; the effect of a feeling of strong love or devotion remains in the astral body long after the occasion that caused it has been forgotten. It is possible, though unusual, to have two sets of vibrations going on strongly in the astral body at the same time—for example, love and anger. At the moment of feeling intense anger a man would not be likely to have any strong affectionate feeling, unless the anger were noble indignation ; in that case the after results would go on side by side, but one at a much higher level than the other, and therefore persisting longer.

7

LAUGHTER

It is very natural for boys and girls to wish to enjoy themselves, to be merry, to read and to hear amusing things, and to laugh at them; that is quite right, and it does no harm. If people could see the vibrations set up by jovial, kindly laughter they would realize at once that while the astral body is disturbed to some extent, it is the same thing as shaking up the liver in riding; it actually does good, not harm. But if the results of some of the less pleasant stories that foul-minded people are in the habit of telling were visible to them they would realize a ghastly difference; such thoughts are altogether evil, and the forms produced by them remain clinging for a long time to the astral body, and attract all kinds of loathsome entities. Those approaching the Masters must be utterly free from this coarseness, as well as from all that is boisterous and rough; and the younger must constantly be on their guard against any relapse into childishness or silliness.

There is sometimes a tendency towards inane giggling, which must be avoided at all costs, as it has a very bad effect on the astral body. It weaves round it a web of grey-brown threads, very unpleasant to look upon, which forms a layer which hinders the entrance of good influences. It is a danger against which young people should sedulously guard themselves. Be as happy and as joyous as you can; the Master likes to see it, and it will help you on your path. But never for a moment let your joyousness be tinged by any sort of roughness or rudeness, never let your laughter become a boisterous guffaw; never let it, on the other hand, degenerate into silly giggling.

There is a definite line of demarcation in this, as in other matters, between what is harmless and what may easily become harmful. The most certain method of determining it is to consider whether the amusement passes beyond the point of delicacy and good taste. The moment that the laughter oversteps these—the moment that there is in it the least touch of boisterousness, the moment that it ceases to be perfect in its refinement, we are passing on to dangerous ground. The inner side of that distinction is that so long as the

ego is fully in control of his astral body, all is well; as soon as he
loses control, the laughter becomes vacuous and meaningless—the
horse is, as it were, running away with its rider. An astral body
thus left unchecked is at the mercy of any passing influence, and may
easily be affected by most undesirable thoughts and feelings. See to
it also that your mirth is ever pure and clean—never tinged for a
moment with a malicious delight in the suffering or discomfiture of
another.‘ If a mortifying accident should happen to someone, do not
stand there laughing idly at the ridiculous side of the incident, but
rush forward at once to help and console. Loving-kindness and
helpfulness must be always your most prominent characteristics.

IDLE WORDS

A clairvoyant who can see the effect upon the higher bodies of
the various undesirable emotions finds no difficulty in understanding
how important it is that they should be controlled. But because most
of us do not see the result we are liable to forget it, and allow ourselves to become careless. The same thing is true of the effect produced
by casual or thoughtless remarks. The Christ in his last incarnation
on earth is reported to have said that for every idle word that men
shall speak, they shall give account on the day of judgment. That
sounds a cruel thing to say, and if the orthodox view of judgment
were correct, it would indeed be unjust and abominable. He did
not mean in the least that every idle word spoken would condemn
a man to eternal torture—there is no such thing as that; but we
know that every word and every thought has its karma, its result,
and when foolish things are repeated again and again, it makes
an atmosphere round the person which does keep out good
influences. To avoid this, constant attention is required. It would
be a superhuman ideal to expect a person never to forget himself for
a moment; but disciples are after all trying to become superhuman,
because the Master is beyond man. If the pupil could live the perfect
life, he would himself already be an Adept; he cannot be that yet,
but if he constantly remembered his ideal he would approach much

nearer to it. Every idle word that he speaks is certainly affecting for the time his relations with the Master ; so let him watch his words with the utmost care.[1]

FORMS MADE BY SPEECH

The pupil should watch the manner of his speech, as well as its matter, so that it may be graceful, beautiful and correct, and free from carelessness and exaggeration. His words should be well chosen and well pronounced. Many people think that in daily life it is not necessary to take the trouble to speak clearly ; it matters much more than they think, because we are all the time building our own sur- roundings, and these react upon us. We fill our rooms and houses with our own thoughts, and then we have to live in them. If, for example, a man allows himself to be overcome by depression, his room becomes charged with that quality, and any sensitive person coming into it becomes conscious of a certain lowering of vitality, a loss of tone. Much more, he himself, who lives in that room much of the time, is perpetually affected by the depression, and cannot easily throw it off. In the same way the man who surrounds himself with unpleasant sound-forms by careless and uncultured speech pro- duces an atmosphere in which these forms constantly react upon him. Because of this perpetual pressure the man is likely to reproduce these unpleasant forms ; if he is not careful he will find himself getting into the habit of speaking roughly and coarsely.

I have heard again and again from school-teachers : " We can do nothing with the children's speech. While we have them here in school we try to correct them, but when they go home they hear the wrong pronunciation of the words, and that always persists, and makes it impossible for us to counteract it." The children are in school for perhaps five hours a day, and are in and about the home most of the remaining time. In that home an atmosphere of undesirable sound-forms may be pressing on them all the time, so that they are absolutely enslaved by it ; there are certain words

[1] See also Chapter XIV, on Right Speech.

they actually cannot say, for they cannot utter a pure sound. You may think that a small thing and unimportant ; it is by no means small, and a number of such things perpetually repeated produce a great effect. It is surely better that we should surround ourselves with beauty than with ugliness, even though it be in etheric matter. It is of great importance to speak correctly, clearly and beautifully, for that leads to refinement inwardly as well as outwardly. If we speak in a coarse and slovenly manner, we degrade the level of our thought ; and such a manner of speech will repel and disgust people whom we wish to help. Those who cannot be accurate in their use of words, cannot be precise in their thinking ; even in morality they will be vaguer, for all these things react one upon another.

Each word as it is uttered makes a little form in etheric matter, just as a thought does in mental matter. Some of those forms are most objectionable. The word "hate", for instance, produces a horrible form, so much so that, having seen its shape, I never use the word. We may say that we dislike a thing, or that we do not care about it, but we should never use the word "hate" more than we can help, for merely to see the form that it makes gives a feeling of acute discomfort. There are words, on the other hand, which produce beautiful forms, words which it is well to recite. All this might be worked out scientifically, and will be some day, I have no doubt, when people have time to do it. It may be said, however, in general, that the words which are connected with desirable qualities produce pleasant forms, and those which are associated with evil qualities produce ugly forms.

Such word-forms are not determined by the thought which accompanies the word ; the thought builds its own form in a higher type of matter. For example, that word "hate" is often used quite casually without any real hatred at all, when speaking, perhaps, of some article of food ; that is a perfectly unnecessary use of the word, and it obviously does not convey any serious emotions ; so that the astral hate-form is not produced ; but the ugly etheric sound-form appears just as though the speaker really meant it. So, clearly, the word itself is not a good word. The same is true of the oaths and obscene words so often used amongst uneducated and uncultured people ; the forms produced by some of these are of a peculiarly horrible nature when seen by clairvoyant sight. But it is unthinkable that anyone aspiring to be a disciple would pollute his lips with these. We often hear people using all sorts of loose slang phrases which in reality have no meaning or legitimate derivation. It is important that all these should be avoided by the student of occultism.

The same thing is true with regard to the habit of exaggeration. People sometimes talk in a most extravagant way. If a thing is a hundred yards distant they say it is " miles off ". If a day comes that is hotter than usual, they say it is " boiling ". Our command of English is poor if we are not able to find words to express different gradations of thought without plunging into these wild, meaningless superlatives. Worst of all, if they wish to convey the idea that something is especially good, they describe it as " awfully " good, which is not only a contradiction in terms, and therefore an utterly silly and meaningless expression, but it is also a shocking misuse of a word which has a solemn connotation of its own which renders its employment in such a sense grotesquely inappropriate. All such abominations should be strictly avoided by one who aspires to become a student of occultism.

We emphasize control of speech from the point of view of regulating the meaning of our words—and quite rightly ; nothing is more necessary ; I wish we could all control the *pronunciation* of our words, and regard that also as an act of self-training. The importance of accuracy and refinement in speech cannot be exaggerated.

Whenever we speak or laugh we make colour as well as sound. If it is the right kind of laughter, hearty and kindly, it has a very pleasant effect, and spreads a feeling of joyousness all round. But if it should be a sneering or sarcastic laugh, a coarse guffaw, a snigger or a giggle, the result is very different, and exceedingly unpleasant. It is remarkable how closely all shades of thought and feeling mirror themselves in other planes. This is very evident when we pass from one country to another, and find the air filled with quite different sound-effects. If one crosses the Channel from England to France, one sees at once that the sound-forms made by the French language are quite different from those produced by the English. It is especially noticeable with regard to certain sounds, because every language has some sounds peculiar to itself, and it is those which are the principal features which distinguish the appearance of one language from that of another.

The colour of the forms produced depends more upon the spirit in which we speak. Two people may speak the same words, and so make broadly the same form, but the forms may have a different spirit behind them. When you are parting with someone you say " Good-bye ". Those words may be accompanied by a real outrush of friendly feeling ; but if you say " Good-bye " in a casual tone, without any special thought or feeling behind it, that produces a totally different effect on the higher planes. One is just a flash in the pan, meaning little, doing little ; the other is a definite outpouring which you give to your friend. It is well to remember that the expression means " God be with you " ; therefore it is a blessing which you are giving. In France we say " Adieu ", " To God I commend you ". If you would think of the meaning of such words whenever you say them, you would do much more good than you do, for then your will and your thought would go with the words, and the blessing would be a real help and not a mere casual flicker.

In all these ways the disciple's speech should be refined and evolved. Remember how it is said in *The Light of Asia* that the King, the Self, is within you, and that whatever comes out of your mouth in his presence should be a golden thought expressed in golden words :

> Govern the lips
> As they were palace doors, the King within ;
> Tranquil and fair and courteous be all words
> Which from that presence win.

FUSS

Especially is it necessary for the aspirant to avoid all fidgetiness or fussiness. Many an energetic and earnest worker spoils most

of his efforts and makes them of no effect by yielding to these failings ;
for he sets up around him such an aura of tremulous vibrations that
no thought or feeling can pass in or out without distortion, and the
very good that he sends out takes with it a shiver that practically
neutralizes it. Be absolutely accurate ; but attain your accuracy by
perfect calmness, never by hurry or fuss.

Another point that it is necessary to impress upon our students
is that in occultism we always mean exactly what we say, neither
more nor less.

When a rule is laid down that nothing unkind or critical must
be said about another, just that is exactly what is meant—not that
when we happen to think of it we should slightly diminish the
number of unkind or critical things that we say every day, but that
they must definitely altogether cease. We are so much in the habit
of hearing various ethical instructions which no one seems to endeavour to put seriously into practice, that we have a habit of thinking
that a perfunctory assent to an idea, or an occasional feeble effort to
approximate to it, is all that religion requires of us. We must put
aside that frame of mind altogether and understand that exact and
literal obedience is required when occult instruction is given, whether
by a Master or by his pupil.[1]

THE VALUE OF ASSOCIATION

Very much help in all these matters is often given to the
aspirant, both probationary and accepted, by the presence of an
older pupil of the Masters. In the early days in India, when a guru
selected his chelas, he formed them into a group and took them
about with him wherever he went. Now and then he taught them,
but often they received no instructions ; yet they made rapid progress, because all the time they were within the aura of the teacher
and were being brought into harmony with it, instead of being
surrounded by ordinary influences. The teacher also assisted them

---

[1] For additional instruction on these lines the reader is referred to *Talks on the Path of
Occultism*.

in the building of character, and always watched the tyros carefully. Our Masters cannot adopt that plan physically, but they have sometimes arranged matters so that some of their elder representatives can draw round themselves a group of the younger neophytes, and attend to them individually, much as a gardener would deal with his plants, raying upon them day and night the influences needed to awaken certain qualities or strengthen weak points. The older helper rarely receives direct instructions with regard to this work; though now and then the Master may make some remark or comment.

The fact that the novices are together in a group also assists their progress; they are influenced in common by high ideals, and this hastens the growth of desirable characteristics. It is probably inevitable in the course of karmic law that one who is aspiring shall be brought into contact with someone more advanced than himself, and receive much benefit through his ability to respond to him; and it is generally the fact that the Master does not advance or raise any person unless he has been with an older student who can guide and help him. There are, however, exceptions, and each Master has his own way of dealing with his catechumens. In one case, it has been said by Dr. Besant, the Master makes a practice of sending his pupils "to the other end of the field", so that they may gain great strength by the development of their powers with the minimum of external assistance. Each individual is treated as is best for him.

It has been asked whether advancement is possible for a lonely student, whose karma has placed him on some remote farm or plantation, or has bound him to some spot where he is not likely to meet anyone already established on the Path. Undoubtedly such a man may make progress, and though his task is harder because he has less physical-plane help, he will learn to rely upon himself, and will probably develop greater will-power and determination just because he is so much alone. It will be well for him to get into correspondence with some older student, who can answer his questions and advise him in his reading, as by that means much time may be saved, and his way may be made smoother for him.

CHAPTER V

ACCEPTANCE

UNION WITH THE MASTER

THOUGH the acceptance of the pupil by the Master produces so great a difference in his life, there is but little more of external ceremony attached to it than there was in the case of probation. If one observes this ceremony with the sight of the causal body, one sees the Master as a glorious globe of living fire, containing a number of concentric shells of colour, his physical body and its counterparts on other planes being in the centre of the glowing mass, which extends to a radius of many hundreds of yards.

In approaching the physical body of the Master, the pupil advances into that glowing globe of finer material, and when he finally reaches the feet of his Master he is already in the heart of that splendid sphere ; and when the Master expands himself to include the aura of the pupil, it is really the central heart of fire which so expands and includes him, for all through the ceremony of acceptance he is already far within the outer ring of that mighty aura. Thus for a few moments they two are one, and not only does the Master's aura affect that of the pupil, but any special characteristics attained by the latter act upon the corresponding centres of the Master's aura, and that flashes out in response.

The inexpressible union of the pupil with the Master which begins during the ceremony of acceptance is a permanent thing, and after that, though the pupil may be far distant from the Master on the physical plane, his higher vehicles are vibrating in common with those of his Teacher. He is all the time being tuned up, and thus growing gradually more and more like his Master, however remote the resemblance may have been in the beginning; and thus he becomes of great service in the world as an open channel by means of which the Master's force may be distributed on the lower planes. By constant meditation upon his guru, and ardent aspiration towards him, the pupil has so affected his own vehicles that they are constantly open towards his Master and expectant of his influence. At all times they are largely preoccupied with that idea, waiting the word of the Master and watching for something from him, so that while they are keenly and sensitively open to him they are to a considerable extent closed to lower influences. Therefore all his higher vehicles, from the astral upwards, are like a cup or funnel, open above but closed at the sides, and almost impervious to influences touching him at the lower levels.

This tuning-up of the pupil continues throughout the period of discipleship. At first his vibrations are many octaves below those of the Master, but they are in tune with them, and are gradually being raised. This is a process that can take place only slowly. It could not be done at once, like the stamping out of a piece of metal with a die, or even comparatively quickly, as one would tune a violin or piano string. Those are inanimate things; but in this case a living being is to be moulded, and in order that the life may be preserved, the slow growth from within must adapt the form to the outside influence, as a gardener might gradually direct the limbs of a tree, or a surgeon with proper appliances might by degrees straighten a crooked leg.

We know that throughout this process the Master is not giving his full attention to each individual pupil, but is working upon thousands of people simultaneously, and all the time doing much higher work as well—playing a great game of chess, as it were, with the nations of the world and with all the different kinds of powers, of angels and men, as pieces on the board. Yet the effect is as though he were watching the pupil and thinking of no one else, for the attention that he can give to one among hundreds is greater than ours when we concentrate it entirely upon one. The Master often leaves to some of his older pupils the work of tuning the lower bodies, though he himself is allowing a constant flow between his vehicles and those of his pupil. It is in this way he does most for his pupils, without their necessarily knowing anything about it.

The accepted pupil thus becomes an outpost of the Master's consciousness—an extension of him, as it where. The Adept sees, hears and feels through him, so that whatever is done in his presence is done in the Master's presence. This does not mean that the Great One is necessarily always conscious of such events at the time when they are going on, though he may be so. He may be absorbed in some other work at the time ; nevertheless the events are in his memory afterwards. What the pupil has experienced with reference to a particular subject will come up in the Master's mind among his own knowledge when he turns his attention to that subject.

When a pupil sends a thought of devotion to his Master, the slight flash which he sends produces an effect like the opening of a great valve, and there is a tremendous downflow of love and power from the Master. If one sends out a thought of devotion to one who is not an Adept, it becomes visible as a fiery stream going to him ; but when such a thought is directed by a pupil to his Master, the pupil is immediately deluged by a stream of fiery love *from* the Master. The Adept's power is flowing outwards always and in all directions like the sunlight ; but the touch of the pupil's thought draws down a prodigious stream of it upon him for the moment. So perfect is the union between them that if there is any serious disturbance in the lower bodies of the pupil it will affect also those of the Master ; and, as such vibration would interfere with the Adept's work on higher planes, when this unfortunately happens he has to drop a veil that shuts the pupil off from himself until such time as the storm settles down.

It is of course sad for the pupil when he has to be cut off in this manner ; but it is absolutely his own doing, and he can end the separation at once as soon as he can control his thoughts and feelings. Usually such an unfortunate incident does not last longer than forty-eight hours ; but I have known cases much worse than that, in which the rift endured for years, and even for the remainder of that incarnation. But these are extreme cases, and very rare, for it is little likely that a person capable of such defection would be received as a pupil at all.

THE ATTITUDE OF THE DISCIPLE

No one is likely to become an accepted pupil unless he has acquired the habit of turning his forces outwards and concentrating his attention and strength upon others, to pour out helpful thoughts and good wishes upon his fellow-men. Opportunities for doing this are constantly offering themselves, not only among those with whom we are brought into close contact, but even among the strangers whom we pass in the street. Sometimes we notice a man who is obviously depressed or suffering : in a flash we can send a strengthening and encouraging thought into his aura. Let me quote once again a passage which I saw a quarter of a century ago in one of the New Thought books :

Knead love into the bread you bake ; wrap strength and courage in the parcel you tie for the woman with the weary face ; hand trust and candour with the coin you pay to the man with the suspicious eyes.

A lovely thought quaintly expressed, but conveying the great truth that every connection is an opportunity, and that every man whom we meet in the most casual manner is a person to be helped. Thus the student of the Good Law goes through life distributing blessings all about him, doing good unobtrusively everywhere, though often the recipient of the blessing and the help may have no idea whence it comes. In such benefactions every man can take his share, the poorest as well as the richest ; all who can think can send out kindly and helpful thoughts, and no such thought has failed, or ever can fail while the laws of the universe hold. You may not see the result, but the result is there, and you know not what fruit may spring from that tiny seed which you sow in passing along your path of peace and love.

If the student has a little knowledge of the resources of nature he can often call them to his aid in work of this description. There are large numbers of nature-spirits, of a certain type, both in the woods and in the water, who are especially suitable for the ensouling of thought forms, and take very great delight in being employed in that work. The student, when walking in the fields and in forests or sailing over the water, may invite such creatures to accompany him— may even draw them into his aura, and carry them along ; and then, when he reaches a city, and begins to project his good thoughts upon those whom he meets, he can ensoul each such thought-form with one of these little helpers. By doing that, he gives radiant joy and a certain amount of evolution to the friendly nature-spirit, and also greatly prolongs the life and activity of his thought-form.

THE DISTRIBUTION OF FORCE

Practically all the ordinary people in the world turn their forces inwards upon themselves, and because they are self-centred their forces are jangling together inside. But the pupil has to turn himself inside out, and maintain a constant attitude of giving in affection and service. We have in the pupil, therefore, a man whose higher vehicles are a funnel open to the highest influences from his Master, while his lower vehicles at the bottom of the funnel have been trained into the constant habit of radiating those influences out upon others. This makes him a perfect instrument for his Master's use, for the translation of His force to the outer planes.

If an Adept in Tibet wanted to distribute some force at the etheric level in New York, it would not be economical to direct the current etherically for that distance ; he would have to transmit his force on much higher levels to the point required, and then excavate a funnel downwards at that point.

Another simile which might be suggested in that of the transmission of electricity at enormous voltages across country, and the stepping of it down through transformers which give great current and low voltage at the place where the power is to be used. But to excavate such a funnel, or to step the force down at New York, would involve a loss to the Adept of nearly half of the energy that he had available for the piece of work to be done. Therefore the pupil on the spot is an invaluable labour-saving apparatus, and he must remember that above all things he must make himself a good channel, because that is most of all what the Master needs from him. Thus the pupil may be regarded in another way as an additional body for the Master's use in the place where he happens to be.

Every human body is in reality a transmitter for the powers of the Self within. Through many ages it has been adapted to carry out the commands of the will in the most economical manner ; for example, if we wish for any reason to move or to overturn a tumbler standing upon the table, it is easy enough to stretch out one's hand and do so. It is also possible to overturn that tumbler by mere force of will without physical contact ; indeed one of the earliest members of the Theosophical Society tried this experiment and actually succeeded, but only at the expense of devoting an hour's strenuous effort to it every day for two years. It is obvious that to use the ordinary physical means is in such a case far more economical.

In the earlier stages of the pupil's relation with his Master, he will often feel that a vast amount of force is poured through him, without his knowing where it is going ; he feels only that a great volume of living fire is rushing through him and flooding his neighbourhood. With a little careful attention he can soon learn to tell in which direction it is going, and a little later he becomes able to follow with his consciousness that rush of the Master's power, and can actually trace it down to the very people who are being affected and helped by it. He himself, however, cannot direct it ; he is being used simply as a channel, yet is at the same time being taught to co-operate in the distribution of the force. Later, there comes a time when the Master, instead of pouring force into his pupil and aiming it at a person in a distant place, tells him to seek out the person and then give him some of the force, for this saves the Master some energy. Whenever and wherever a pupil can do a little of the Master's work, he will always give it to him, and as the pupil increases in usefulness, more and more of the work is put into his hands, so as to relive, by however slight an amount, the strain upon the Master. We think much, and rightly so, about the work that we can do down here; but all that we can imagine and carry out is as nothing to what he is doing through us. There is always a gentle radiation through the pupil, even though he may not be conscious of it, yet the same pupil will feel it distinctly whenever an unusual amount of force is being sent.

This transmission of force from a particular Master is generally confined to his pupils, but any person who is seriously trying to live a life of service, purity and refinement may be used as a channel for force. It might well happen that in any given place there was no pupil quite fitted for a certain kind of outpouring; but there might be some other person who, though not so far advanced, could yet be employed for that particular purpose. In such a case the Master would probably use him. Many varieties of force are poured out by the Master for different purposes; sometimes one person is suitable, and sometimes another. Watching the case of two pupils side by side, one sees that one is used always for one type of force and the other for another kind.

This outpouring is physical as well as astral, mental and buddhic, and on the physical plane it issues mainly through the hands and feet. On this account—as well as for general reasons—very great care must be taken about cleanliness. If the physical body of the person selected failed for a moment in this important matter, the Master could not utilize him, because the man would not be a suitable channel. It would be like pouring pure water through a dirty pipe—it would be fouled on the way. Therefore those who are in close relation with the Master are exceedingly vigilant about perfect bodily cleanliness. Let us take care, then, that we shall be fit in this respect if we are needed.

Another point about which we need to be watchful if we wish to be of use is to avoid distortion, especially of the feet. Not long ago I stayed for a few weeks in a community where it is the custom to walk barefooted, and I was horrified to see the twisted and crippled appearance of the feet of many of the students, and to observe how seriously this deformity interfered with their usefulness as channels of the Master's force. The natural course for that force under ordinary conditions is to fill the whole body of the pupil and rush out through the extremities ; but in cases where unhygienic foot-gear has produced permanent malformation the Adept can utilize only the upper half of the body ; and as that imposes upon him the additional trouble of constructing each time a sort of temporary dam or barrier in the neighbourhood of the diaphragm of the pupil, it inevitably follows that others who are free from this disfigurement are employed far more frequently.

THE TRANSMISSION OF MESSAGES

Sometimes the Master sends a definite message through his pupil to a third party. I remember once being told to deliver such a message to a very highly intellectual member whom I did not know very well. I felt a little embarrassment in approaching him on such a subject, but of course I had to do it ; so I said to the recipient : " I have been told by my Master to give you this message, and I am simply doing as I am told. I am perfectly aware that I cannot give you any evidence that this is a message from the Master, and I must leave you to attach to it just as much importance as you feel disposed. I have no alternative but to carry out my instructions." I was of course conscious of the contents of the message, because I had had to take it down ; and I aver that, on the face of it, it was a perfectly simple and friendly message, such as might have been sent by any kindly person to another, without appearing to bear any special significance whatever. But evidently appearances were deceptive ; the old gentleman to whom I delivered it looked much startled, and said : " You need not take any trouble to try to persuade me that that is a message from your Master : I know it instantly from the wording ; it would have been absolutely impossible for you to know the meaning of several of the references that he makes." But to this day I have no idea what he meant.

It is, however, but rarely that a message is given in such a form as that. There seems to be much misconception on this subject, so it

8

may be useful to explain exactly how messages are usually conveyed from higher to lower planes. We shall understand this more easily if we consider the relation between these planes, the difficulties in the way of communication between them, and the various methods by which these difficulties are overcome.

SENSITIVENESS, MEDIUMSHIP AND PSYCHIC POWERS

In the ordinary man of the world, who has made no special study of these matters and no effort to develop the powers of the soul these planes are as separate worlds, and there is no conscious communication between them. When he is what he calls " awake ", his consciousness works through his physical brain, and when his body is asleep it works through his astral vehicle. If, therefore, a dead man or a kamadeva wishes to communicate with such a man, there are two ways in which he can do it. He can meet the man face to face in the astral world and converse with him just as though they were both in physical life ; or he can in any one of various ways manifest himself upon the physical plane, and set up some kind of communication there.

The first method is obviously both easier and more satisfactory ; but the drawback is that the average man brings through no reliable recollection from his astral to his physical life ; so that efforts to inspire and guide him are usually only very partially successful. Every man meets astral friends every night of his life ; and conversations and discussions take place between them precisely as they do in the daytime in this denser world ; the " living " man rarely remembers these in his waking consciousness, but his thoughts and actions may be, and often are, considerably influenced by advice given and suggestions made in this way, though when awake he is quite ignorant of their source, and supposes the ideas thus presented to his mind to be his own.

The astral entity who wishes to communicate, therefore, frequently adopts the second method, and tries to produce effects upon the physical plane. This again can be done in two ways. The first of these is by causing certain physical sounds or movements which can be interpreted according to a pre-arranged code. Raps can be produced upon a table, or the table can be tilted at selected letters as someone repeats the alphabet, or the Morse telegraphic code may be employed if both parties happen to know it. Or the pointer of an ouija board can be moved from letter to letter so as to spell out a message.

Another way, less crude and tedious but more dangerous to the physical participant, is the employment by the astral entity of some of the organs of his friend on this plane. He can seize upon the vocal cords of the latter, and speak through him; he can use the hand of the " living " man to write messages or make drawings of which his physical instrument knows nothing. When the " dead " man speaks through the " living ", the latter is usually in a condition of trance; but the hand can be used for writing or drawing while its legitimate owner is wide awake, reading a book or conversing with his friends.

Not every one can be thus utilized by astral entities—only those who are specially amenable to such influences. Such persons are often described as psychics, mediums or sensitives; perhaps the last of these titles is the most appropriate in the cases which we are considering. But however sensitive a person may be to influences from another plane, he has a strongly defined personality of his own which usually cannot be entirely repressed. There are many degrees of sensitivity to influences from higher planes. Some people are born with this quality; others acquire it by effort; in both cases it can be developed and intensified by practice. That is what is usually meant in spiritualistic circles by " sitting for development "; someone who is by nature readily impressible is advised to render himself as negative as possible, and to sit day after day for hours in that attitude. Naturally, he becomes more and more impressible, and if some astral entity comes and acts upon him day after day, they become accustomed to each other, and the transference of ideas is greatly facilitated.

At a certain stage in that process the physical body of the victim is usually entranced—which means that the ego no longer controls his vehicles, but for the time hands them over to the astral influence. The vehicles, however, still bear the strong impress of the ego, so that, although the intelligence which is using them is quite different, they will nevertheless move to a considerable extent along their accustomed ruts. The sentiments of the communicating entity may be of the most exalted kind, but if the sensitive happens to be uneducated, ungrammatical or slangy, the expression of those exalted sentiments on the physical plane will be likely to exhibit those characteristics in a very marked manner. When we hear of Julius Caesar or Shakespeare or the Apostle St. John manifesting at a séance, we generally find that they have somehow vastly deteriorated since the time of their last earth-life ; and naturally and rightly enough we decided that these great men of old are not really present at all, but that the whole thing is merely an impudent impersonation. That is no doubt a perfectly just conclusion ; but what we sometimes forget is that, even if such communication were genuine, it would still in ninety-nine cases out of a hundred be subject to exactly the same disabilities.

There is a condition of trance-control so perfect that the defects inherent in the personality of the instrument are entirely overcome ; but such complete control is very rare indeed. When it exists we may have a strikingly accurate reproduction of the voice and intonation and the habitual expressions of the dead man, or an exact imitation of his handwriting ; but even in such an extreme case we are far from having an absolute guarantee that we are dealing with the person whose name is given. In these higher planes thought-reading, thought-transference of all kinds, is so exceedingly easy that there is comparatively little information which can be regarded as in any sense private or exclusive.

All this so-called development is exceedingly bad for the poor sensitive ; more and more, as he grows in susceptibility of this kind, the ego loses his grasp of his vehicles. He becomes increasingly amenable to astral influences, but he has no guarantee whatever as to their nature, which means that he is just as readily impressible by evil as by good. And the promise frequently given, that some

" spirit-guide " will protect him, is of little value, as the power of such guides is very limited. He is in the position of one who lies bound and helpless by the roadside, at the mercy of the next passer-by, who may of course be a good Samaritan, who will release him from his bonds and minister to his needs, but may also be a robber, who will take from him all that has been left to him ; and perhaps robbers are on the whole more common than good Samaritans. From my own point of view, based upon no inconsiderable experience, I should strongly warn my brethren against engaging in any kind of mediumship.

The title of medium might, I think, well be reserved for those through whom physical phenomena are produced—people from whom what is now technically termed ectoplasm can be withdrawn, so that materialization may take place, and heavy objects of various kinds can be moved.

Another and very different kind of development is that which may legitimately be denominated psychic, for *psyche* in Greek means " the soul ". The soul has its powers as well as the body ; though perhaps it would be more accurate to say that all powers which a man possesses are the powers of the soul, though they manifest on different planes. It is after all not the body which sees or hears, which writes or draws or paints ; it is always the man himself working through the body. And when a man develops these psychic powers it really means only that he has learnt to function through other vehicles than the physical and that he can to some extent bring the results through into his waking consciousness.

It is the point last mentioned which creates the difficulty in almost every case. Any man, functioning on the astral plane during the sleep of his physical body or after the death of that body, is aware of his astral surroundings, but it does not follow that he will remember them when he wakes. The difficulty therefore is not in having the experiences, but in being able to impress them upon the physical brain ; the power to do that can be acquired only by long-continued effort. There seems to be a general impression that the possession of such powers indicates high moral and spiritual development, but this is not necessarily so. A sufficiently strenuous and persevering effort will unfold these powers in anyone, quite irrespective of his moral character; but it is true that they usually develop spontaneously when a man reaches a certain stage of spiritual advancement.

It is generally in that way that these powers come to the pupils of the Masters; and though they are not without their especial dangers, they are certainly on the whole very useful and valuable. But it is necessary that those to whom they come should try to understand them—to comprehend something of their mechanism; they must not suppose that, even if the powers come to them as the result of general advancement, the recipients are thereby freed from the ordinary laws under which such faculties work. There are many difficulties connected with the bringing through clear recollection, and these exist for us just as they do for the spiritualistic sensitive, though our long course of careful study ought to fit us to meet them and to understand them better than he does.

Above all, we must not forget that we also have our personalities, which are likely to be even stronger than those of our neighbours, just because we have been trying to develop strength and definiteness of character. Of course, we have also been trying for years to dominate the personality by the individuality, but that does not alter the fact that we are likely to be colourful persons with decided characteristics, and that whatever comes through us is liable to be modified by those precise characteristics.

Let me try to illustrate what I mean by quoting one or two instances which have come under my personal observation. I remember one lady who was an exceedingly good clairvoyant, capable of looking back into the past, and describing historical events with great accuracy and wealth of detail. She was a very devout Christian, and I think she was never quite able to feel that any other religion could be as full an exposition of the truth as her own. She might be said (using the word in no invidious sense) to have a strong prejudice in favour of Christianity. The result of that upon her clairvoyance was very striking—in fact, almost amusing sometimes.

She might be describing, let us say, a scene in ancient Rome ; so long as nothing directly connected with religion came into her purview, the description would be quite accurate, but the moment that it appeared that one of the characters in the scene was a Christian she immediately displayed a remarkably strong bias in his favour. Nothing that he did or said could be wrong, whereas anything whatever that was said or done against him was always indicative of the greatest wickedness. When this factor was introduced her clairvoyance became absolutely unreliable. One supposes that she must have seen the facts as they occurred, but the account she gave of them and the interpretation which she placed upon them were certainly entirely untrue.

Another lady whom I knew had a brilliantly poetical imagination, which induced her in ordinary conversation to magnify everything which she related—not in the slightest degree intentionally to falsify it, but simply so to embroider it as to make it in every way greater and more beautiful than the actual fact had been—quite a happy attitude of mind, of course, in many ways, but somewhat fatal to scientific observation. The same thing occurred with regard to her rememberance and description of a scene on other planes, whether it were contemporaneous or something from past history. A quite ordinary little ceremony on the physical plane, attended perhaps by some friendly devas and a few dead relations of the parties concerned, would in her report of it be magnified into a tremendous initiation attended by all the great Adepts and most of the celebrated characters of history, and blessed by the presence of a whole army of Archangels.

One may see from these small examples how necessary it is for the budding clairvoyant to watch himself very carefully and to allow a liberal discount from his early impressions. It must never be forgotten that one has to become accustomed to the use of faculties on these higher planes just as a man has to familiarize himself with the use of new tools of any kind in this physical world. The little child learns only by degrees to understand perspective : he has his eyes from the first, but he must learn how to use them. The man who has the misfortune to be blind can learn to read by the Braille system with great ease and rapidity, but most of us who have the use of our eyes would find it practically impossible to distinguish one letter of that system from another without a long and tiresome training.

Just so a man whose astral faculties are beginning to open finds it at first a practical impossibility to describe what he sees and hears ; everything appears so different, and he finds what he would probably call his sight acting in all sorts of unexpected directions. It is only after years of experience that he becomes fully reliable ; and even then it is only a mere reflection of what he sees that he can bring through into the lower consciousness. There is always a side of any astral happening which cannot be expressed in physical words ; and as the man rises to higher levels more and more of these additional sides or aspects confront him, and he finds it less and less within his power to give even the slightest idea of his experiences, and even what he *is* able to bring through is certain to be coloured by his own idiosyncrasies.

MESSAGES FROM ADEPTS

Many of us have been long meditating daily upon our great Masters—some of us for years ; we have drawn ourselves near to them by the intensity of our reverence and devotion, and it often happens to the more fortunate among us to come into personal touch with them and sometimes to be charged by them with messages for less fortunate brethren. Anyone who is honoured by being charged with such a message will, I am sure, make every effort to transmit it with painstaking accuracy, but he must remember that he is by no means free from the general law in such matters, and he must be very definitely on his guard lest his own predilections or dislikes should in any way colour what he is directed to say. You may think that that is impossible—that a Master would take the trouble to ensure the accurate delivery of any message which he sent. But you must remember that the great Adepts themselves work under universal law, and that they cannot alter its provisions for our convenience. There are cases, such as that which I have just mentioned, in which a direct charge of great importance is dictated word by word, and written down on the physical plane at the time by the recipient : but such cases are exceedingly rare. Let me try to describe, as far as physical words will do it, what usually takes place when a Master conveys a message through one of his disciples.

In the first place let it be understood that an Adept habitually keeps his consciousness focussed upon a very high plane—usually that which we call Nirvana. He can of course in an instant bring it down to any level where he wishes to work; but to descend below the causal body involves a limitation which it is rarely worth his while to undertake. The pupil when out of his body functions at different levels according to his development ; but anyone who is likely to be entrusted with a message would probably be using at least his causal body, and it often happens that communications are exchanged at that level. To understand this transference of ideas, therefore, we must try to see what form such a communication would take.

Here on the physical plane we may put our thought or our emotion into spoken words; we know that such words are not used in the higher life, but that the emotions and thoughts take definite floating forms on the astral and mental planes respectively. As a rule each thought and each emotion makes its own separate form, though when they are mixed we find forms in which the colours are curiously blended. Suppose that we try to raise ourselves in imagination to that high part of the mental plane on which the ego functions in his causal body, and let us see how his ideas express themselves there. As usual, language fails us ; but one principal point of difference is that the ego does not use words and sentences at all, nor does he express such things in a succession of thoughts. He does not appear to *think about* a subject in our sense of the word at all ; he never argues it out and thereby arrives at a conclusion as we do down here.

When a subject comes before him he sees it and knows all about it ; if he wishes to convey an idea to another it is as though he threw at him a kind of ball which somehow includes knowledge and inferences all in one. Nor does he in the least confine himself to projecting a single idea. The thought of an Adept showers upon his pupil a kind of hailstorm of lovely little spheres, each of which is an idea with its relation to other ideas quite clearly worked out ; but if the pupil is fortunate enough to remember and clever enough to translate such a hailstorm, he is likely to find that it may need twenty pages of foolscap to express that one moment's deluge, and even then of course the expression is necessarily imperfect.

Furthermore, it has to be recognized that no words have been given to him—only ideas ; and therefore he must of necessity express those ideas in his own language. The ideas are the Master's, if he is fortunate enough to have caught and interpreted them accurately ; but the form of expression is entirely his own. Therefore his idiosyncrasies will certainly appear, and people reading the message will say : " But surely that is so-and-so's style "—referring to the intermediary to whom the message was confided. In saying so they are of course quite right, but they must not allow that obvious fact to blind them to the spirit or the importance of the message.

Long ago Madame Blavatsky, referring to the letters which were at that time (1888) frequently received from the Adepts, wrote :

> It is hardly one out of a hundred occult letters that is ever written by the hand of the Master in whose name and on whose behalf they are sent, as the Masters have neither need nor leisure to write them ; and when a master says " I wrote that letter," it means only that every word in it was dictated by him and impressed under his direct supervision. Generally they make their chela, whether near or far away, write (or precipitate) them, by impressing upon his mind the idea they wish expressed, and if necessary aiding him in the picture-printing process of precipitation. It depends entirely upon the chela's state of development, how accurately the ideas may be transmitted and the writing-model imitated.[1]

When the pupil has for years been accustomed to transmit messages for the Master he will attain by constant practice a far greater facility and accuracy in translation ; but that is because he has learnt to allow for his own personal equation, so that he is able practically to rule it out. Even so, modes of expression which he is in the habit of using are likely to occur, simply because they are to him the best way of expressing certain ideas; but when a person of the development and extensive experience of Dr. Besant (for

---

[1] *Lucifer*, Vol. III, p. 93.

example) conveys a message, we may be quite certain that its sense is accurate and that the form of its expression is the best that can be attained on this plane.

THE PERSONAL EQUATION

For those of us who have not yet attained to that level the personal equation is certain to intrude itself. Unfortunately, it often does so not only with regard to the style of the communication (which, after all, is not so very important, and can easily be discounted) but also with regard to its substance. To understand why and how this is so, we must consider for a moment the constitution and development of the man through whom the messages come.

Our older students will remember that in the book *Man Visible and Invisible* I gave a number of illustrations of the astral and mental bodies of men at various stages of their progress. Those illustrations, however, gave only the exterior appearance of those bodies—that part of each vehicle which is always in relation with the astral or mental world round the man, and is therefore kept in a condition of fairly constant activity. We must remember that these ovoids of astral and mental matter are only superficially vitalized, and that in the case of the average man the surface layer which is thus affected is usually thin. There is always a large proportion in each vehicle which is not yet vivified—a heavy core which takes almost no part in the outer activities of the vehicle, and is indeed but little moved by them. But though this mass of comparatively inert matter is scarcely influenced by the more awakened portion, it is quite capable of acting upon the latter in certain ways.

We have spoken of the personality as being in fact a fragment of the ego working through these lower vehicles—the mental, astral and physical bodies. A fairly full account of the method and detail of this working will be found in Chapter VIII of this book, in *The Inner Life*, under the heading " Lost Souls ", and in *Talks on the Path of Occultism*, Vol. II, Fragment III, Chapter 2. It is explained there that the ego is by no means fully alert as yet, but that in many cases what I suppose we must call a large portion of him (absurd as it sounds) is not yet in activity. It is the Monad which vivifies the ego, but in all of us as yet the ego is only partially awakened. Exactly in the same way it is the ego which animates the personality, but that work also is very far from being perfectly done as yet ; and because of these facts certain conditions are set up which it behoves us to take careful note. In some exalted moment an inrush of power from the ego may temporarily raise the standard of the personality, while on the other hand a steady pressure from the unused portion of the astral or mental body may for the time appreciably lower it.

This lethargic mass of unilluminated matter has a certain life and tendencies of its own, which assert themselves when the more active part of the personality is somewhat in abeyance, and that happens more especially when the man himself is not actively using those bodies. These qualities naturally vary with different people, but an intense egotism is almost always prominent. The thoughts and impressions generated by this sluggish kernel are often those of conceit and self-glorification, and also of instinctive self-preservation in the presence of any danger, whether real or imaginery. Before we reach the flashing glories of the developed man (see *Man Visible and Invisible*, Plate xxi) there is a long period of slow unfoldment during which this heavy core is being gradually permeated by the light, being warmed and thawed into glowing response. But it is a slow process to escape from this subtle domination of the personality. It will of course be gradually eliminated as the man brings the whole of his nature under control, but meanwhile he will be very wise to doubt most seriously any communications which glorify the personality, or suggest to him that he alone is chosen out of all mankind to receive some stupendous revelation which is to revolutionize the world.

Some such promise is the regular stock-in-trade of the communicating spirit in many private inspirational seances ; but we must not therefore assume intentional deceit on the part of that spirit. He is very often so strongly impressed by certain great facts which loom large before him in the astral life that he feels that, if only these could be adequately presented to the world, its attitude would indeed be wholly changed—forgetting that the same ideas were promulgated again and again during his physical life-time, and that he himself did not take the slightest notice of them. It illustrates the old remark of Dives to Abraham : " If one went to them from the dead they would repent " ; and the result shows the wisdom of Abraham's reply : " If they hear not Moses and the prophets, neither will they be persuaded even though one rose from the dead." It is precisely the insidious but constant pressure of this subconscious self which lays a man (otherwise of average common sense) open to extraordinary self-deception, so that he is able to accept without protest flattery which without that influence he would at once see to be ridiculous.

It was to this strange undeveloped subconsciousness that M. Coué appealed with much success. One of its peculiarities is that it seems always to resent any effort of the awakened part of the personality to impress it by means of the will. Being indolent and prejudiced, it sets itself always against any change, any attempt to arouse it and set it to work. Therefore M. Coué especially advised his patients not to use their will at all, for that would only awaken opposition, but simply and quietly to repeat a suggestion until this subconscious self absorbed it. It will be recollected that one of the methods used to impose such an impression upon another was to make it during the sleep of his physical body. Even the auto-suggestion was to be done as nearly as possible in the same way ; the patient was adjured to sink into slumber softly murmuring : " Every day and in every way I am growing better and better." And such is the power of a constantly reiterated insinuation, that the subconscious self presently became fully charged with this idea (which readily harmonized with its irrepressible egotism) and radiated it steadily upon the more active consciousness until definite results were produced. So the undeveloped mass, which to the ignorant may prove a danger and a source of weakness, may actually be used by the wise man to help him on his upward way.

The moral of all this is that ignorance is always dangerous, and that even the noblest intentions cannot always atone for lack of scientific knowledge. Any sportive or scheming entity can beguile a man who is little acquainted with the hidden laws of nature, while he who has studied them can avoid many pitfalls. Yet even he should not presume upon his knowledge, for unceasing vigilance is the price of accuracy. Much advice has been given as to this, and assuredly we shall do well to heed it. Avoid all personal feeling— pride most of all ; distrust profoundly all glorification of the individual, for " ambition is the first curse " and " the power which the disciple shall covet is that which shall make him appear as nothing in the eyes of men." " Be humble if thou wouldst attain to wisdom : be humbler still when wisdom thou hast mastered." He who forgets himself utterly, and devotes his life wholly to the service of others, will be saved thereby from many dangers ; his heart will be pure as crystal, so that the light of the Logos may shine through it unsullied ; his whole nature will respond so truly to the vibrations of his Master that thoughts and messages from higher planes will flow through him undistorted, uncontaminated by any lower touch. So shall he serve our Masters best, by serving the humanity which they love.

TESTING THOUGHT

Another most valuable privilege which the accepted pupil enjoys is that of laying his thought on any subject beside that of his Master, and comparing them. It will be readily understood how the frequent use of this power will keep the pupil's thought running along noble and liberal lines—how he will constantly be able to correct any mistakes, any tendencies towards prejudice or lack of understanding. There may be various ways in which he can exercise this power ; my own method was always to lie down in meditation and endeavour to reach up into the consciousness of the Master just as far as I possibly could. When I had reached the highest point that was for the time possible to me, I suddenly turned and looked back, as it were, upon the subject in question, and instantly received an impression of how it appeared to the Master. It was probably very far from being a perfect impression, but at least it showed me what he thought on the matter, as far as I was able to enter into his thought.

Care, however, must be taken that this wonderful privilege is not misused. It is given to us as a power of ultimate reference in questions of great difficulty, or in the cases where we have no sufficient ground for judgment, and yet have to come to some decision; but it is by no means intended to save us the trouble of thinking, or to be applied to the decision of ordinary everyday questions which we are perfectly competent to settle for ourselves.

Those who meditate long upon a Master and form a strong thought-image of him, presently find that that thought-image is definitely vivified by that Master, so that they receive through it an unmistakable outpouring of spiritual force. This is as it should be; this is precisely the object of such meditation; and through it the pupil comes to know the influence so well that he can always recognise it. There have been cases, though they are happily rare, in which some evil entity has personated as Master in order to deceive a student; but such an attempt can succeed only if there is in the latter some subtle weakness, such as conceit, ambition, jealousy or selfishness, which an insidious tempter can arouse and foster until it becomes a fatal bar to spiritual progress. Unless the roots of such qualities are sternly and thoroughly eliminated, the aspirant is never free from the possibility of deception; but if he be truly humble and selfless he need have no fear.

The candidate for Acceptance must necessarily watch himself closely. If he has not received any direct hint from his Master or from some older pupil as to the special failings which he must try to avoid, he will do his best to observe these for himself, and having once decided upon them or been told of them, he will exercise unceasing vigilance against them. At the same time he should be warned on no account to overdo his introspection and allow himself to become morbid. The safest of all lines for him to take is to concentrate his attention on the helping of others; if his mind is full of that thought he will instinctively move in the right direction. The desire to fit himself thoroughly for that work will impel him to brush all obstacles out of the way, so that without consciously thinking of his own development at all, he will yet find that it is taking place.

RELAXATION

It is not expected that a pupil shall be ever actively thinking of nothing else but the Master; but it *is* expected that the form of the Master shall be always in the background of his mind, always within immediate reach, always there when needed in the vicissitudes of life. Our minds, like bowstrings, cannot be kept always taut; reasonable relaxation and change of thought is one of the necessities of mental health. But the pupil should be exceedingly careful that there is no slightest tinge of impurity or unkindness about his relaxation; no thought should ever be permitted, even for a moment, which the pupil would be ashamed that his Master should see.

There is no harm whatever in reading a good novel for the sake of diversion; the thought-forms engendered by it would not in any way interfere with the current of the Master's thought; but there are many novels full of evil insinuation, novels which bring impure thought-forms before the mind, novels which glorify crime, and others which concentrate the thought of their readers on the most unsavoury problems of life, or vividly depict scenes of hatred and cruelty; all such should be rigorously avoided. In the same way, there is no harm in taking part in or watching all ordinary games which are fairly played; but any which are rough and boisterous, any in which any sort of cruelty is involved, any in which there is likelihood of injury to man or beast—all these are absolutely barred.

CALM AND BALANCE

In all the work which the disciple has to do he must be careful to preserve calm and balance, and that in two ways. Over-work, which is not uncommon among the young and enthusiastic, shows lack of wisdom.   Each of us should do as much as he can, but there is a limit which it is not wise to exceed.   I have heard Dr. Besant say : " What I have not time to do is not my work."   Yet no one labours more strenuously and unceasingly than she.   If we use our forces reasonably for the task of today, we ought to be stronger to face the duties which tomorrow brings ; to overstrain overselves to-day so that we shall be useless tomorrow is not really intelligent service, for we spoil our power for future work in order to gratify to-day's unbalanced enthusiasm.   Of course emergencies occasionally arise in which prudence must be cast aside in order that some piece of work may be finished in time, but the wise craftsman will try to look ahead sufficiently to avoid unnecessary crises of that sort.

The second way in which the disciple must endeavour to pre-serve calm and balance is with regard to his own interior attitude. A certain amount of fluctuation in his feelings is inevitable, but he must try to minimize it.   All sorts of exterior influences are always playing upon us—some astral or mental, some purely physical ; and though we are usually entirely unconscious of them, nevertheless they affect us more or less.   On the physical plane the temperature, the states of the weather, the amount of moisture in the atmosphere, over-fatigue, the condition of one's digestive organs—all these things and many more are factors in our feeling of general well-being.   And that feeling in turn affects not only our happiness but our capacity for work.

Equally without our knowledge, we are liable to be affected by astral conditions, which vary in different parts of the world just as climates, temperatures and physical surroundings do.   Sometimes in the life of the outer world an unpleasant companion attaches himself to us, and is dismissed only with difficulty ; in the astral world it is far less easy to rid oneself of some parasitically-disposed degenerate or even of some unfortunate defunct person drowned in the depths of despair.   Such a one, clinging convulsively to a man, may drain away much of his vitality and flood him with gloom and depression, without being in the slightest degree helped thereby.   We may be quite unaware of such an entity, and even if we know of it, it is often

9

no easy matter to relieve his distress or (if that be impossible) to shake off the incubus of his presence. There are unconscious vampires on the astral plane just as there are on the physical, and in both cases they are most difficult to help.

The general development of the pupil makes him readily responsive to all these influences, whether he is aware of them or not; so he is likely to find himself occasionally inexplicably elated or depressed.

The astral elemental immensely enjoys violent alternations of feeling, and does all that he can to encourage them; but the disciple should not allow himself to be the playground of all these changing moods. He should endeavour to maintain a steady level of joyous serenity, unruffled by passing agitations.

Sometimes he will have the good karma to encounter some great encouragement, some definite stimulation of his progress, such as was afforded, for example, by the opportunity to attend the magnificent Jubilee Convention at Adyar.[1] That was indeed an occasion to be remembered for the extraordinary stimulus and help which it gave to all those who opened their hearts to its influence. Such a happening may well be a milestone on the upward path of the student, from which he may date the opening of additional power, the attainment of a fuller realization of what brotherhood really means.

He will, however, do well to remember that after a splendid outpouring, an unusual upliftment of that sort, there necessarily comes a certain reaction. There is nothing in the least alarming or unnatural about that. It is a manifestation of a law of Nature, of which we see constant examples in everyday life. Many of us, for example, live rather sedentary lives, doing a great deal of reading and writing; probably most of us do not give our physical bodies quite enough exercise—not as much as they need. Then that fact suddenly occurs to us, and we make a great spurt. We play some violent games, perhaps, or go off for a long walk or something of that sort. As long as we do not overdo it, that is very good. But

---

[1] This was the fiftieth International Convention and was held at the World Headquarters of the Society, attended by 2,500 delegates from all parts of the world.

when we have done it, when we have played our game or had our walk, a feeling of lassitude comes over us, and we want to sit down and rest. That, again, is quite right and quite natural. We have been perhaps a little overstraining a number of muscles which we do not generally use, or at least we do not use them so violently, and consequently they are tired and need relaxation. Therefore we have rather a limp feeling ; we sit down or lie down, and after half-an-hour's or an hour's repose, under ordinary circumstances we are all right again.

But during that half-hour of quiet which we have to take, we must remember that we are in a passive condition ; and therefore if there happen to be disease-germs in the air, as there generally are, we are a little more likely to be affected by them just at that time than at any other. The same thing is true at other levels, and when we have had a great upliftment and stimulation, our various vehicles have been strained a little more than they are accustomed to be. I do not say that it is a bad thing for us in any way ; it has been a very good thing for us ; but still the fact remains that our various bodies have done more than they generally do, and consequently there comes this period when they need relief from the strain.

There are various ways in which that period of rest has its little dangers. The relaxation, the slipping back from the height at which we have been living, brings first of all a certain risk that we may slip back a trifle too far—that, letting ourselves subside somewhat from that exalted spiritual condition, we may glide further down into materiality than in ordinary life ; so that some little casual temptation, which in a general way would have no effect upon us, may possibly catch us unawares. That is one possibility against which we may not be on our guard—some little temptation which usually we should hardly notice. In that slight reaction of fatigue we might feel a little more self-indulgent than we should normally be, and so we might make some quite foolish mistake which commonly we should not make.

There is a correspondence to the disease-germ, too. While we are resting there are all sorts of thought-forms floating about, some

pleasant enough and some distinctly unpleasant ; many of them, at
any rate, below the level at which our thought ordinarily works. We
should be more likely to be affected by those during that reaction
period.

THE DARK POWERS

There are other considerations about which it is just as well
that we should know something. At such a time of upliftment
as that of which we have spoken, we receive a very unusual outpouring of spiritual force from on high, from the Great White
Brotherhood, from our individual Masters and teachers. There is
an obscure law in Nature which produces this rather curious result,
that whenever there is a great outrush of higher and grander forces,
there is also a corresponding efflux of undesirable energy. It may
seem strange, but it undoubtedly is so ; it has been put sometimes that
when the Great Ones, working on the side of evolution, permit
themselves to give an unusual benediction, in some curious kind of
balance or fairness, they must allow a similar outflow of force on
the other side. We have heard much of Darker Powers, of black
magicians, of Brothers of the Shadow. These men are following an
absolutely different line from ours, a line which brings them into
collision with the Masters of the Wisdom, with the Hierarchy which
directs the world and the solar system. Naturally that opposition acts
not only upon those great Adepts, but upon us, their humble followers.

I do not wish to devote much space to these people in this book.
I have written of them at considerable length in *Talks on the Path of
Occultism* (vol. III, chapter 2). I have little to add to what is there stated,
except to say that one theory, on which they justify to themselves
their amazing proceedings, is that the Logos does not really wish for
union—that his intention in evolution is the development of each
individual to the highest possible level. (You will note, by the way—
though *they* would never admit   it—that that level is not very high,
after all, because their scheme keeps them working at the strengthening of the ego, and will not carry them on to the buddhic and

nirvanic planes, which are planes of union.) They say : " You think you see about you signs of evolution towards union ; you think that is the will of the Logos. On the contrary, that is a temptation which the Logos is putting in your way. Instead of wanting you to become one, he wants you to assert your individuality in spite of all this which tempts you to be absorbed into an undistinguished unity."

People who really believe that find themselves in conflict with us and with our Masters at every point and all the way through ; we follow our own Masters, who know much more about the Will of the Logos than anyone taking that wrong line can ever come to know, because they can attain union with him, which is impracticable for the advocates of separateness.

Therefore it comes that these men oppose us ; they attempt to obtain recruits ; like everyone else, they want to convert others to their own opinions, and if we are developing and refining ourselves a little more than the average man in some ways, we are the very people of whom they want to get hold. Many of the more intellectual of them are as little enmeshed in materiality as any great ascetic. They quite agree that man should put aside lower things and aim at the higher ; but they aim at an intensified individuality which in the end can only come to grief. So they are very likely to try to influence us, to intensify the individuality in us, to awaken a subtle conceit in us. Remember that it is part of their creed to be utterly unscrupulous ; to them scrupulosity would seem a foolish and despicable weakness, so they will play the meanest tricks.

There is one of our special dangers. The more advanced we can become, the better prey we should be for these Brothers of the Shadow if they could get hold of us. But they cannot get hold of us, they cannot touch us, as long as we can keep ourselves in full community of thought with our Masters ; as long as we can keep ourselves steadfastly along the line of unselfishness, of the constant outpouring of love.

Our strength against these Darker Powers is our union with our Masters, and our power to keep ourselves in their attitude— open always towards influences from above, but resolutely closed against all separative agencies which may try to affect us. Anything which tends to accentuate separateness is simply playing into the hands of the enemy ; and this is true in small things as well as in those which we think greater. So we must put aside all silly little jealousies and animosities ; every time that we yield ourselves to them we make ourselves weak spots in the Theosophical citadel, breaches in its defences ; each time we indulge our lower nature by letting it have a gleeful little orgy of pride and spite, of feeling itself offended by some perfectly innocent brother, we are to just that extent traitors to our Masters. We might think : " Surely our Masters will save us from any such downfall as that." They will not, because they cannot interfere with our liberty ; we must learn to stand alone. Besides, we do not want to give our Masters the trouble of watching over us as a nurse watches over a little toddling child. The Adepts are the busiest people in the world ; they deal with egos in blocks ; they deal with souls by the million, not with personalities one by one. Still, if in real extremity one calls upon a Master, a response certainly comes. We should be very sorry to cause the Master even that moment's trouble if we could possibly help it, but when *really* necessary the aid does come.

In the early days of this Society, while Madame Blavatsky was still alive, we had a member who was in many ways a man of tremendous power. If he had chosen to become a Black Magician he would have been a very effective specimen. Sometimes he was slightly unscrupulous ; he had a passion for knowledge ; he would have done almost anything—even something a little shady—to gain further information. He was a doctor of medicine, and in attending upon one of our members he discovered her to be a clairvoyant of rather rare powers in certain ways. Finding this, when she was convalescent he asked her to join him in certain experiments. He said to her quite openly on the physical plane : " You have a very wonderful power ; if you will allow me to mesmerize you, to put you into a trance, I am sure that you can attain heights which I myself can never touch, and in that way we should gain much knowledge which at present is out of our reach." The lady refused—I think quite rightly ; for such domination is a most dangerous thing, and should certainly not be undertaken except under exceptional conditions and with elaborate safeguards.

At any rate, she refused absolutely. The doctor was very much dissatisfied and declined to take " No " for an answer ; but for the time he went his way. That same night he materialized in her bedroom and began to attempt mesmeric passes. Not unnaturally she was intensely angry ; she felt a great sense of flaming outrage that he should dare to intrude upon her, that he should try to force upon her what she had definitely and after due consideration declined ; and she set herself to fight against his influence with all her strength. But she quickly realized that her mental power was nothing as compared to his ; that her will was being slowly but surely overborne ; so, knowing that she was fighting a losing battle, she called upon her Master (the Master Kuthumi) for help.

The result was not only instantaneous, but it astonished her beyond words. Remember that she was filled with the most violent and passionate sense of outrage. In a flash, in a moment, as she made the call, she saw the doctor disappearing in the far distance. That was perhaps not quite so wonderful ; but what struck her, what she never forgot, was that in one moment her whole feeling was absolutely changed. The anger was gone, the sense of outrage was gone, and all that she felt towards the disappearing doctor was profound regret that a man who had such wonderful powers should misuse them in that way. So, you see, when there is a real extremity help is at hand : but I think none of us will call for it unless we are absolutely forced to do so.

Think of others and not of yourself ; think of loyalty and love to your Master, and how you can serve him best by spreading his influence among your brethren ; then you need not be afraid that you will lose instead of gaining by any wonderful inspiration that has come to you.

THE CERTAINTY OF SUCCESS

The pupil must make up his mind that with regard to his effort towards self-improvement he will never allow himself to be discouraged by failure, even though it be often repeated. However many times he may have failed in his .effort, however many falls he may have on the path which he sets before himself, there is exactly the same reason for getting up and going on after the thousandth fall that there was after the first. In the physical plane there are many things which are frankly impossible ; but that is not the case in the higher worlds. We cannot lift a ton weight without machinery, but in the higher worlds it is possible with perseverance to lift the weight of our many imperfections. The reason for this is obvious if we think. Human muscles are not so constructed as to be able to lift a ton, and no conceivable training of them could enable them to do it, because the force behind them is limited. In spiritual matters, the man has behind him the whole divine power on which he can draw, and so little by little and by repeated efforts he will become strong enough to overcome any obstacle.

People often say : " I can deal with things on the physical, but on the astral and mental I can do very little ; it is so difficult." That is the reverse of the truth. They are not accustomed to thinking and working in that finer matter, and so they believe that they cannot. But as soon as their will is set, they will find that things will follow the direction of that will in a way impossible in the physical world.

Some pupils have found themselves much helped in this work by the use of a talisman or amulet. That may be a very real aid, since the physical nature has to be dealt with and brought into subjection, as well as the mind and the emotions, and it is without doubt the hardest to influence ; a talisman strongly charged with magnetism for a particular purpose by someone who knows how to do it may be an invaluable help, as I have explained at considerable length in *The Hidden Side of Things*. Many people hold themselves superior to such aids, and say that they need no help ; but for myself, I have found the task so arduous that I am glad to avail myself of any assistance that may be offered to me.

CHAPTER VI

OTHER PRESENTATIONS

THE MASTERS AND THE BROTHERHOOD

ALL this while, the Adept, besides using his pupil as an apprentice, has been preparing him for presentation to the Great White Brotherhood for Initiation. The whole object of the existence of that Brotherhood is to promote the work of evolution, and the Master knows that when the pupil is ready for the stupendous honour of being received as a member of it, he will be of very much more use in the world than before. Therefore it is his wish to raise his pupil to that level as soon as possible. In the Oriental books on the subject, written thousands of years ago, are to be found many accounts of this preparatory period of instruction ; and when reference has been made to it in the earlier Theosophical literature it has been called the Probationary Path—the term referring not to being put upon probation by any individual Adept, but to a course of general training preparatory to Initiation. I myself used the term in *Invisible Helpers*, but have lately avoided it on account of the confusion caused by the employment of the same word in two distinct senses.

The method really adopted is readily comprehensible, and is in fact much like that of some of our older Universities. If a student wishes to take a degree at one of those, he must first pass the entrance examination of the university and then be admitted to one of the colleges. The Head of that College is technically responsible for his progress, and may be regarded as his tutor-in-chief. The man will have to work to a large extent by himself, but the Head of his College is expected to see that he is properly prepared before he is presented to take his degree. The Head does not give the degree; it is conferred by that abstraction called the university—usually at the hands of its Vice-Chancellor. It is the university, not the Head of the College, that arranges the examination and confers the various degrees; the work of the Head of the College is to see that the candidate is duly prepared, and generally to be to some extent responsible for him. In the process of such preparation he may, as a private gentleman, enter into whatever social or other relations with his pupil he may think proper; but all that is not the business of the university.

Just in the same way the Great White Brotherhood has nothing to do with the relations between a Master and his pupil; that is a matter solely for the private consideration of the Master himself. The Initiation is given by an appointed member of the Brotherhood in the name of the One Initiator; that is the only way in which an Initiation can be obtained. Whenever an Adept considers that one of his pupils is fit for the first Initiation, he gives notice of that fact and presents him for it; the Brotherhood asks only whether the man is ready for Initiation, and not what is the relationship between him and any Adept. It is not their affair whether he is at the stage of probation, acceptance or sonship. At the same time it is true that a candidate for Initiation must be proposed and seconded by two of the higher members of the Brotherhood—that is to say, by two who have reached the level of Adeptship; and it is certain that no Master would propose a man for the tests of Initiation unless he had with regard to him the certainty of his fitness which could only come from very close identification with his consciousness.

The Probationary Path is thus a stage leading up to the Path Proper, which begins at the first Initiation. In the Oriental books both these Paths are described quite impersonally, as though no private Masters existed. The questions are first raised: " How is a man living in the ordinary world brought to this Probationary Path, and how does he come to know that such a thing exists ? "

FOUR WAYS TO THE PATH

In the books we are told that there are four ways, any one of which may bring a man to the commencement of the Path of development. First, by being in the presence of, and getting to know, those who are already interested along that line. Some of us, for example, may have been monks or nuns in the Middle Ages. We may have come into contact in that life with an abbot or abbess who had deep experience of the inner world—a person like St. Theresa. We may, looking up to that leader, have earnestly wished that such experience should come to us; and our wish for that may have been quite unselfish. It may be that we did not think of the importance that would come to us or of the satisfaction of achievement, but simply of the joy of helping others, as we saw the abbot able to help others through his deeper discernment. Such a feeling in that life would certainly bring us in the next incarnation into touch with teaching on the subject.

It happens that, in lands which have the European culture, almost the only way in which we can get the inner teaching put clearly before us is by coming into the Theosophical Society, or by reading Theosophical works. There have been mystical or spiritualistic works which have given some information, which have gone a long way, but there are none, so far as I know, which state the case so clearly, so scientifically, as the Theosophical literature has done. I know of no other book which contains such a wealth of information as *The Secret Doctrine*.

There are, of course, the sacred books of the Hindus and of other nations, and there is a great deal on this subject in those, but it is not put in a way which makes it easy for us, with our training, to assimilate it or to appreciate it. When, having read Theosophical books, we take up some of those beautiful translations of Oriental works, we can see our Theosophy in them. In the Christian Bible (though that is in many places not well translated from our point of view) we shall find a great deal of Theosophy; but before we can find it we must know the system. When we have studied Theosophy we see at once how many texts support it, and cannot rationally be explained without it ; we see how Church ceremonies, before apparently meaningless, leap into life under the illumination of the teaching, and become vivid and full of interest. Yet I never heard of anyone who was able to deduce the Theosophical system from either the texts or the ceremonies.

So one way of approaching the Path is by being with those who are already treading it. Another way is by reading or hearing about it. All this teaching came to me in 1882 through Mr. Sinnett's book *The Occult World* ; and immediately after that I read his second book *Esoteric Buddhism*. I knew at once instinctively that what was written was true, and I accepted it ; and to hear and to read about it at once fired me with the desire and the determined intention to know more, to learn all I could on the subject, to pursue it all over the world if necessary until I found it. Shortly after that I gave up my position in the Church of England and went out to India, because it seemed that more could be done there.

Those are two ways in which people are led to the Path—by reading and hearing of it, and by being in close association with those who are already treading it. The third way which is mentioned in Oriental books is by intellectual development ; by sheer force of hard thinking a man may come to grasp some of these principles, though I think that method is rare. Again, they tell us of a fourth way—that by the long practice of virtue men may come to the beginning of the Path—that a man may so develop the soul by steadily practising the right so far as he knows it that eventually more and more of the light will open before him.

THE BUDDHIST CLASSIFICATION

Forty years ago, when the Qualifications for the Path were first put before me from the Esoteric Buddhist point of view, they were given as follows : the first of them, Discrimination, called by the Hindus *Viveka*, was described as *Manodvāravajjana*, which means the opening of the doors of the mind, or perhaps escaping by the door of the mind. That is a very interesting way of putting it, since Discrimination arises from the fact that our minds have been opened in such a way that we can understand what is real and what unreal, what is desirable and what undesirable, and can distinguish between the pairs of opposites.

The second qualification, Desirelessness, known as *Vairāgya* among the Hindus, was taught to me as *Parikamma*, meaning preparation for action, the idea being that we must prepare ourselves for action in the occult world by learning to do right purely for right's sake. This involves the attainment of a condition of higher indifference in which one certainly no longer cares for the results of action ; and so it comes to mean the same thing as Desirelessness, though it is put from a different point of view.

The Six Points of Good Conduct, called *Shatsampatti* in the Hindu scheme, were given as *Upāchāro*, which means attention to conduct. For the convenience of the student who would like to compare the Six Points with those given in *At the Feet of the Master*, I will reprint here what I said about them in *Invisible Helpers*.

These are called in Pali :

(*a*) *Sama* (quietude)—that purity and calmness of thought which comes from perfect control of the mind—a qualification exceedingly difficult of attainment, and yet most necessary, for unless the mind moves only in obedience to the guidance of the will, it cannot be a perfect instrument for the Master's work in the future. This qualification is a very comprehensive one, and includes within itself both the self-control and the calmness necessary for astral work.

(*b*) *Dama* (subjugation)—a similar mastery over, and therefore purity in, one's actions and words—a quality which again follows necessarily from its predecessor.

(*c*) *Uparati* (cessation)—explained as a cessation from bigotry or from belief in the necessity of any act or ceremony prescribed by a particular religion—so leading the aspirant to independence of thought and to a wide and generous tolerance.

(*d*) *Titikkha* (endurance or forbearance)—by which is meant the readiness to bear with cheerfulness whatever one's karma may bring upon one, and to part with anything and everything worldly whenever it may be necessary. It also includes the idea of complete absence of resentment for wrong, the man knowing that those who do him wrong are but instruments of his own karma.

(*e*) *Samādhāna* (intentness)—one-pointedness, involving the incapability of being turned aside from one's path by temptation.

(f) *Saddhā* (faith)—confidence in one's Master and oneself : confidence, that is, that the Master is a competent teacher, and that, however diffident the pupil may feel as to his own powers he has yet within him that divine spark which, when fanned into a flame, will one day enable him to achieve even as his Master has done.

The fourth qualification in the Hindu classification is called *Mumukshutva*, usually translated as an ardent longing for liberation from the wheel of births and deaths, while among the Buddhists the name given to it is *Anuloma*, which means direct order or succession, signifying that its attainment follows as a natural consequence from the other three.

HINDU YOGA

The series of qualifications described above is at once seen to be quite in accord with those given in *At the Feet of the Master*, which in turn have exactly the same framework as those mentioned in the books ascribed in India to Shankarāchārya and his followers, for the use of candidates aiming at yoga. The term yoga, which has long been used in India, means union, and as that is generally considered to imply union with the Divine, it is in fact unity. But the expression refers in all the different schools of yoga in India not only to the distant goal of union, but also to the methods of training prescribed as leading to that goal ; therefore some say that the meaning of yoga is meditation, which plays a large part in most of the systems.

It must not be assumed, however, that meditation is the only or even the principal means to yoga, for there have been and still are many different schools, each having its own special methods. Professor Ernest Wood has described the seven principal schools of yoga in *Raja Yoga : The Occult Training of the Hindus*,[1] and has shown how they belong each to one of the seven Rays, so that they must be regarded as complementary, and not as rival methods of practice. Each great Teacher expounded a method suited to one type of ego—a fact so well known among the Hindus that they are always liberal and tolerant in their thought, and consider it perfectly right for each man to follow the method which suits his temperament.

[1] Out of print.

This book explains that in each school there are certain characteristics similar to those which prevail in the teaching of our Masters; there is always a preliminary training—accompanied by the requirement of high moral attainments—before the candidate can enter the Path Proper, and on reaching that Path he is always advised to see a master or guru. In the school of Patanjali, for example, which is the first to be treated, as it is the oldest of which we have any written record, there are ten commandments, the first five of which are negative (prohibiting injury to others, untruth, theft, incontinence and greed) and the second five positive (enjoining cleanliness, contentment, effort, study and devotion).

In the preliminary course of training there are three requirements—*tapas* or effort, *svādhyāya* or study of one's own nature with the aid of the Scriptures, and *Ishvara-pranidhāna* or devotion to God at all times; these the author compares respectively with our three qualifications of *shatsampatti* or good conduct, which involves the use of the will in a number of efforts, *viveka* or discrimination, which implies understanding of the true and the false, inside and outside oneself, and *vairāgya* or desirelessness, since personal emotions can best be transcended by devotion. After developing these preliminary requirements the candidate on the path uses his will to master and employ every part of his nature in a series of steps, physical, etheric, astral, mental and beyond; and because of this the school is described as of the first Ray, on which the use of the will predominates.

The second school of yoga is that of Shri Krishna, particularly expounded in the great poem the *Bhagavad-Gītā*, which has been translated with such accuracy and beauty by Dr. Besant, and also in a freer rendering by Sir Edwin Arnold under the title of *The Song Celestial*. This teaches above all else the doctrine of love. The disciple Arjuna, to whom the Guru spoke, was a great lover of mankind; according to the scripture this great soldier sank down upon the floor of his chariot before the battle of Kurukshetra began, full of sorrow because he loved his enemies and could not bear to injure them. The teacher Shri Krishna then explained to him, amid much philosophical teaching, that the greatest thing in life is service, that God himself is the greatest server—for he keeps the wheel of life revolving, not because any benefit can possibly accrue to him in consequence, but for the sake of the world—and that men should follow his example and work for the welfare of mankind. Many Great Ones, he said, had reached perfection by following this path of life, by doing their duty without personal desire. To love without ceasing is the way of the second Ray ; in the *Gītā* it is shown how this love should be directed to men and other beings in karma yoga (the yoga by action or work) and to God in bhakti yoga (the yoga by devotion).

Once more three preliminary teachings are given. To reach the love-wisdom a candidate must practise devotion or reverence, inquiry or investigation, and service—the first involving right emotion, the second right thought and understanding, and the third right use of the will in practical life—which again are compared to our first three qualifications. It is particularly interesting to notice that the Teacher says that when the candidate has prepared himself in this triple way, " The Wise Ones, who know the essence of things, will teach you the Wisdom "—in other words the aspirant will find the Master.

The third school, that of Shankarāchārya, as already mentioned, presents the qualifications in the order in which we have them, placing *viveka* or discrimination first. It is intended for those people whose temperament leads them to want to understand what they are about—not only what service they ought to perform, but in what way their contribution fits into the scheme of things and the development of mankind. It must be noted that the Master Kuthumi, in presenting these qualifications, has interpreted them all newly in the light of love.

The fourth school is that of *hatha yoga*. Rightly understood, this involves a severe physical purification and training, intended to bring the body into a perfect state of health, orderly functioning and refinement, so as to enable the ego using it to attain as much as is possible for him in the present incarnation. To this end there are many practices, including breathing exercises, intended to act upon the nervous system and the etheric double as well as upon those parts of the dense body usually trained in courses of physical culture. Unfortunately very much of what appears in the popular literature on this subject reflects only a superstitious distortion of the real teaching, and describes various repellent forms of subjugation and mortification of the body which were common also in Europe a few centuries ago ; but in all the Sanskrit books dealing with *hatha yoga* it is clearly stated that the object of the physical practices is to bring the body into the highest state of health and efficiency.

The fifth school, denominated *laya yoga*, aims at awakening the higher faculties of man through a knowledge of kundalini, the " serpent-power ", which in most people lies latent at the base of the spine, and of the seven chakras or force-centres through which the awakened power is guided. Of these centres and this force I have already written to some extent in *The Inner Life* and *The Hidden Side of Things*. I have now gathered this material together, made some additions to it, and published a monograph on the subject with large coloured illustrations of the seven chakras and of the courses of the various prānas or streams of vitality.[1] The methods of this and the previous school are not, however, recommended to Western students, or indeed to anyone who is not specially directed by a competent teacher to practise them. They are suitable only for those who have the Oriental physical heredity, and can live as simply and peacefully as do some Orientals ; for others they are not only unlikely to be successful, but are distinctly dangerous to health, and even to life. I have known many sad cases of disease and madness to result from attempts on these lines, especially in America.

The sixth school is that of bhakti or devotion. This is also taught to a large extent in the *Bhagavad-Gītā* ; indeed, we find it in every religion among those true devotees who put their trust entirely in the Divine—who do not pray for personal favours, but

---

[1] See the author's book *The Chakras*, issued by The Theosophical Publishing House, Adyar, Madras.

are quite convinced that God is perfect master of his world, that he knows what he is doing, and that therefore all is well; they are therefore more than content, they are thrilled with ecstasy, if they can but have the opportunity and the privilege to serve and obey him in any way.

MANTRAS

Lastly we have the seventh school, which in India is called *mantra yoga*. It may be well to expound its principle here at somewhat greater length than the others, for the Ray of which it is one of the principal expressions is just now becoming dominant in the world, and is playing a large and increasing part among us in both East and West.

The word *mantra* is Sanskrit, and is practically equivalent to our word charm or spell. The majority of mantras used in India for good purposes are verses from the Vedas, pronounced with intention according to the traditional methods, which are the outcome of practical occult knowledge. There are also many mantras employed by men who follow the Tantras, and those are just as often used for evil as for good; so we find afloat in India a great number of them, both desirable and undesirable. If we are to classify them from our Western point of view, I should say that there are five main types of these mantras :

1. Those that work simply by faith.
2. Those that work by association.
3. Those that work by agreement or covenant.
4. Those that work by their meaning.
5. Those that work by their sound, without reference to meaning.

THE EFFECT OF FAITH

1. The first class produce their effect simply because of the strong conviction of the operator that the result must follow, and because of the faith of the person upon whom they are operating. If

both men are quite sure that something will happen—say the cure of a wound or a disease—then that thing *does* happen ; and in some cases the faith of only one of the parties seems to be sufficient. In England, and indeed among the peasants in all countries, quite a number of such charms are being used in country places. People have little forms of words, generally semi-religious in character, which have been handed down to them by their forefathers, and these are supposed to produce definite results. They often seem the merest nonsense ; the wording is frequently not even coherent. They are probably corruptions of certain forms of words, either in English or in some cases Latin or French. They do not work by sound, for they have none of the sonority indispensable to the true mantra ; but when recited over patients under certain conditions they are at times unquestionably effective. In such cases it must be faith in the ancient formula which produces the result.

Many similar charms found in Oriental countries appear to act through faith. I can give one example from my personal knowledge which I suspect to be of that nature. Once when I was in the interior of Ceylon I was bitten rather badly in the hand by a dog. The wound was bleeding considerably. A casual passer-by, an agricultural labourer by the look of him, rushed up, snatched a leaf off the nearest shrub, pressed it on the wound and muttered some words which I could not understand ; and the wound immediately stopped bleeding. This charm, therefore, undoubtedly worked, and certainly not through any faith of mine, for I had no idea of what the man was going to do. As is always the case in the East, the man would not take any money for the exercise of his powers. So far as I was able to hear the words, I should say that they were incoherent, or if coherent were at any rate neither Sinhalese, which would have been the man's own language, nor Sanskrit. I have been told that there are similar charms against snake-bite in Ceylon, and they also appear to work—again by faith, I imagine ; everyone concerned is sure that something is going to happen, and so it does happen.

There is a variant of this type in which success is achieved by the strength of will of the operator. As he speaks his word or makes his sign he is utterly determined that a given result shall follow, and accordingly it does follow. I have seen Prince Harisinghji Rupsinghji of Kathiawar cure instantaneously a man suffering from the sting of a scorpion. The man was already pallid and half fainting from fright, writhing and groaning in acute pain, and scarcely able to drag himself along with the assistance of two friends; the Prince made over the wound the sign of the five-pointed star, spoke sharply one Sanskrit word, and in a moment the victim, who had sunk to the ground, staggered to his feet, declaring himself well and entirely free from pain, and then proceeded to prostrate himself before the Prince in gratitude.

ASSOCIATION OF THOUGHT

2. There are mantras which work by association. Certain forms of words bring with them definite ideas, and quite change the current of our thoughts and feelings. An example of this is the National Anthem of a country. As soon as we hear that strain we straighten ourselves up instinctively and pour out our loyalty and goodwill towards the land and its ruler. And this evokes a definite response, for, according to the law, force so outpoured unselfishly must call down a corresponding descent of power from on high. This response comes through certain types of Angels connected with the work of the First Ray, and the attention of these is attracted whenever the National Anthem is sung, and they pour out their blessing upon and through the people whose loyalty has been thereby stimulated.

Another example, though far less powerful, of a similar type of mantra is "The Voice that breathed o'er Eden"; we cannot hear that hymn without thinking strongly of a wedding, and all the festive feeling of goodwill usually connected with such a function. Various Christmas hymns and carols also invoke in our minds a very definite stream of thought. The war-cries which played so prominent a part in the battles of mediaeval times were mantras of this type. There are a number of such forms which instantly call up corresponding ideas, and they produce results because of their associations, and not because of anything inherent in themselves.

ANGELIC CO-OPERATION

3. There are certain mantras which work by agreement or by covenant. Most religions appear to have some examples of this type. The great Muhammadan call from the minaret partakes of this character, although it has also something about it of the type which we have last considered. It is a declaration of faith : " There is no God but God " (or, as some have translated it, " There is nothing but God ", which is an eternal truth) " and Muhammad is the Prophet of God." It is interesting to see the effect produced upon the people by these words. It is far more than the mere thought of their meaning, for it calls up in those who hear it a fiery faith, an outburst of devotion, which is quite beautiful in its way, and very characteristic of Muhammadanism. This might be a mere instance of association, but for the fact that Angels of a certain type are evoked by the call, and it is their action which causes much of the enthusiasm which is exhibited.

It is perhaps in the Christian religion that we find the best examples of this third type of mantra, as those who know anything of the Services of the Church will realize. The greatest of them all is *Hoc Corpus est Meum*, " This is My Body " ; for the Christ himself has made a covenant with his Church that whenever that call is uttered, whenever those words are pronounced in any language by one of his duly ordained Priests, he will respond thereto. But this power is given under conditions, given only to those who are prepared by another mantra of the same type to receive it—a mantra also prescribed by Christ himself—the words " Receive ye the Holy Ghost."

The power which with these words he gave to his disciples just before he left them has been handed down with the same words in an unbroken chain for nigh two thousand years, and constitutes what is called the Apostolic Succession. Whenever a Priest who has been duly ordained in that Succession pronounces with intention those other words " This is My Body ", a certain wonderful change is thereby brought about in the bread over which he speaks them, so that though its outward appearance remains the same its higher principles or counterparts are superseded by the very life of the Christ himself, so that it becomes just as truly his vehicle as was the body which he wore in Palestine.

There is no doubt of the working of this mantra " This is My Body ", for its action can be seen today by those who have eyes to see.   Lord Tennyson tells us in *The Idylls of the King* that Galahad, describing the celebration of the Eucharist, said :

> I saw the fiery face as of a child
> That smote itself into the bread.

And just so any clairvoyant who watches the offering of that same Holy Sacrifice today may see the counterpart of the bread flash out into a line of living light when the same sacred mantra is spoken. All the branches of the Christian Church—the Roman Catholic, the Greek Orthodox, the Anglican and the Liberal Catholic Churches— that celebrate the Holy Eucharist at all in the form which was laid down by the Christ, use those Words as part of their Liturgy, and in all of them that wonderful result is produced.   All these branches of the Church, too, invoke the angelic Hosts to assist in the Service, and that is done not only by a particular form of words, but also (when the Service is sung) by a particular form of music, by an arrangement of sounds which has persisted with but slight variation from an early period in the history of the Church.   The Angels of a special type take those words as a call, and at once attend to play their part in the Service which is to be held.[1]

THE EFFECT OF REPETITION

4.   We come now to a class of mantras which act by virtue of the meaning of the words repeated.   A man recites a certain form of

---

[1] For a full account of the working of this most marvellous mantra, see *The Science of the Sacraments*.

words with firm confidence over and over again, so that their meaning beats very strongly upon his brain and upon his mental body ; and if he is trying, for instance, to do a certain piece of occult work, such a repetition will greatly strengthen his will. Such mantras can be used in many different ways. As far as the man is concerned, they produce one of two effects ; either they strengthen his will to do that which he is trying to do, or they impress upon him the absolute conviction that it will be done. Mantras of this type appear in the daily meditations prescribed for the Hindus, and in most occult schools ; the repetition of certain sentences at fixed points during the day tends to impress the ideas contained in the sentences strongly upon the mind. " More radiant than the Sun, purer than the Snow, subtler than the Ether, is the Self, the Spirit within my heart. I am that Self ; that Self am I ", is a good example of this type of mantra, and it is of course just as effective when thought as when spoken aloud.

BLESSINGS

Under this heading should come the various types of blessings such as are given in the Church, in the Temple, in the Mosque, in Freemasonry, and by the pupils of our Masters. Blessings may be arranged in two sections—those which a man gives from himself, and those which are given through him as an official by higher power. The first kind of blessing is merely an expression of an earnest good wish. A typical instance of this is the blessing some-times given by a father to his son, either on the death-bed of the former, or when the latter is about to start on some long and possibly dangerous journey. The blessing of the dying Isaac to his sons Esau and Jacob is a good illustration, though in that particular case com-plications were introduced by the scandalous duplicity of Jacob. Readers of the Scripture account of this incident will remember that Isaac was fully persuaded of the effectiveness of his blessing, and when he discovered the deceit which had been practised upon him, he was unable to reverse the wish which he had expressed.

The question then arises, does a blessing of this nature bring any result, and if so how is that result produced ? The only reply that can be given is that this will depend upon the earnestness of the good wish and the amount of spiritual force put into it. The blessing makes a thought-form which attaches itself to the person who is blessed ; the size, strength and persistence of that thought-form depend upon the will-power of the person giving the benediction. If the words were uttered as a matter of form, without much feeling or intention behind them, the effect would be slight and transient ; on the other hand, if they came from a full heart and were uttered with definite determination, their effect would be deep and lasting.

The second type of blessing is that which is uttered by an official appointed for the purpose through whom power flows from some higher source. A good example of this is the benediction with which most Church services conclude. This may not be given by any one whose ecclesiastical rank is lower than that of Priest ; and to this extent the blessing may be said to partake of the character of mantras of the third class, since the power of giving a definite blessing is one of those conferred upon the Priest at his ordination. In this case he is simply a channel for the power from on high, and if it should unfortunately happen that he speaks it merely as a matter of course and as part of his ritual, that would make no difference to the spiritual power outpoured.

The blessing flows equally over all, but the amount of the influences which any individual can obtain from it depends upon his receptivity. If he is full of love and devotion, he may be very greatly helped and uplifted ; if he is carelessly thinking of some other matter, he will gain only the benefit of the impact of a higher vibration. It will be noted that when a Bishop is present at a service he always pronounces the benediction. The reason for that is that at his Consecration his higher principles are opened up much beyond those of the Priest ; therefore power at those higher levels can be poured through him. The same general principle holds in Freemasonry also, for it is only either an Installed Master or an ordained Chaplain who pronounces the words of blessing in the course of the closing of the Lodge.

We have already seen that one who has been accepted as a pupil of a Master has thereby become a channel for his influence ; and while that influence is always flowing through the pupil, he can certainly direct its force for the moment upon any person, as he wishes. In the same way, one who is an Initiate can give the blessing of the Brotherhood, which is in truth that of the King who is its Head.

THE POWER OF SOUND

5. We may now consider the type of mantra which works only by its sound. The vibration which the sound sets in motion impinges upon the various bodies of man, and tends to bring them into harmony with it. A sound in the first place is an undulation in the air, and every musical sound has a number of overtones which it sets in motion as well. Four or five or more overtones are detected and recognized in music, but the oscillations extend a great deal further than the ear can follow. Corresponding waves are set up in higher and finer matter altogether, and therefore the chanting of a note or series of notes produces effects upon the higher vehicles. There are sounds (I suppose we must still call them sounds), overtones, which are too fine to affect the air ; nevertheless they set etheric matter in motion, and that etheric matter communicates its oscillations to the man who recites the mantra and also to other people around him, and if he is directing his will towards any particular person, to that person the vibration will assuredly go. Thus the mantras which work by sound may produce decidedly material results on the physical plane, though there are other and finer waves sent forth at the same time which may affect the higher vehicles.

Such a mantra usually consists of several ordered sounds, very resonant and sonorous in character. Sometimes a single syllable only is used, as in the Sacred Word, *Om* ; but there are several ways of saying that, and they produce quite different results according to the notes upon which its syllables are chanted, and the way in which they are pronounced. For some purposes we emphasize and prolong the open sound ; we combine the A U into O, strengthen that and carry it on for perhaps half the time of recitation, and then change to the M sound.   But for other purposes the O should be quite short, and the humming inside the head and in the centres, which is a very powerful sound, should be prolonged. The results of these two methods differ greatly. When the O is prolonged we are affecting one another and the surrounding world, but with the long M almost the entire effect produced acts upon ourselves. Sometimes the three letters A U M are sounded separately. Again, it may be taken on many different notes in succession, in a sort of *arpeggio*.   I have heard that according to the Indian books there are supposed to be about one hundred and seventy ways of pronouncing the Word, each with its different effect, and it is thought to be the most powerful of all mantras.

This Hindu sacred word corresponds to the Egyptian *amen*. From that word also was made the *aion* of the Greeks and the *aivum* in Latin. The word *aeon* is one derivative of it.   It has been said that *Om* is the word which represents the name of the Logos, the Ineffable Name, in our fifth root race, and that the word used in a similar way in the fourth root race was Tau. Swami T. Subba Row once told us that these substituted words, which are given in each root race, are all syllables of a great word which will be complete in the seventh root race.

The special effect of this word when properly sounded at the beginning of meditation or in a meeting is always like a call to attention.   It arranges the particles of the subtle bodies in much the same way as an electric current acts upon the atoms in a bar of iron. Before the passing of such a current, the ultimate atoms in the metal lie pointing in various directions, but when the bar is magnetized by the electric current, they all turn over and lean in one direction. Just so, at the sound of the sacred word every particle in us responds, and we are then in the best condition to benefit by the meditation or study which is to follow.   At the same time it acts as a call to other beings—human and non-human—who at once gather round, some with understanding of the meaning and power of the word, and others brought by the strangely attractive sound.

This matter of sound is one that penetrates very deeply. " By the Word of the Lord were the Heavens made " in the first place. The Logos or Word is the first Emanation from the Infinite, and that quite certainly is far more than a mere figure of speech. It represents a fact, although that Emanation takes place at a level where there could not be anything such as we mean by sound, for there would be no air to convey it. Yet that which corresponds to and acts like sound is the power which is employed to create the Universe.

I do not know that we can hope to have any understanding on this plane, in this world down here, of what is meant by that Creative Word. " He spake, and it was done." God said : " Let there be Light, and there was Light." This was the first Expression of the Deity ; the Eternal Thought concealed in darkness comes forth as the Creative Word. Perhaps because of this great Truth, words sung or spoken down here invoke higher power—power out of all proportion to the level to which they themselves belong. I am sure that there is another side of this whole question of sound which our minds cannot reach at present ; we can only faintly adumbrate it. But at least we can see that the power of sound is a very great and wonderful thing.

All mantras that depend upon the power of sound are valuable only in the language in which they have been arranged. If we translate such a one into another language, we shall have another and quite different group of sounds. Broadly speaking, the good mantra which is intended to harmonize the body and to produce beneficient results consists largely of long open vowels. We find this in our own Sacred Word, and the same is true of the Amen of the Egyptians, which has been handed down into the Christian Church. It is, by the way, best sounded on two notes. The Church has its traditional way of taking it on two notes a semitone apart—usually F sharp and G.

Mantras which are used for evil purposes contain nearly always short vowels and consonants of a tearing and disruptive character, such as *hrim, kshrang* or *phut*. These uncouth exclamations are delivered with a furious energy and spitefulness which certainly makes them terribly powerful for evil. Sometimes all the vowels in turn are inserted into these cacophonous combinations of consonants, and their utterances conclude with some peculiarly explosive curses which it seems impossible to express in any ordinary system of letters. In Oriental countries, where they know something about these things, I fear that the mantra is often used for evil purposes. I have come across a good deal of that in connection with Voodoo and Obeah ceremonies, of which I saw something both in the West Indies and South America, and I know that there is much hatred put into such spells and incantations.

Our connection with mantras will be only with those of a beneficient and kindly nature, and not with the maleficient. But good and ill alike have the same method of working; they are all intended to produce vibrations in the subtle bodies, either of the reciter or of those at whom he aims the mantra. Sometimes they are intended to impose entirely new rates of oscillation. It strikes Western minds oddly that people should be recommended to recite a mantra three thousand times. Our first feeling is: How can we find time? We say that time is money; that Oriental says that time is naught; it is a difference in the point of view. The Oriental methods and ideas are often unsuited to our Western lives; but none the less they have their value for those for whom they are intended.

The Brahmana practically spends his life in religious recitations, for every act that he performs all through the day is always accompanied by some text or pious thought. It is a life lived absolutely in religion, or rather it is supposed to be such. In many cases today it is an outer form only, a sort of shell; but men still recite the words, even though they may not put the old life and energy into them. They have plenty of time; they can well afford to repeat a phrase a hundred and eight times a day; and the object of their doing so is perfectly clear.

The Christ is said to have warned his disciples not to use vain repetitions when they prayed, as did the heathen; and from that text the deduction has been made that all repetitions are useless. They assuredly would be so in an invocation addressed to the Deity, for they would imply that he had not heard the first request ! They would be (or should be) unnecessary for disciples—for men who have already made some progress along the path of development; to formulate an intention clearly and to express it once strongly should surely be sufficient for them. But the ordinary man of the world has by no means reached that stage; it often needs a long course of steady hammering to impress a new vibration upon him, and so for him repetitions are far from useless, for they are deliberately intended to produce definite results. The constant impinging of these sounds (and of the various undulations which they set up) upon the different vehicles does tend steadily to bring those vehicles into harmony with a particular set of ideas.

This tuning-up of vibrations is analogous to the work done by an Indian guru upon his pupils, which has already been mentioned in Chapter IV. All the time the waves radiating from his astral body are playing upon their astral bodies, the waves from his mental and causal bodies are playing upon theirs; and the result is that, because his vibrations are by the hypothesis stronger than those of his pupils, he gradually brings them into closer and closer harmony with himself, if they are in any way capable of being so tuned. The constant recitation of a mantra is intended to tune up the particular part of the mental and astral bodies at which it is aimed, and there is no doubt at all that it can and does produce powerful results.

The same methods are prescribed in Christian lands. One may often see a Roman Catholic reciting his " Aves " and " Pater-nosters " many times over. Generally he just mutters them, and so they are of little use to him, except for the thoughts that they may suggest to him. In India mantras are always chanted, and the chanted mantra does produce an effect. That is one reason why the older langu-ages are better in this respect than modern tongues. Modern languages are generally spoken quickly and abruptly, and only the Italian, Spanish and Greek peasants seem to speak in the old way in long, musical cadences. In the Liberal Catholic Church, however, we especially recommended that its Service shall always be in the language of the country, because we find that far more devotion is aroused in the people if they understand clearly what is being said and can join intelligently in the ceremonies. But there can be no question that the Latin is more sonorous. Many mantras of this nature have no special meaning, are little more than a mere collection of vowels. In the *Pistis Sophia*, the well-known Gnostic treatise, there are a number of such meaningless mantras, marked in a way that must have indicated chanting.

Such rolling sonorous sounds as we find in the Indian mantras impose their rates of vibrations gradually on the various bodies, and so can be used to economize force. Anything whatever that we do by a mantra we could do by our own will without the mantra; but the mantra is like a piece of labour-saving machinery. It sets up the required vibrations, doing part of the work for us and making it easier in consequence; we may therefore regard it as a means for economizing force.

Another point with regard to mantras which is stressed in the Indian books is that students are forbidden to use them in the presence of coarse or evil-minded people, because the power of a mantra will often intensify evil as well as good. If there were a person present who could not answer to the vibrations in their higher form, he might well receive a lower octave, which would be quite likely to strengthen the evil in him. We should never use a mantra where there are people who are likely to be injured by it.

Madame Blavatsky told us, I remember, that a mantra might be recited not for oneself at all, but with a special view to someone whom it was thought it might help. In this way we might recite the Sacred Word or the Gayatri, or any of those beautiful Buddhist mantras which flow so sweetly, thinking strongly of a special person and projecting towards him the force of the mantra. But she advised us to use these things with care. Again, she gave a caution that no one should attempt to use a mantra which is too high for him. None such will be given to us by our teachers; but I would say this, as a caution to neophytes, that if the reciting even of the Sacred Word in any particular way should produce headache or a feeling of nausea or faintness, it should be stopped at once. We should go on working at the development of our characters, and try it again in a few months. In using the Word, we are invoking great forces, and if we are not yet quite up to their level they may not be harmonious, and the result may be not invariably good.

In addition to the effect of the vibration of the chanted sound, many of these mantras resemble our third type in having powers associated with them. For example, certain Angels are connected with the Gayatri and the Tisarana, though they belong to very different types.

The Gayatri is perhaps the greatest and most beautiful of all the ancient mantras. It has been chanted all over India from time immemorial, and the Deva kingdom has learnt to understand it and respond to it in a very striking manner—a manner which is in itself most significant, as showing that, in an antiquity so remote that the very memory of it has been forgotten, the altruistic use of such mantras was fully comprehended and practised. It begins always with the sacred word *Om*, and with the enumeration of the planes upon which its action is desired—the three worlds in which man lives, the physical, the astral and the mental ; and as each plane is mentioned, the Devas belonging to that plane flock round the singer with joyous enthusiasm to do the work which by the recitation of the mantra he is about to give them. Students will remember that in India Shiva is sometimes called Nilakantha, the Blue-Throated, and that there is a legend connected with that title. It is interesting to note that some of the Angels who respond when the Gayatri is chanted bear that characteristic of the blue throat, and are clearly first-ray in type.

This wonderful mantra is an invocation to the Sun—of course really to the Solar Logos, who stands behind that grandest of all symbols ; and the great shaft of light which immediately pours down upon and into the reciter comes as though from the physical Sun, in whatever direction that Sun may happen to be. This shaft of light is white tinged with gold, and shot with that electric blue which is so often seen in connection with any manifestation of the power of the first Ray ; but when it has filled the very soul of the reciter it promptly shoots from him again in seven great rays of cones having the colours of the spectrum. It is as though the singer acts as a prism : yet the colour-rays which dart forth are of a shape the reverse of what we usually find in such cases. Commonly when we send out rays of spiritual force they spring forth from a point in the body— the heart, the brain, or some other centre ; and as they shoot out they steadily broaden fanwise, as do those shining from a lighthouse. But these rays start from a basis wider than the man himself—a basis which is the circumference of his aura ; and instead of widening out they decrease to a point, just as do the rays of a conventional star except that they are of course cones of light instead of mere triangles.

Another remarkable feature is that these seven rays do not radiate in a circle in all directions, but only in a semi-circle in the direction which the reciter is facing. Furthermore, these rays have a curious appearance of solidifying as they grow narrower, until they end in a point of blinding light. And a still more curious pheno- menon is that these points act as though they were living ; if a man happens to come in the way of one of them, that point curves with incredible rapidity and touches his heart and his brain, causing them to glow momentarily in response. Each ray appears to be able to produce this result on an indefinite number of people in succession ; in testing it on a closely-packed crowd we found that the rays appa- rently divided the crowd between them, each acting on the section that happened to be in front of it, and not interfering with any other section.

As to the question of the language of the mantra, it seems to be of minor importance. The repetition of the words in English,[1] having a clear intention behind them, produced the full effects. The recitation of the same thing in Sanskrit with the same intention brought about

---

[1] The literal rendering of this celebrated versicle into English is : " Om : We adore the res- plendent glory of *Savitri* our Lord ; may He inspire our devotion and understanding." But in the course of ages it has come to imply to the devout Hindu very much more than is conveyed by the mere words.

A Sanskrit scholar tells me that, while the ordinary word for the sun is *Surya*, this especial title *Savitri* is used always to imply the Sun (that is to say the Solar Logos) as inspirer or encourager. It seems to have a signification closely allied to the word Paraclete, which is often, but very unsatis- factorily, translated as the Comforter. (See *The Hidden Side of Christian Festivals*, p. 202.) My friend also emphasizes the fact that this is not a prayer to the Logos to *give* us wisdom or devotion, but the expression of an earnest aspiration and resolve that His influence shall so act upon us as to call out and to strengthen that which already exists within us.

an identical result, but in addition built round the radiating shafts a sound-form re embling a wonderfully intricate kind of carved wooden frame-work ; it provided us with something which might be imaged as a sevenfold gun through which the rays were shooting out. This sound-form extended only for a short distance, and did not seem to make any difference at all to the power or size of the rays.

When the Buddhist Tisarana is chanted the Angels that come are those especially associated with the Yellow Robe, and they bring with them a wonderful peace and joyousness, for although they are so peaceful they are amongst the most joyous in the world.

When we speak of Angels as " appearing " we must remember all the dimensions of space. They have not to " come " in the sense of starting from somewhere far away—from a far-distant heaven, for example. I do not know whether I shall make the matter hopelessly puzzling if I put it that the great forces representing the Logos manifest in those particular forms in answer to the Invocation. They are always there, always ready, but they turn themselves outward in response to the call.

That is the whole history of that sort of prayer and its answer. We have only to think strongly of an idea, and that which ensouls it or represents it will manifest itself to us. Any strong thought of devotion brings an instant response ; the Universe would be dead if it did not. It is in the natural law that the response must come ; the appeal and the reply are like the obverse and the reverse of a coin ; the answer is only the other side of the request, just as we say of karma that the effect is the other side of the cause. There is a wonderful unity in nature, but people enfold themselves so thickly in their personalities that they do not know anything about it. It is only a question of opening ourselves up. One can quite easily see that when we are able to yield ourselves to nature, we can practically command nature, because by the attitude we take we can call forth its forces, and everything works with us. This is clearly explained in *Light on the Path.* We must recognize the forces of nature, and open ourselves up to them ; and because these powers are flowing with us, everything that before was difficult becomes so much easier.

There is yet another section of the whole subject of mantras as to which I myself have very little information. There is the power not only of sound but of words as such, as numbers, and even of letters. We do not trouble about these things in modern days, but in the Sanskrit and also in the Hebrew alphabet every letter has its assigned value, not only of number, but also of power and colour. I have known clairvoyants who see ordinary Roman letters as printed in our books as each of a different colour, A being always red, let us say, B always blue, C yellow, D green, and so on. I have never had any such experience myself; I suppose my mind does not work in that way. Similarly, there are psychics who always see the days of the week as of different colours. That is not my experience; I am not sensitive in that way either, nor do I understand what is meant. That may perhaps be connected with astrological influences; I do not know. This aspect of things is also connected with mantras, and there is a school of mantrists who give to each letter a numerical value, quite independent of its position in the alphabet; and they will tell you that if they add up the values which they assign to the letters of a given word or sentence, and so arrive at a certain total, and if the same total can be made by adding the letters of another word or group of words, the same mantric effect will be produced by the two sentences. But about that I know nothing.

The mantra is usually a short, strong formula, and when for any purpose we want to produce a decided effect, that is the kind of form that our adjuration must take. If we wish to affect people profoundly and rapidly when speaking to them, we must use sentences which are short and strong, not long and rambling; they must follow the line of the military command or of the mantra; and there must be a definite climax. Suppose we wish to help a person who is frightened. We may formulate within ourselves such words as: "I am strong, strong, strong; I am part of God, and God is strength, so I am full of that strength"; and the repetition of the idea will bring the divine strength within us to the surface, and we shall be able to inspire others with our courage. In this as in all other lines, knowledge is power ; if we wish to work to the best advantage we must understand, and if we wish to understand we must study. The wise man knows how to live in peace and happiness, because his life is in harmony with God's life. Comprehending all, he sympathizes with all ; he has cast selfishness behind him for ever, and he lives but to help and to bless.

THE REQUIREMENTS NEVER CHANGE

In considering the different systems described above it must not be imagined that their methods are mutually exclusive. Each plan contains something of nearly all the others ; they are defined by that which dominates in each case. Nor should it be supposed that any of them are strictly necessary. What is required is that which lies beneath all of them—the development of character, purification of life and devotion to service so strongly emphasized in *At the Feet of the Master*.

From this comparison of the different systems it will be seen that the qualifications which the aspirant must develop preparatory to the first great Initiation are fundamentally the same, however much they may appear to differ at first glance. Certainly for twenty-five centuries, and probably for a long time before that, this quite systematic procedure has been followed with regard to the evolution of those special persons who persist in struggling ahead ; and although at certain times circumstances are more favourable for Initiation than at others, the requirements remain the same, and we must be careful not to fall into the erroneous thought that the qualifications have been in any way reduced. We thus find that these different lines all bring us to the same point of Initiation.

PART III
THE GREAT INITIATIONS

CHAPTER VII

THE FIRST INITIATION

THE ONE INITIATOR

MOST people when they think of Initiation have in mind a step to be gained for themselves. They think of the Initiate as a man who has developed himself very highly, and has become a great and glorious figure, as compared with the man of the outer world. That is true ; but the whole question will be better understood if we try to look down on it from a higher point of view. The importance of Initiation does not lie in the exaltation of an individual, but in the fact that he has now become definitely one with a great Order, the Communion of Saints, as it is very beautifully put in the Christian Church, though few ever pay attention to the real meaning of those words.

The stupendous reality that lies behind Initiation into the Brotherhood will be better understood after we have considered the organization of the Occult Hierarchy and the work of the Masters, to be dealt with in later chapters. The Candidate has now become more than an individual man, because he is a unit in a tremendous force. On every planet the Solar Logos has his Representative, acting as his Viceroy. On our globe the title given to this great Official is the Lord of the World. He is the Head of the Brotherhood ; and the Brotherhood is not only a body of Men each of whom has his own duties to perform ; it is also a stupendous unity—a fully flexible instrument in the Lord's hand, a mighty weapon that he can wield. There is a marvellous and incomprehensible plan by which the One, having become many, is now becoming One again, not that any unit in the whole scheme will lose the least fraction of his individuality or power as a unit, but that he has added to it something a thousand times greater ; he is part of the Lord, part of the body that he wears, the weapon that he uses, the organ upon which he plays, the implement with which he does his work.

In all the world there is but One Initiator, but in the case of the first and second Initiations it is open to him to depute some other Adept to perform the ceremony for him, though even then that Officient turns and calls upon the Lord at the critical moment of the conferring of the degree. This is a very wonderful moment in the candidate's spiritual life, as was explained by the Master Kuthumi, when accepting a pupil not long ago. He said to him :

" Now that you have attained the immediate goal of your aspiration, I would exhort you at once to turn your attention to the far greater requirements of the next step. That for which you have now to prepare, the ' entering upon the stream ' which the Christians call salvation, will be the salient point in the long line of your earthly existences, the culmination of seven hundred lives. Ages ago, by individualization, you entered the human kingdom ; in a future which I trust is not remote, you will quit it by the door of Adeptship, and become a Superman ; between these two extremes is no point of greater importance than that Initiation towards which you should now turn your thoughts. Not only will it make you safe forever, but it will admit you to that Brotherhood which exists from eternity unto eternity—the Brotherhood which helps the world.

" Think then with how great care so wondrous an event should be approached. I would have you keep the glory and the beauty of it constantly before your mind, that you may live in the light of its ideals. Your body is young for so mighty an effort, but you have a rare and splendid opportunity ; I want you to take it to the full."

THE BROTHERHOOD

When an ego is initiated he becomes part of the closest organization in the world ; he is now one with the vast sea of consciousness of the Great White Brotherhood. For a long time the new Initiate will not be able to understand all that this union implies, and he must penetrate far into the sanctuaries before he can realize how close is the link, and how great is that consciousness of the King himself, which all Brothers to a certain extent share with him. It is incomprehensible and inexpressible down here ; metaphysical and subtle it is beyond words, but nevertheless a glorious reality, real to such an extent that when we begin to grasp it everything else seems unreal.

We have seen how the accepted pupil may lay his thought beside that of the Master ; so now may the Initiate put his thought beside that of the Brotherhood and draw into himself just as much of that tremendous consciousness as he at his level is able to appreciate ; and ever as he draws it into himself he will be able to receive more of it, and his own consciousness will widen out so that narrowness of thought will become impossible for him. And just as the accepted pupil must take care not to cause disturbance in the lower vehicles of the Master, lest he should interfere with the perfection of his work, so must a member of the Brotherhood never introduce anything discordant into that mighty consciousness, which is acting as a whole.

He must remember that not by any means the whole of the Brotherhood is doing the same work as our Masters. Many of them are engaged in other labours which require the utmost concentration and the most perfect calm, and if some of the younger members should sometimes forget their high calling, and cause ripples of annoyance to disturb the Brotherhood, it would affect the work of those Greater Ones. Our own Masters might perhaps overlook that, and be willing to endure a little occasional worry of that kind for the sake of the future when the new member will be making really great use of the powers of the Brotherhood ; but we can quite understand that those who have nothing to do with the training of individuals might say : " Our work is being disturbed, and it is better that those who have such immature personalities should stay outside." They would say that nothing was lost, that progress can be made just as well outside, and that pupils could go on making themselves better and stronger and wiser before gaining Initiation.

So wonderful is the expansion of the Initiate's consciousness that it is most apt to speak of the change as a new birth. He begins to lead a new life "as a little child", the life of the Christ; and the Christ, the intuitional or buddhic consciousness, is born within his heart. He has also now the power to give the blessing of the Brotherhood—a tremendous and overwhelming force, which he is able to give or send to anyone, as he judges to be most appropriate and useful. The power of the Brotherhood will flow through him just as much as he will let it flow; it is for him to use the power and to remember that he has the entire responsibility of directing it for whatever purpose he may choose. The benediction given by the Officient at Initiation means: "I bless you; I pour my force and benison into you; see that you in your turn constantly pour out this good-will upon others."

The more confidence the new Initiate has the greater will be the flow of force through him. If he feels the least hesitation, or is weighed down by the responsibility of letting such a tremendous power flow through him, he will not be able to use this wonderful gift to the full; but if he has that qualification of *Shraddhā*—perfect trust in his Master and in the Brotherhood, and the utter certainty that because he is one with them all things are possible to him—he may go through the world as a veritable angel of light, shedding joy and benediction around his path.

The consciousness of the Great White Brotherhood is an indescribably wonderful thing. It is like a great calm shining ocean, so strangely one that the least thrill of consciousness flashes from end to end of it instantaneously, and yet to each member it seems to be absolutely his own individual consciousness, though with a weight and a power and a wisdom behind it that no single human consciousness could ever have. This magnificent sea of "cosmic consciousness" of the Brotherhood is something so great, so wonderful, that there is nothing else in the world like it: even those who belong to it by virtue of having passed the first great Initiation can catch only glimpses of it, can remember only a little of it here and there. It can be felt fully only on the nirvanic plane, on which the

Brotherhood primarily exists, though it has its manifestation on the lower planes, even down to the physical world.

As the band of pupils is all one in the Master, so is the Brotherhood all one in its Lord. The members may freely discuss a point among themselves, yet it is as though different aspects of a case presented themselves, in the same mind, and were by that mind weighed one against the other ; but one is all the time in the presence of a tremendous, an almost awful serenity, a certainty which nothing can ever disturb. And yet somehow in all that every suggestion is welcomed ; indeed, there is the sensation that the whole Brotherhood is alertly and eagerly waiting for each individual's contributions to the subject before it. There is nothing down here to which this consciousness can be adequately compared ; to touch it is to come into contact with something new and strange, yet inexpressibly wonderful and beautiful, something which needs no evidence and no comparison, but asserts itself to be of a higher and unknown world.

Though individualities are so strangely merged in this, yet are they at the same time sharply separated, for the assent of each Brother is required to every decision of importance. The rule of the King is absolute, yet he carries his vast council with him, and is at every moment willing to consider any point that occurs to any member of it. But this great governing body differs utterly from any parliament of earth. Those who stand above the rest in positions of authority have not been elected, nor have they been appointed by some party organization ; they hold their positions because they have won them —won them by superior development and greater wisdom. None doubts the decision of his superior, because he knows that he really *is* a superior—that he has greater insight and a fuller power to decide. There is, there can be, no shadow of compulsion that these Supermen shall think or act alike ; yet is their confidence in their mighty organization so perfect that it is unthinkable that in the long run they should differ ; it is only in the case of such a Brotherhood under such a King that we can fully realize the beautiful wording of one of the Collects of the Church of England : " In His service is perfect freedom."

FAILURES

In such an organization there should surely be no possibility of failure or trouble of any sort ; and yet, because humanity is frail, and because not all members of this great Brotherhood are yet Supermen, failures do sometimes occur, although they are very rare. " Great ones fall back even from the threshold, unable to sustain the weight of their responsibility, unable to pass on ", as is said in *Light on the Path*, and only the attainment of Adeptship ensures perfect safety. The Initiator tells the candidate that now he has entered upon the stream he is safe for ever ; but although that is so, it is still possible for him to delay his progress to a most serious extent, if he yields to any of the temptations that still beset his path. To be safe for ever is usually taken to betoken the certainty of passing onward with the present life-wave—of not being left behind at the " day of judgment " which comes in the middle of the fifth Round, when the Christ who has descended into matter decides what souls can and what souls cannot be carried on to final attainment in this chain of worlds. There is no eternal condemnation ; it is, as the Christ said simply aeonian ; there are some who cannot go on in this age or dispensation, but they will follow along in the next, precisely as a child who is too dull to succeed in this year's class will drift comfortably along in next year's, and will probably even be at the head of it.

When the sad and terrible thing does occur—when there is a failure of any sort among Initiates, a thrill of pain runs through the whole of that vast consciousness, for the separation of one from the rest is of the nature of a veritable surgical operation, tearing the heart-strings of all. Only with the uttermost regret does the Brotherhood ever thus sever a member from itself, and even when it does so the erring Brother is not finally cut off, however far he may stray. He will be brought back again some time, somehow, somewhere ; there is a link that cannot be broken, although we know little of the weary road of trial and suffering that he must tread before he can again weld it together with the rest.

The Voice of the Silence remains within him, and though he leave the path utterly, yet one day it will resound, and rend him asunder, and separate his passions from his divine possibilities. Then with pain and desperate cries from the deserted lower self, he will return.[1]

Others there be who fall away only for a short time, through some outburst of such feeling as is quite impossible for the Brotherhood to endure. Then, just as a Master may drop a temporary veil between himself and an erring disciple, so the Brotherhood finds it necessary to make for a time a sort of cyst round one of its members who fails it. The whole force of the Brotherhood is turned upon one who is failing in that way, so that, if it be at all possible they may prevent him from overstepping the boundary. But sometimes, even in spite of all the strength which the Brotherhood is permitted by the law of karma to use, a member still declines to give up his petty personal attitude of supposed injury, or offence, or whatever it may be ; then they must encyst him for a while until he learns better.

THE INITIATOR'S CHARGE

The formula of Initiation has been unchanged throughout the ages, yet there is a certain elasticity about it. The Initiator's Charge to the candidate is always the same so far as the first part of it goes, but almost invariably there is a second and personal part which consists practically of advice to the particular candidate who is going through. This is usually called the private part of the Charge. I have also seen instances in which an image is made of the candidate's worst enemy and he is asked how he would deal with him, whether he is fully prepared to forgive him absolutely, and even help him. In some cases also questions are asked as to the work already done by the candidate, and those who have been helped by him are sometimes invited to come forward and bear witness.

The Initiator's Charge explains the work of the Brotherhood in the world, and the responsibility which rests on each member individually, for each has to share in the bearing of the great

[1] *Light on the Path*, Part I, Rule 21.

burden of the sorrows of the world. Each must be ready to help both by service and by counsel, for it is one Brotherhood, acting under one Law and one Head, and each Brother has the privilege of putting any local knowledge or special faculty that he may possess at the disposition of the Brotherhood for the furtherance of any department of their great work of aiding the progress of humanity. Although the rule of the King is absolute, no decision of importance is taken without the consent of even the youngest member of the Brotherhood. Each is a representative of the Brotherhood in whatever part of the world he may be, and each is pledged to be at the disposal of the Brotherhood, to go wherever he is sent, to work in any way that is required. While younger members will naturally implicitly obey the Heads, they may yet help by local knowledge, and may always suggest anything that seems to them of possible use.

Each Brother living in the world must remember that he is a centre through which the force of the King may be sent for the helping of those who are in need, and that any older Brother may at any time use him as a channel for his blessing. Therefore each younger Brother should always be ready to be so used at any moment, for he never can tell when his services may be required. The life of the Brother should be one of entire devotion to others ; he should watch eagerly and incessantly for every opportunity of rendering service, and let such service be his keenest joy. He must remember that the honour of the Brotherhood is in his hands, and he must see to it that no word or act of his shall ever sully it in the eyes of men, or cause them to think of it one whit less highly.

He must not think that, because he has entered the stream, trial and struggle will cease for him ; on the contrary, he will have to make still greater efforts, but he will have greater strength to make them. His power will be far greater than before : but in exactly the same proportion his responsibility is greater also. He must remember that it is not he, a separated self, who has gained a step which has lifted him above his fellows ; rather he should rejoice that humanity through him has risen a little, has freed itself to this small extent from its chains, has come into this much more of its own. The blessing of the Brotherhood is ever with him ; but it will descend upon him precisely in the measure in which he passes it on to others : for this is the eternal law.

That is part of the Charge which is always given.

THE LENGTH OF THE CEREMONY

The time occupied by the ceremony of Initiation varies according to several considerations, one of which is the amount of knowledge that the candidate brings with him. Some traditions put the period as three days and nights, but it is often finished in much less time. One at which I was present took two nights and a day of seclusion, but others have been condensed into one night, by leaving much that used to be included to be finished later by the higher pupils of the Masters. Some of the old Initiations lasted so long because the candidates had to be instructed in astral work. There are also buddhic experiences which must be realized, for a certain amount of development of the buddhic vehicle is required for Initiation, as some of the teachings which must be given at that level could not otherwise be understood. But when the Initiator knows that the candidate has already some buddhic development it has several times been left to older pupils to carry the candidates through the buddhic experiences on the following night, or whenever it could be arranged.

The actual ceremony of Initiation takes less than six hours, but a certain amount of time is given to the candidates both before and afterwards. Generally it is an occasion of great rejoicing, at any rate among all the younger members. It is a victory for all when another neophyte is admitted, when one more is safe for ever.

SONSHIP

We have already spoken of the close relation between an accepted pupil and his Master ; all the time this intimacy has been steadily growing, and it usually happens that when the pupil is approaching the portal of Initiation the Master considers that the time is ripe for him to draw the chela into a still deeper union. He is then called the Son of the Master, and the link is such that not only the lower mind but also the ego in the causal body of the pupil is enfolded within that of the Adept, and the latter can no longer draw a veil to cut off the neophyte.

A wise Frenchman once said : " *Dans tous les amours, il y a un qui aime et un qui se laisse être aimé.*" [In all love, there is one who loves and one who lets himself be loved.] This is profoundly true in nine cases out of ten in human love. Often the reason for it is that one of the two souls concerned is greater and more developed than the other, and therefore capable of a far deeper love ; the younger soul appreciates that wealth of affection, and returns it to the extent of his capacity, but his best effort falls far short of the wonderful gift poured out so easily and naturally by his elder. Always that must be the case with regard to the Master and his pupil.

Another point. The affection with which we meet in ordinary life is not infrequently unstable, fluctuating, capable of ready dis-couragement ; it may be alienated by coldness, unkindness, lack of response ; it may even be changed into dislike if its object violates our canons of conduct, or acts in some ways that horrifies or disgusts us. But there is a truer and a deeper affection that nothing can shake—a love which recks nothing of response, which is utterly unaffected by neglect, indifference or even unworthiness, on the part of its object—which would indeed feel bitter anguish and regret if that object committed a crime or disgraced himself in any way, but would never for a moment decrease in strength, would lose not a single degree of its fervency *whatever* the loved one might do.

Of that nature is the love of God for his world ; of that nature also must be the love of the Master for those to whom he gives the ineffable privilege of Sonship. He trusts them wholly ; he voluntarily resigns the power to separate them from himself, because only by that utter and unbreakable union with them is he enabled to share with them his own nature to the very fullest extent of their power of response—only by this sacrifice of himself can he give them the utmost which a pupil can receive from a Master.

Thus it may truly be said that he puts himself at the mercy of his pupil. Just think of the awful responsibility which that throws upon us !

Rare though it be, such love is found sometimes among men in this our physical world too ; but when it exists, it has always that same quality and that same result ; it places the higher in the hands of the lower, so that the supremest love is ever also the supremest sacrifice. Yet this utter sacrifice, this utmost resignation of the self brings with it a keener joy than aught else on earth can confer, for such love alone is god-like, such self-surrender bears the man into the very heart of Christ. Indeed is it true that such " love shall cover the multitude of sins,"[1] that " her sins, which are many, are forgiven, for she loved much."[2]

There is a beautiful reference to this state of closest union in *Light on the Path*, where it is written : " ' My Peace I give unto you ' can only be said by the Master to the beloved disciples who are as himself." And so these are they who have the inestimable privilege of being able to pass on that peace to others in all its fullness. Any accepted pupil of the Master has the right and the duty to bless in his Name, and a splendid outpouring of the Master's power will assuredly follow his effort to do so. Especially should he give that blessing mentally whenever he enters a house : " May the blessing of the Master rest on this house and on all who live therein." But the Son of the Master can give the very touch of his intimate presence, a fuller and a greater peace. He who is a Son of the Master either is or soon will be a member of the Great White Brotherhood also ; and that, as we have said, gives the power to wield an even greater blessing, though both are appropriate, each in its place.

I well remember giving each of those on different occasions to a great Angel of the neighbourhood with whom I have the honour to be well acquainted. Passing close to his territories in a vessel I gave him once as a greeting the full blessing of my Master, and it was indeed beautiful to see the way in which he received it, bowing

[1] I Peter, iv, 8.
[2] Luke, vii, 47.

profoundly and showing his appreciation by a lovely soft glow of holiness and uttermost devotion. Another day under similar circumstances I gave him the blessing of the Brotherhood, and instantly every power of that great Angel flashed out in glad response, and the whole of his territory lit up. It was as though a soldier had leapt to attention, as though everything, not only within himself but in all the thousands of minor creatures working under him, had suddenly been vivified and raised to its highest power. All nature instantly responded. You see, my Master, however deeply reverenced by him, is not his Master, but my King *is* his King, for there is but One.

THE LEVEL OF INITIATION

The question as to whether a man is approaching fitness for Initiation involves three separate sets of considerations, all depending upon one another. The first is as to whether he is in possession of a sufficient amount of the necessary qualifications, as laid down in *At the Feet of the Master*, and that means that he must have a minimum of all, and very much more than a minimum of some of them. To illustrate this, think for a moment of the method adopted in marking papers at certain examinations. It is determined beforehand by the examiners that no candidate shall be allowed to pass, who falls below a certain minimum in each of the subjects ; but the percentage required in each subject is very low—say twenty-five per cent. Anyone who fails to secure twenty-five per cent of the marks in any subject will fail ; but nevertheless one who secures exactly that amount in each of the subjects will not succeed, for not only are separate minima set for the different subjects, but there is also a total minimum—let us say forty per cent. One therefore who falls as low as twenty-five or thirty per cent in one or two of his subjects must make very much more than that in several other subjects in order to attain the average required.

This is precisely the method adopted in Occultism ; there must be a certain amount of each of these qualifications present in the successful candidate, but he must have very thoroughly developed some of them. A candidate cannot succeed if he be entirely lacking in discrimination ; yet if he shows much less of that than he should, an overflowing flood of love may perhaps be accepted as atoning for it. Secondly, the ego must have so trained his lower vehicles that he can function perfectly through them when he wishes to do so ; he must have effected what in our earlier Theosophical literature was called the junction of the lower and the higher self ; and thirdly, he must be strong enough to stand the great strain involved, which extends even to the physical body.

As to the level of progress at which he will be initiated, there is room for very great variety. It would be a mistake to suppose that all Initiates are equal in development, just as it would be unsafe to assume that all men who have taken the degree of Master of Arts are equal in knowledge. It is quite possible that a candidate might have done exceedingly well in many of the qualities required, and be far beyond the total minimum, and yet be seriously deficient and below the minimum standard in one subject ; it would then, of course, be necessary for him to wait till he had the minimum in that neglected subject, and no doubt while he was acquiring that he would be developing the others still further.

It is therefore obvious that while there is a certain attainment required for Initiation, some of those who are presented for it may have achieved far more than that in some directions. We see, too, that there is likely to be considerable variation in the interval between Initiations. One man who has just now been able to take the first may nevertheless possess a considerable share of the qualifications for the second ; therefore for him the interval between the two might be unusually short. On the other hand, a candidate who had only just sufficient strength in all directions to enable him to pass through the first, would have slowly to develop within himself all the additional faculties and knowledge necessary for the second, so his interval would probably belong.

THE PRESENT OPPORTUNITY

We have now entered upon a period in the world's history in which progress at all levels of evolution can be very rapid. Rapid progress is, however, a very decided strain—a thing which few aspirants sufficiently realize. The student of occultism who sets before himself the idea of hastening his development will do well to remember that one of the necessities is good physical health. He wishes to make in one life the progress which under ordinary circumstances would be distributed over twenty or more, and as the amount that has to be done is the same in either case (for no reduction whatever has been made in the standard of the requirements for Initiation) it is obvious that he must work all his vehicles very much harder if he is to succeed.

It is possible on the physical plane to shorten the period of study usually assigned to any given examination ; but a man can do it only by putting a far greater tax upon his brain, his attention, his eyesight, his power of endurance ; and we all know how fatally easy it is for him to strain himself in any one of these directions, and thereby seriously to injure his physical health. Similar conditions attend upon the efforts to hasten spiritual evolution ; it can be done, and it has been done, and it is a very fine thing for any man to do, always with this proviso, that he must watch very carefully against overstrain, lest in the ultimate he should delay his development instead of advancing it. It is not sufficient to have good physical health at the beginning of one's endeavour ; it is also necessary to preserve it until the end, for the progress itself is but a means to an end, and we try to develop ourselves not that we may become great and wise, but that we may have the power and the knowledge to work for humanity to the best effect. We must never forget that Occultism is above all the apotheosis of common sense.

YOUNG INITIATES

It is always the ego who is initiated ; the age of the physical body which it happens to be holding at a given time has little to do with the case. In all cases when young people have been initiated, elder members of the Brotherhood living near to them or in touch with them in the physical body have undertaken to assist and guide them,

This is necessary, because of the great responsibility that Initiation brings along with its expansion of consciousness and additional faculty and power. A wrong action or a false step on the part of an Initiate involves bigger karmic consequences than a similar action on the part of one who is not a member of the Brotherhood. Therefore perhaps it will be well to include here a few directions for these younger people.

Each one should ever remember that he was initiated because in past lives, and perhaps in the present one, he has helped the world to a certain requisite degree, and it is hoped that he will continue in that path and become an ever larger channel for the life of the Logos. It is because of the probability of his increased usefulness that he is admitted to Initiation, and at the ceremony he takes the pledge, not only as the ego but as the Monad, that he will make it his life-work to pour himself out in blessing, even as the Logos is continually streaming forth his love. He must therefore each day and hour keep this pledge in mind and subserve all things to it. His karma from the past gives him various personal characteristics and impulses; he must take heed lest these drive him to think of himself and his own well-being, rather than of the greater self and the welfare of the world.

Before he can undertake the larger work awaiting him, the youthful Initiate has often to prepare himself by an ordinary training in college and university. In that case he will be plunged into circumstances of vigorous activity and many self-centred interests. Life surrounds him with many temptations, and with occasions tending to make him forget his pledge to the Brotherhood. Through them all he must have a clearly defined attitude, that he has thrown in his lot with the aims of the Brotherhood. In that life in the world on every occasion, whether of study, recreation or amusement, he must definitely hold the thought : " Is this that I am going to do likely to make me better equipped for the Master's work, or a better channel to spread love and happiness ? "

He must always remember that the Brotherhood has the first claim on his services, and must never put himself in any position which makes it impossible for him to fulfil his duty to it. It is not intended that he should live the life of a hermit; but while he lives that life in society which will give him the growth he requires, he must all the time watch to see whether it is making him more of a channel for the Logos. Henceforth for him any experience, however pleasant and harmless, which cannot make him a fuller channel of the Logos, or give an opportunity for service, is valueless to him, and is so much waste of time. He should try to take advantage of every opportunity to help that he sees, and to learn such things as will make him useful.

THE INITIATE BROTHER TO ALL

When the pupil takes the great step of Initiation and becomes a member of the Brotherhood, he also becomes, in a far greater and more special sense than before, the brother of every one of his fellow-men. This does not mean that he must direct their lives, and try to guide them with criticism. It is not his business in life to criticize but to encourage; but if he sees reason to make any suggestion, he must do it with the very greatest care and courtesy. The world does not see the higher members of the Brotherhood; therefore it is apt to judge that organization by the junior members who come within its purview. That is what is meant by the remark in the Charge at Initiation, that the neophyte holds the honour of the Brotherhood in his hands.

It is his duty to stream forth love and benediction, so that every place in which he happens to be is happier because of his presence. He must therefore steadily turn outwards. Henceforth it does not matter to him what judgment the world gives on his actions, but only what judgment the Brotherhood gives. Whether he is popular or unpopular with the world matters not at all, if through all his conduct he has been loyal to the ideals placed before him. Some senior members of the Brotherhood may desire to use him at any moment, wherever he happens to be, and sometimes without his knowing it in the brain-consciousness, but he cannot be used if, at the moment when he is needed, he is found brooding over his own affairs and turned inwards, not outwards to the world. The supreme need for him is the building of character, so that, when his Master looks at him he will find him thinking of the world's welfare, and not whether that world is giving him happiness or misery.

CHAPTER VIII

THE EGO

THE BIRTH OF THE EGO

IN order that the further steps on the Path may be clearly understood, it is necessary at this point to consider the ego, and the way
in which he has awakened and put forth his powers to bring the
personality into harmony with himself, and to reach up to the buddhic
plane and realize his unity with all that lives.

In *Man Visible and Invisible* and *The Christian Creed* I published
a diagram which I reproduce here, illustrating the three Outpourings of the Divine Life in our evolutionary scheme. At the top
of the diagram appear three circles symbolizing the three Aspects of
the Logos, the three Persons of the Blessed Trinity; and from each
of them a line runs down, crossing at right angles the horizontal lines
which signify the seven planes of nature. That from the lowest circle
(the Third Aspect) is drawn straight down the middle of the
diagram, growing heavier and darker as it descends, showing how
the Holy Spirit vivifies the matter of the various planes, first build
ing their respective atoms, and then aggregating those atoms into
elements.

Into that matter so vivified the Second Outpouring comes
down from the circle typifying God the Son, and the Divine Life of
which that Outpouring consists draws that matter together into
forms which it can inhabit, and thus incarnates and makes bodies or
vehicles for itself. At its lowest level of materiality that Life ensouls
the mineral kingdom, and as it evolves it gradually becomes definite
enough to ensoul the vegetable kingdom, and still later the animal.

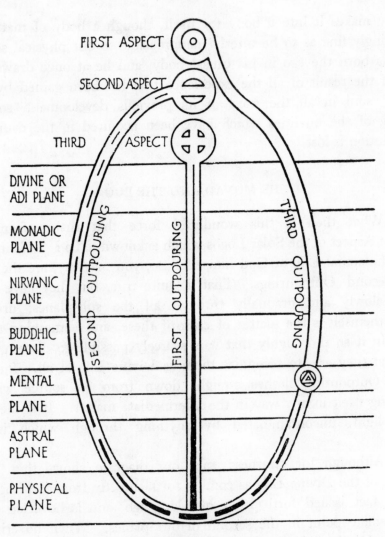

FIRST ASPECT

SECOND ASPECT

THIRD   ASPECT

DIVINE OR
ADI PLANE

MONADIC
PLANE

NIRVANIC
PLANE

BUDDHIC
PLANE

MENTAL
PLANE

ASTRAL
PLANE

PHYSICAL
PLANE

SECOND OUTPOURING

FIRST OUTPOURING

THIRD OUTPOURING

DIAGRAM 2

When it has risen to the highest level of the animal kingdom a very remarkable change takes place, and an entirely new factor is introduced—that of the Third Outpouring, which comes from the highest circle, the First Aspect of the Logos, commonly called God the Father.

That force which has hitherto been the ensouler now becomes in its turn the ensouled, and the new force from the First Person seizes upon what has heretofore been the soul of the animal, and actually makes it into a body for itself, though a body of matter so exceedingly fine as to be utterly inappreciable to our physical senses. Thus is born the ego in his causal body, and he at once draws into himself the result of all the experience that has been gained by that animal soul in all the æons of its previous development, so that nothing of the qualities which have been acquired in the course of its evolution is lost.

THE MONAD AND THE EGO

What then is this wonderful force that rushes from the Highest Aspect of the Solar Logos which is known to us ? It is in very truth the actual Life of God himself. So, you may say, are the First and Second Outpourings. That is quite true, but they have come down slowly and gradually through all the sub-planes, drawing round themselves the matter of each of these, and enmeshing themselves in it so thoroughly that it is scarcely possible to discern them for what they are, to recognize them as Divine Life at all. But this Third Outpouring flashes straight down from its source without involving itself in any way in the intermediate matter. It is the pure white light, uncontaminated by anything through which it has passed.

Although for clearness' sake our diagram shows this Third Stream of the Divine Life as coming forth directly from the Logos, it has in fact issued forth from him long ago, and is hovering at an intermediate point in the second of our planes. When hovering at that level it is called the Monad, and perhaps the least misleading manner in which we can image it to ourselves is to think of it as a part of God—a part, but of That which cannot be divided—a paradox, truly, to our mortal intellect ; yet enshrining an eternal truth which is far beyond our comprehension.

The general method of this descent of Spirit into matter seems to be always the same, though the diverse conditions of the different planes naturally produce many variations in detail. The Logos Himself puts down the Monad—a tiny fragment of Himself—into a level far below his own ; of course such a descent must mean a most serious limitation, though it is all too far above the utmost reach of our consciousness to be described or understood. In exactly the same way the Monad puts down a tiny fragment of himself which becomes the ego ; and in that case also the limitation is enormously increased. The very same thing happens once more when the ego repeats the operation and projects a minute portion of himself into the mental, the astral and the physical bodies of the man—a fragment which we call the personality.

This last tiny fragment is the point of consciousness which those of us who are clairvoyant can see moving about within the man. According to one system of symbology this is seen as " the golden man the size of a thumb ", who dwells in the heart ; but many of us see it rather in the form of a star. I think I have always seen it myself as a brilliant star of light. A man may keep this star of consciousness where he will—that is to say, in any one of the seven principal centres of the body. Which of these is most natural to a man depends largely upon his type or Ray, and I think also upon his race and sub-race. We of the fifth sub-race of the fifth root race nearly always keep that consciousness in the brain, in the centre dependent upon the pituitary body. There are, however, men of other races to whom it comes more natural to keep it habitually in the heart, the throat or the solar plexus.

This star of consciousness is the representative of the ego down here in these lower planes, and as it manifests through those vehicles we call it personality ; and that is the man as he is known to his friends down here.

COMMUNICATION WITH THE PERSONALITY

But though that personality is absolutely part of the ego— though the only life and power in it are those of the Ego—it nevertheless often forgets those facts, and comes to regard itself as an entirely separate entity, and works down here for its own ends. It has always a line of communication with the ego (often called in our books the *antahkarana*), but it generally makes no effort to use it. In the case of ordinary people who have never studied these matters, the personality is to all intents and purposes the man, and the ego manifests himself only very rarely and partially.

Man's evolution in its earlier stages consists in the opening up of this line of communication, so that the ego may be increasingly able to assert himself through it, and finally entirely to dominate the personality, so that it may have no separate thought or will, but may be merely (as it should be) an expression of the ego, on these lower planes. It must, of course, be understood that the ego, belonging as he does to an altogether higher plane, can never *fully* express himself down here ; the most for which we can hope is that the personality will contain nothing which is not intended by the ego—that it will express as much of him as can be expressed in this lower world.

The absolutely untrained man has practically no communication with the ego ; the Initiate has full communication ; consequently we find (as we should expect) that there are men among us at all stages between these two extremes. It must be remembered that the ego himself is only in process of development, and that we have therefore to deal with egos in very different stages of advancement. In any case an ego is in a great many ways something enormously bigger than a personality can ever be. Though, as has been said, he is but a fragment of the Monad, he is yet complete as an ego in his causal body, even when his powers are undeveloped ; whereas there is but a touch of his life in the personality.

It is also true that life at his level is an infinitely larger and more vivid thing than what we know as life down here. Just as it is evolution for the personality to learn to express the ego more fully, so is it evolution for the ego to learn to express the Monad more fully. An undeveloped personality forgets all about this connection with the ego and feels himself quite independent. It can hardly be possible for an ego at his much higher level to be unaware of his link with the Monad ; certainly some egos are far more awake to the necessities of their evolution than others—which is only another way of saying that there are older and younger egos, and that the older are striving more earnestly than the younger to unfold their latent possibilities.

IN HIS OWN WORLD

We are apt to think that the only development possible for an ego is through the personality ; but that is not so—or rather it is so only in connection with one small set of qualities. As I have explained at length in *Man Visible and Invisible*, the causal body of an undeveloped man is almost colourless. As in the process of his evolution he develops good qualities which can find corresponding vibrations in the matter of the causal body, the colours expressive of these qualities begin to show themselves ; and presently the causal body, instead of being empty, is full of active pulsating life. So much more of the ego can now manifest through it that it has to increase enormously in size ; it extends further and further from its physical centre until the man is able to enfold hundreds and even thousands of persons within himself, and so to exercise a vast influence for good.

But all this, wonderful though it be, is only one side of his development. He has quite other lines of progress of which we down here know nothing ; he is living a life of his own among his peers, among the great Arupadevas, among all kinds of splendid Angels, in a world far beyond our ken. The young ego probably is but little awake as yet to all that glorious life, just as a baby in arms knows little of the interests of the world surrounding him ; but as his consciousness gradually unfolds, he awakens to all this magnificence, he becomes fascinated by its vividness and beauty.

At the same time he himself becomes a glorious object, and gives us for the first time some idea of what God means man to be. Among such beings thoughts no longer take form and float about as they do at lower levels, but pass like lightning-flashes from one to another. Here we have no newly acquired vehicles, gradually coming under control and learning by degrees more or less feebly to express the soul within ; but we are face to face with one body older than the hills, an actual expression of the Divine Glory which ever rests behind it, and shines through it more and more in the gradual unfolding of its powers.

Here we deal no longer with outward forms, but we see the things in themselves, the reality which lies behind the imperfect expression. Here cause and effect are one, clearly visible in their unity, like two sides of the same coin. Here we have left the concrete for the abstract ; we have no longer the multiplicity of forms, but the idea which lies behind all those forms. Here the essence of everything is available ; we no longer study details ; we no longer talk round a subject or endeavour to explain ; we take up the essence or the idea of the subject and move it as a whole, as one moves a piece when playing chess. What down here would be a system of philosophy, needing many volumes to explain it, is there a single definite object —a thought which can be thrown down as one throws a card upon the table. An opera or an oratorio, which here would occupy a full orchestra for many hours in the rendering, is there a single mighty chord ; the methods of a whole school of painting are condensed into one magnificent idea ; and ideas such as these are the intellectual counters which are used by egos in their converse one with another.

It is not easy to explain in physical words the differences which exist between egos, since all of them are in many ways much greater than anything to which we are accustomed down here. An ego who is already on the Path, and is nearing Adeptship, has much in common with the great Angels, and radiates spiritual influences of prodigious power.

HIS INTEREST IN THE PERSONALITY

Can we wonder, then, that the ego throws himself energetically into the whirl of intense activity of his own plane, and that it seems to him immensely more interesting and important than the faint

far-distant struggles of a cramped and half-formed personality, veiled
in the dense obscurity of a lower world ?

In the physical life of the ordinary man of the world there is
little of interest to the ego, and it is only now and then that something
of real importance occurs, that may for a moment attract his attention, so that from it he draws whatever is worth taking. The
ordinary man lives in patches ; more than half the time he is not
awake to the real and higher life at all. Some of us are apt to complain that our egos take very little notice of us ; let us ask ourselves
how much notice we have taken of them. How often for example, in
any given day, have we even thought of the ego ? If we wish to attract
his attention we must make the personality useful to him. As soon
as we begin to devote the greater part of our thought to higher things
(and that is equivalent to saying, as soon as we really begin to live),
the ego will be likely to take somewhat more notice of us.

The ego knows that certain necessary parts of his evolution
can be achieved only through the personality, and in its mental,
astral and physical bodies ; he knows, therefore, that he must some
time attend to it, must take it in hand and bring it under his control.
But we can well understand that the task may often seem uninviting,
that a given personality may appear anything but attractive or hopeful. If we look at many of the personalities around us—their physical bodies poisoned with meat, alcohol and tobacco, their astral
bodies reeking with greed and sensuality, and their mental bodies
having no interests beyond business, or perhaps horse-racing and
prize-fighting—it is not difficult to see why an ego, surveying them
from his lofty height, might decide to postpone his serious effort to
another incarnation, in the hope that the next set of vehicles might
be more amenable to influence than those upon which his horrified
gaze then rested. We can imagine that he might say to himself : " I
can do nothing with that ; I will take my chance of getting something
better next time ; it can hardly be worse, and meantime I have much
more important business to do up here."

A similar thing not infrequently happens in the early stages of
a new incarnation. From the birth of the child the ego is hovering

over it, and in some cases he begins to try to influence its development while it is still very young. As a general rule he pays little
attention to it until about the age of seven, by which time the work
of the karmic elemental should be practically over. Children differ
so widely that it is not surprising to find that the relation between
the egos and the personalities involved differs widely also. Some
child-personalities are quick and responsive, some are dull or
wayward ; when the latter characteristics are prominent the ego
often withdraws his active interest for the time, hoping that as the
childish body grows, it may become cleverer or more responsive.

Such a decision may seem to us unwise, because if the ego
neglects his present personality it is unlikely that the next will be an
improvement upon it ; and if he allows the child-body to develop
without his influence, the undesirable qualities which have been
manifested may quite possibly grow stronger instead of dying out.
But we are hardly in a position to judge, since our knowledge of the
problem is so imperfect, and we can see nothing of the higher business to which he is devoting himself.

From this it will be seen how impossible it is to judge with any
precision the position in evolution of anyone whom we see only on
the physical plane. In one case karmic causes may have produced
a very fair personality, having an ego of only moderate advancement
behind it ; while in another case those causes may have given rise to
an inferior or defective personality, belonging to a comparatively
advanced ego. A good illustration of this appears among the stories
of the life of the Lord Buddha. A man came to him one day, as
people in trouble were wont to do, and told him that he had great
difficulty with his meditation, which he could scarcely succeed in doing
at all. Then the Buddha told him that there was a very simple reason
for it—that in a previous life he had foolishly been in the habit of
annoying certain holy men and disturbing their meditations. Yet
that man may have been more advanced as an ego than some of his
companions whose meditations were well done.

When the ego does decide to turn the full force of his energy
upon the personality, the change which he can produce is marvellous.

No one who has not personally investigated the matter can imagine how wonderful, how rapid, how radical, such a change may be when conditions are favourable—that is, when the ego is reasonably strong, and the personality not incurably vicious—more especially when a determined effort is made by the personality on its side to become a perfect expression of the ego, and make itself attractive to him.

THE ATTITUDE OF THE PERSONALITY

The difficulty of this subject is greatly enhanced by the fact that it is necessary for us to regard it simultaneously from two points of view. Most of us down here are very emphatically personalities, and think and act almost exclusively as such; yet we know all the time that in reality we are egos, and those of us who by many years of meditation have rendered ourselves more sensitive to finer influences are often conscious of the intervention of this Higher Self. The more we can make a habit of identifying ourselves with the ego, the more clearly and sanely shall we view the problems of life; but in so far as we feel ourselves to be still personalities looking up to our Higher Selves, it is obviously our duty and our interest to open ourselves to them, to reach up towards them, and persistently to set up within ourselves such vibrations as will be of use to them. At least let us be sure that we do not stand in the way of the ego, that we always do our best for him according to our lights.

Since selfishness is the intensification of the personality, our first step should be to get rid of that. Then we must keep our minds filled with high thoughts; for if they are continually occupied with lower matters (even though those lower matters may be quite estimable in their way), the ego cannot readily use them as channels of expression. When he makes a tentative effort, when he puts down an exploratory finger, let us receive him with enthusiasm and hasten to obey his behests, that he may take possession of our minds more and more, and so come into his inheritance as far as these lower planes are concerned. Thus shall we bring ourselves ever nearer to the goal that we wish to reach; thus shall we set our feet upon the Path which leads directly to that first Initiation in which the lower and the higher become one, or rather the greater has absorbed the lesser, so that there should now be nothing in the personality which is not a representation of the ego; the lower is now merely an expression of the higher.

The personality may have had a great many unpleasant qualities of his own, such as jealousy, anger and depression, but they have all been cast off, and now he merely reproduces that which comes from above. The ego having brought the lower self into harmony with himself is now reaching upwards into the buddhic plane, the plane of unity. It is only in this way that the man can begin to cast off the delusion of self which stands in the way of his further progress, and that is why the buddhic experience is necessary at the first Initiation, if it has not been had before. In many cases it has come earlier, because the higher emotions, showing themselves in the astral body, have reflected themselves in the buddhic vehicle and aroused it, and consequently there is some awakening before Initiation.

REALIZATION OF UNITY

All that lives is really one, and it is the duty of those who enter the Brotherhood to know that as a fact. We are taught that the Self is one, and we try to understand what that means; but it is quite a different thing when we see it for ourselves, as the candidate does when he enters the buddhic plane. It is as if in physical life we were each living at the bottom of a well, from which we may look up at the sunlight in the world above; and just as the light shines down into the depth of many wells, and yet ever remains the one light, so does the Light of the One illumine the darkness of our hearts. The Initiate has climbed out of the well of the personality, and sees that the light which he thought to be himself is in very truth the Infinite Light of all.

While living in the causal body, the ego already acknowledged the Divine Consciousness in all; when he looked upon another ego his consciousness leapt up as it were to recognize the Divine in him.

But on the buddhic plane it no longer leaps to greet him from with-out, for it is already enshrined within his heart. He *is* that con-sciousness and it is *his*. There is no longer the " you " and the " I ", for both are one—facets of something that transcends and yet includes them both.

Yet in all this strange advance there is no loss of the sense of individuality, even though there is an utter loss of the sense of separate-ness. That seems a paradox, while yet it is obviously true. The man remembers all that lies behind him. He is himself, the same man who did this action or that in the far-off past. He is in no way changed, except that now he is much more than he was then, and feels that he includes within himself many other manifestations as well. If here and now a hundred of us could simultaneously raise our consciousness into the intuitional world, we should all be one consciousness, but to each man that would seem to be his own, absolutely unchanged, except that now it included all the others as well.

To each it would seem that it was he who had absorbed or included all those others, so we are here manifestly in the presence of a kind of illusion, and a little further realization makes it clear to us that we are all facets of a greater consciousness, and that what we have hitherto thought to be *our* qualities, *our* intellect, *our* energies have all the time been His qualities, His intellect, His energy. We have arrived at the realization in actual fact of the time-honoured formula : " Thou art That." It is one thing to talk about this down here and to grasp it, or to think that we grasp it, intellectually ; but it is quite another to enter into the marvellous world and *know* it with a certainty that can never again be shaken.

When this buddhic consciousness fully impresses the physical brain, it gives a new value to all the actions and relations of life. We no longer *look upon* a person or object, no matter with what degree of kindliness or sympathy ; we simply *are* that person or object, and we know him or it as we know the thought of our own brain or the movement of our own hand. We appreciate his motives as our own motives, even though we may perfectly understand that another part of ourselves, possessing more knowledge or a different view-point, might act quite differently.

Yet it must not be supposed that when a man enters upon the lowest sub-division of the intuitional world he at once becomes *fully* conscious of his unity with all that lives. That perfection of sense comes only as the result of much toil and trouble, when he has reached the highest sub-division of this realm of unity. To enter that plane at all is to experience an enormous extension of consciousness, to realize himself as one with many others; but before him there opens a time of effort, of self-development, analogous at that level to what we do down here when by meditation we try to open our consciousness to the plane next above us. Step by step, sub-plane by sub-plane, the aspirant must win his way; for even at that level exertion is still necessary if progress is to be made.

Having passed the first Initiation and consciously entered the buddhic plane, this work of developing himself on sub-plane after sub-plane now lies before the candidate, in order that he may get rid of the three great fetters, as they are technically called, which embarrass his further progress. He is now definitely on the Path of Holiness, and is described in the Buddhist system as the *Sotāpatti* or *Sovan*, " he who has entered the stream "; while among the Hindus he is called the *Parivrājaka*, which means " the wanderer ", one who no longer feels that any place in the three lower worlds is his abiding-place of refuge.

CHAPTER IX

THE SECOND AND THIRD INITIATIONS

THE FIRST THREE FETTERS

THE candidate who has passed the first Initiation has entered definitely upon the Path Proper—the Path that leads to Adeptship, to the portal leading out of the human kingdom into that of the Superman. Looking at this Path from below, one might wonder that the aspirant is not exhausted after his labours leading to the first Initiation, that he does not shrink back discouraged by the dizzy heights that he sees rising before him on the relentless ever-ascending Path. But he has drunk at the fount of life, and his strength is as the strength of ten because his heart is pure, and the glory of the ideal humanity, which he sees with ever-increasing clearness, has for him an attraction and inspiration with which no material stimulus or interest can ever compare.

The first stage of his journey ends in the second Initiation, to achieve which he must cast off three *Samyojana* or fetters, which are:

1. *Sakkāyaditthi*—the delusion of self.
2. *Vichikicchā*—doubt or uncertainty.
3. *Silabbataparāmāsa*—superstition.

The first of these is the " I am I " consciousness which, as connected with the *personality*, is nothing but an illusion, and must be thrown aside at the very first step of the real upward path. But to cast off this fetter completely means even more than this, for it involves the realization of the fact that the individuality also is in very truth one with the all, that he can therefore never have any interests opposed to those of his brethren, and that he is most truly progressing when he most assists the progress of others.

As to the second fetter, a word of caution is necessary. People who have been trained in western habits of thought are, unhappily, so familiar with the idea that a blind, unreasoning adhesion to certain dogmas may be claimed from a disciple of any religion, school or sect, that on hearing that in Occultism *doubt* is considered to be an obstacle to progress, they are likely to suppose that this Path also requires from its followers the same unquestioning faith as do many modern superstitions. No idea could be more entirely false.

It is true that doubt (or rather uncertainty) on some questions is a bar to spiritual progress, but the antidote to that doubt is not blind faith (which is itself considered a fetter, as will presently be seen), but the certainty of conviction founded on individual experiment or mathematical reasoning. While a child doubts the accuracy of the multiplication table, he can hardly acquire proficiency in the higher mathematics ; but his doubts can be satisfactorily cleared up only by his attaining a comprehension, founded on reasoning or experiment, that the statements contained in the table are true. He believes that twice two are four, not merely because he has been told so, but because it has become to him a self-evident fact. And this is exactly the method, and the only method, of resolving doubt known to Occultism.

Vichikicchā has been defined as doubt of the doctrines of karma and reincarnation, and of the efficacy of the method of attaining the highest good by this Path of Holiness ; but the knowledge of these things also brings with it a vivid realization that the world is God's school for man, and that His plan is the evolution of the immortal life through the perishing forms, and is wonderful and beneficent in every part. As he casts off his second fetter, the Initiate arrives at absolute certainty, based either upon personal first-hand knowledge or upon reason, that the occult teaching upon these points is true.

The third fetter, superstition, has been described as including all kinds of unreasoning and mistaken belief, and all dependence upon outward rites and ceremonies to purify the heart. He sees that all the methods of help offered to us by the great religions—prayers, sacraments, pilgrimages, fastings, and the observation of manifold rites and ceremonies—are helps and no more ; that the wise man will adopt such of them as he finds useful to him, but will never trust to any of them alone as sufficient to attain salvation. He knows definitely that within himself deliverance must be sought, and that however valuable these aids may be in developing his will, his wisdom and his love, they can never take the place of that personal effort by which alone he can achieve. The man who has cast off this fetter realizes that there is no one form of religion which is a necessity for all men, but that through any and all alike, and even outside of them, the path to the highest may be found.

These three fetters are in a coherent series. The difference between individuality and personality being fully understood, it is then possible to some extent to appreciate the actual course of reincarnation, and so to dispel all doubt on that head. This done, the knowledge of the spiritual permanence of the true ego brings reliance on one's own spiritual strength, and so dispels superstition.

SUBDIVISIONS OF THE STEPS

Each stage of the Path Proper is divided into four steps. The first is its *maggo* or way, during which the student is striving to cast off the fetters. The second is its *phala*, literally fruit or result, when the man finds the result of his efforts showing themselves more and more. Thirdly comes its *bhavagga* or consummation, the period when, the result having culminated, he is able to fulfil satisfactorily the work belonging to the step on which he now firmly stands. The fourth is its *gotrabhu*, which means the time when he has arrived at a fit state to receive the next Initiation.

That the candidate may become *gotrabhu*, we see that complete and entire freedom from the fetters of his stage on the Path is absolutely essential. Before the man can proceed to the second Initiation, the Initiator chosen by the King demands evidence as to how the candidate has used the powers acquired by him at the first Initiation, and one of the most beautiful features of the ceremony is the part when those who have been helped by the candidate come forward to give their testimony. It is also requisite for this Initiation that the candidate shall have developed the power to function freely in his mental body, for although the ceremony of the first Initiation is held on the astral plane, that of the second takes place in the lower mental world.

It may seem difficult to reconcile that statement with the fact that the Initiations are described as occurring in a certain hall or garden : but really there is no discrepancy. If the Lord Maitreya acts as Initiator, the ceremony is usually performed either in his garden or in his great room. He himself is present in his physical body and so in many cases is the Lord Vaivasvata Manu, who lives close by. All others present are usually in the astral vehicle in the case of the first Initiation, but in the mental body in the case of the second. The Great Ones present focus their consciousness with perfect ease at whatever level is required, but there is of course on the astral and the mental planes a perfect counterpart of everything on the physical, and so the accounts given are perfectly correct, and the positions taken up in relation to physical objects are just as there described.

MENTAL DEVELOPMENT

The second Initiation rapidly continues the development of the mental body, and at or near this point the pupil learns to use the *māyāvi-rūpa*, which is sometimes translated as the body of illusion. This is a temporary astral body made by one who is able to function in his mental body. When a man travels in the astral plane, he usually does so in the astral body ; and if it were necessary for him to show himself on the physical plane while he was functioning in his astral body, he would have to materialize a physical body round it. This is sometimes done, though not frequently, because it involves a great expenditure of force. Similarly, if he were working in his mental body and desired to manifest himself on the astral plane, he would need to materialize a temporary astral body, which is the *māyāvi-rūpa*. When he had finished his work, he would withdraw to the mental plane once more, and the temporary body would vanish, its materials returning to the general circulation of astral matter whence they had been drawn by the pupil's will.

Up to the time of the first Initiation the man works at night in his astral body ; but as soon as it is perfectly under control and he is able to use it fully, work in the mental body is begun.   When that body in turn is completely organized, it is a far more flexible vehicle than the astral body, and much that is impossible on the astral plane can be accomplished therein.   With the power to form the *māyāvi-rūpa*, the man is able to pass instantly from the mental plane to the astral and back, and to use at all times the greater power and keener sense of the mental plane, and it is only necessary to form the astral materialization when he wants to become visible to people in the astral world.   It is necessary that the Master shall first show His pupil how to make the *māyāvi-rūpa*, after which, although it is not at first an easy matter, he can do it for himself.

A very great expansion and development of the mental body takes place in connection with this second Initiation, but it is usually some years before the effects of this can show themselves in the physical brain.   As they begin to do so they unquestionably put a great strain upon that brain, as it cannot be instantaneously tuned to the necessary pitch.

THE DANGER-POINT

The period after the taking of the second Initiation is in many ways the most dangerous on the Path, although at any point until the fifth Initiation is passed there is the possibility of falling back, or of spending many incarnations wandering about.   But it is at this stage especially that, if there is any weakness in a candidate's character, it will show itself.   It should be impossible for a man who has raised himself to this height to fall back ; but unfortunately experience has shown us that even this does sometimes happen.   In nearly all cases the danger comes through pride ; if there is the least tinge of pride in the man's nature, he is in serious risk of a fall.   What we talk about down here as intellect is the merest reflection of the real thing ; yet some of us are proud of that, proud of our intellect and insight. So when a man gets even a remote glimpse of what his intellect is going to be in the future there is serious danger, and if he once starts on that line he will have a terribly hard time getting back again. Nothing but unceasing and increasing vigilance can enable him to pass through this stage successfully, and it must be his constant endeavour to kill out every trace of pride, selfishness and prejudice.

When we know these things from behind, we find sudden and curious illumination thrown upon various texts of the Bible. This danger-point in the life of the Initiate is indicated in the Gospel story by the temptation in the wilderness which followed the Baptism of Christ by John. The forty days in the wilderness symbolize the period during which the expansion of the mental body given in the second Initiation is being worked down into the physical brain, though for the ordinary candidate not forty days but forty years might well be required for its accomplishment. In the life of Jesus it was the period when his brain was being adapted to the incoming Christ. Then the devil, who in the symbolism represents the lower nature, comes to tempt the Initiate, first to use his powers for the satisfaction of his own needs : " If thou be the Son of God, command that these stones be made bread." Then he is tempted to cast himself down from a pinnacle of the temple, thus performing a miracle which would astound the populace. And lastly he is shown all the kingdoms of the world and the glory of them, and the devil says : " All these things will I give thee, if thou wilt fall down and worship me "—he is tempted to use his powers to gratify his own ambition. Each of these temptations represents a different form of pride.

Just as the first great Initiation corresponds to a new birth, so may the second Initiation be justly compared to the baptism of the Holy Ghost and of Fire ; for it is the power of the Third Person of the Blessed Trinity that is outpoured at that moment, descending in what may but inadequately be described as a flood of fire, a flaming

tide of living light.   The man at this stage is spoken of among the
Buddhists as a *Sakadāgāmin*, the man who returns but once, which
means that he who has reached that level should need but one more
incarnation before attaining Arhatship, the fourth Initiation, after
which there is no compulsory physical rebirth.   The Hindu name
for this second step is the *Kutichaka*, the man who builds a hut, he
who has reached a place of peace.

At this stage no additional fetters are cast off, but it is usually
a period of considerable psychic and intellectual advancement.   If
what are commonly called psychic faculties have not been previously
acquired, it is the tradition that they should be developed at this
stage, as without them it would seem practically impossible to assimilate the knowledge which must now be given, or to do the higher
work for humanity in which the Initiate is now privileged to assist.
He must have the astral consciousness at his command during his
physical waking life, and during sleep the heaven-world will be open
before him—for the consciousness of a man when away from his
physical body is always one stage higher than it is while he is still
burdened with the house of flesh.   Dr. Besant, however, in her
Initiation, the Perfecting of Man, supplies us with an alternative interpretation of this ; she says that before a man can come to the third
Initiation he must learn to bring the spirit of intuition (buddhi)
down to his physical consciousness, so that it may abide in him and
guide him.   Then she adds :

> This process is usually called " the development of psychic faculties ",
> and it is so, in the true meaning of the word " psychic ".   But it does not mean the
> development of clairvoyance and clairaudience, which depend on a different process.[1]

THE THIRD INITIATION

When the candidate has passed through the four sub-stages
of the second Initiation, and has once more become *Gotrabhu*, he is
ready for the third Initiation, to become the *Anāgāmin*, which means
literally " he who does not return ", for it is expected of him that he
will attain the next Initiation in the same incarnation.   The Hindu

[1] *Op. cit.*, p. 82.

name for this stage is the *Hamsa*, which means a swan, but the word is also considered to be a form of the sentence *So-ham*, " That am I ". There is a tradition, too, that the swan is able to separate milk from water, and the sage is similarly able to realize the true value for living beings of the phenomena of life.

This Initiation is typified in the Christian symbolism by the Transfiguration of the Christ. He went up " into an high mountain apart, and was transfigured " before his disciples : " His face did shine as the sun, and his raiment was white as light," " exceeding white as snow, so as no fuller on earth can white them ". This description suggests the Augoeides, the glorified man, and it is no inaccurate picture of what happens at this Initiation, for just as the second Initiation is principally concerned with the quickening of the lower mental body, so at this stage the causal body is especially developed. The ego is brought more closely into touch with the Monad, and is thus transfigured in very truth. Even the personality is affected by that wondrous outpouring. The higher and the lower self became one at the first Initiation, and that unity is never lost, but the development of the higher self that now takes place can never be mirrored in the lower worlds of form, although the two are one to the greatest possible extent.

The Gospel story tells also that at the Transfiguration there appeared Moses and Elijah, the chief figures of the old dispensation ; one the greatest of the Jewish prophets, the other representing the Jewish law. Thus the two dispensations or methods of approach to truth, that of the following of the law and that of the inspiration of prophecy, are represented as with him who was about to establish a new dispensation, that of the Gospel ; and all these symbols have meanings referring to the actual facts of the third Initiation.

Another symbol relating to the same step appears in the Gospel story of the presentation of the Christ to his Father in the Temple. In the traditional account this is somewhat out of place, for the Christ is then presented as a little child. At this stage of the man's progress he has to be brought before the spiritual King of the

World, the mighty Head of the Occult Hierarchy, who, at this third step, either confers the Initiation himself, or deputes one of His pupils, the three Lords of the Flame who came with him from Venus, to do so; and in the latter event the man is presented to the King soon after the Initiation has taken place. Thus the Christ is brought into the presence of his Father; the buddhi in the Initiate is raised until it becomes one with its origin on the nirvanic plane, and a very wonderful union between the first and the second principles in man is then effected.

THE FOURTH AND FIFTH FETTERS

The *Anāgāmin* enjoys, while moving through the round of his daily work, all the splendid possibilities given by the full possession of the faculties of the higher mental plane, and when he leaves his physical vehicle at night he enters once more into the wonderfully widened consciousness that belongs to the buddhic plane. While in this state he has to throw off any lingering remains of what are called the fourth and fifth fetters, *kāmarāga* and *patigha*, attachment to the enjoyment of sensation, typified by earthly love, and all possibility of anger or hatred. The aspirant must free himself from the possibility of being enslaved in any way by external things. It is not by any means that he will not feel the attraction of what is pleasant or beautiful or clean, nor the repulsion for the opposites of these things. He will still take them into account in the course of his work; but he will not let them be a deciding element in duty, and will override them entirely on those emergent occasions when it is necessary for his work.

Here we must guard against a possible misconception—one with which we frequently meet. The purest and noblest human love never dies away—is *never* in anyway diminished by occult training; on the contrary, it is increased and widened until it embraces all with the same degree of fervour which at first was lavished on one or two only. But the student does in time rise above all considerations connected with the mere *personality* of those around him, and so is free from all the injustice and partiality which ordinary love so often brings in its train.

Nor should it for a moment be supposed that in gaining this wide affection for all, he loses the especial love for his-closer friends. The unusually perfect link between Ananda and the Lord Buddha, as between St. John and the Christ, is on record to prove that, on the contrary, this is enormously intensified; and the tie between a Master and his pupils is far stronger than any earthly bond. For, the affection which flourishes upon the Path of Holiness is an affection between egos, not merely between personalities; therefore it is strong and permanent, without fear of diminution or fluctuation, for it is that "perfect love which casteth out fear".

CHAPTER X

THE HIGHER INITIATIONS

THE ARHAT

DURING the stages following the first, second and third Initiations the candidate is gradually developing the buddhic consciousness ; but at the fourth Initiation he enters the nirvanic plane, and from then onward he is engaged in climbing steadily through that, or rather through that division of it, consisting of its five lower sub-planes, on which the human ego has being. This Initiation is in one way a midway point, as it is usually said that seven lives are occupied on the average at normal times between the first and the fourth Initiations, and seven lives also between the fourth and the fifth ; but these figures are capable of very great reduction or increase, as I have said before, and the actual period of time employed is in most cases not very great, since usually the lives are taken in immediate succession, without interludes in the heaven-world.

The candidate who has passed the fourth Initiation is spoken of in Buddhist terminology as the *Arhat*, which means the worthy, the capable, the venerable or perfect, and in the Eastern books very many beautiful things are said about him, for they know at what a high level of evolution he stands. The Hindus call him the *Paramahamsa*, the one above or beyond the *Hamsa*.

CHRISTIAN SYMBOLOGY

In Christian symbology the fourth Initiation is indicated by the suffering in the garden of Gethsemane, the Crucifixion and the

Resurrection of the Christ; though since there are certain preliminary stages it may be more completely symbolized by the various events that are said to have taken place during Holy Week. The first event in the series was that the Christ raised Lazarus from the dead; and this is always commemorated on the Saturday before Palm Sunday, though according to the Gospel narrative it took place a week or two earlier. On the Sunday there was the triumphal entry into Jerusalem; on Monday and Tuesday the delivery of a number of addresses in the Temple; on Wednesday the betrayal by Judas Iscariot; on Thursday the Founding of the Holy Eucharist; on the night between Thursday and Friday the trials before Pilate and Herod; and on Good Friday the Crucifixion. Holy Saturday was spent in preaching to the spirits in prison, and at midnight on Saturday, or rather at the first moment on Sunday morning, Christ rose from the dead, triumphant for evermore.

All these details of the Christ-drama have a relation to what really happens in connection with the fourth Initiation. The Christ did something unusual and wonderful in the raising of Lazarus on the Saturday, and it was very largely as a result of that that he enjoyed his one earthly triumph soon after, for all the people came together when they heard of the raising of the dead man. They waited for him, and when he came out from the house to go on the way to Jerusalem they received him with an ovation and a great display of feeling, and treated him as in the East they still treat anyone whom they think to be holy; so he was escorted by the people with great enthusiasm into Jerusalem, and having won that little earthly recognition, he naturally took the opportunity of teaching them, and gave the addresses in the Temple, to which great crowds came to see and hear him. This is symbolical of what really takes place. The Initiate attracts some attention, and gains a certain amount of popularity and recognition. Then there is always the traitor to turn upon him and distort what he has said and done, so that it appears to be evil; as Ruysbroek put it:

Sometimes these unhappy ones are deprived of the good things of earth, of their friends and relations, and are deserted by all creatures; their holiness is mistrusted and despised, men put a bad construction on all the works of their life, and they are rejected and disdained by all those who surrounded them ; and sometimes they are afflicted with diverse diseases.

Then follows a shower of obloquy and abuse, and his rejection by the world. After that comes the scene in the garden of Gethsemane when the Christ feels himself utterly forsaken ; and then he is held up to derision and crucified. Finally there is the cry from the cross : " My God, my God, why hast thou forsaken me ? "

Madame Blavatsky held a theory, which she expounded in *The Secret Doctrine*, which I am not able personally to verify, that the real meaning of those words was : " My God, how thou dost glorify me ! " I do not know which of the two renderings is the more accurate, but there is great truth in both of them. It is one of the features of the fourth Initiation that the man shall be left entirely alone. First he has to stand alone on the physical plane ; all his friends turn against him through some misunderstanding ; it all comes right afterwards but for the time the man is left with the feeling that all the world is against him.

Perhaps that is not so great a trial, but there is another and inner side to it ; for he has also to experience for a moment the condition called *Avichi*, which means " the waveless ", that which is without vibration. The state of *Avichi* is not, as has been popularly supposed, some kind of hell, but it is a condition in which the man stands absolutely alone in space, and feels cut off from all life, even from that of the Logos ; and it is without doubt the most ghastly experience that it is possible for any human being to have. It is said to last only for a moment, but to those who have felt its supreme horror it seemed an eternity, for at that level time and space do not exist. That appalling trial has, I think, two objects—first, that the candidate may be able fully to sympathize with those to whom *Avichi* comes as a result of their actions ; and secondly, that he may learn to stand absolutely apart from everything external, triumphant in his utter certainty that he *is* one with the Logos and that this overwhelming consternation, caused by the sensation of isolation from him, is nothing but an illusion and a temptation. Some have collapsed before this terrible test, and have had to go back and begin over again their climb towards the higher Initiation ; but for the man who can stand firm through its awful nightmare it is indeed a wonderful experience, however formidable, so that while to the trial itself the interpretation " Why hast thou forsaken me ? " might be applicable, " How thou dost glorify me ! " would well express the feeling of the man who comes forth from it victorious.

This Initiation differs from all the others in that it has this strange double aspect of suffering and victory. Each of the earlier Initiations was symbolized in the Christian system by one definite fact, the Birth, the Baptism, the Transfiguration ; but in order to represent this fourth Initiation a series of events has been found necessary. The Crucifixion and all the varied sufferings of which it was the culmination were employed to typify one side of this Initiation, while the Resurrection with its triumph over death represents the other side. Always at this stage there is suffering, physical, astral and mental ; always there is the condemnation by the world, and the apparent failure ; always there is the splendid triumph upon higher planes—which, however, remains unknown to the outer world. The peculiar type of suffering which invariably accompanies this Initiation clears off any arrears of karma which may still stand in the Initiate's way ; and the patience and joyousness with which he endures them have great value in the strengthening of his character, and help to determine the extent of his usefulness in the work which lies before him.

The Crucifixion and Resurrection which symbolize the actual Initiation are thus described in an ancient Egyptian formula :

Then shall the candidate be bound upon the wooden cross, he shall die, he shall be buried, and shall descend into the underworld ; after the third day he shall be brought back from the dead.

Only after three clear days and nights and part of a fourth had passed was the still entranced candidate of those ancient days raised from the sarcophagus in which he had lain, and borne into the outer air at the eastern side of the pyramid or temple, so that the first rays of the rising sun might fall upon his face and awaken him from his long sleep.

There is an old proverb, " No cross, no crown ", which may be taken to mean that without man's descent into matter, his binding on the cross of matter, it would have been impossible for him to gain the resurrection and receive the crown of glory ; but by the limitation and through the sorrow and trouble he has gained the victory. It is impossible for us to describe that resurrection ; all words that we can employ seem to sully its splendour, and any attempt at description seems almost blasphemy ; but this much may be said, that a complete triumph has been obtained over all sorrows, troubles and difficulties, temptations and trials, and it is his for ever because he has conquered by knowledge and inner strength. We may recall how the Lord Buddha proclaimed his freedom :

> Many a house of life
> Hath held me—seeking ever him who wrought
> These prisons of the senses, sorrow-fraught ;
> Sore was my ceaseless strife !

> But now,
> Thou builder of this tabernacle—thou !
> I know thee ! Never shalt thou build again
> These walls of pain,
> Nor raise the roof-tree of deceits, nor lay
> Fresh rafters on the clay ;
> Broken thy house is, and the ridge-pole split !
> Delusion fashioned it !
> Safe pass I thence—deliverance to obtain.

NIRVANA

For the Arhat henceforth the consciousness of the buddhic plane is his while still in the physical body, and when he leaves that body in sleep or trance, he passes at once into the unutterable glory of the nirvanic plane. At his Initiation he must have at least one glimpse of that nirvanic consciousness, just as at the first Initiation there must be a momentary experience of the buddhic, and now his daily effort will be to reach further and further up into the nirvanic plane. It is a task of prodigious difficulty, but gradually he will find himself able to work upwards into that ineffable splendour.

The entry into it is utterly bewildering, and it brings as its first sensation an intense vividness of life, surprising even to him who is familiar with the buddhic plane. The surprise has been his before, though in a lesser measure, whenever he mounted for the first time from one plane to another. Even when we rise first in full and clear consciousness from the physical plane to the astral, we find the new life to be so much wider than any that we have hitherto known that we exclaim : " I thought I knew what life was, but I have never known before ! " When we pass into the mental plane, we find the same feeling redoubled ; the astral was wonderful, but it was nothing to the mental world. When we pass into the higher mental plane, again we have the same experience. At every step the same surprise comes over again, and no thought beforehand can prepare one for it, because it is always far more stupendous than anything that we can imagine, and life on all those higher planes is an intensity of bliss for which no words exist.

European Orientalists have translated Nirvana as annihilation, because the word means " blown out ", as the light of a candle is extinguished by a breath. Nothing could be a more complete antithesis to the truth, except in the sense that it is certainly the annihilation of all that down here we know as man, because there he is no longer man, but God in man, a God among other Gods, though less than they.

Try to imagine the whole universe filled with and consisting of an immense torrent of living light, the whole moving, moving onward, without relativity, a resistless onward sweep of a vast sea of light, light with a purpose (if that is comprehensible) tremendously concentrated, but absolutely without strain or effort—words fail. At first we feel nothing but the bliss of it, and see nothing but the intensity of the light ; but gradually we begin to realize that even in this dazzling brightness there are brighter spots (nuclei, as it were) through which the light obtains a new quality that enables it to become perceptible on lower planes, whose inhabitants without this aid would be altogether beneath the possibility of sensing its effulgence. Then by degrees we begin to comprehend that these subsidiary suns are the Great Ones, the Planetary Spirits, great Angels, Karmic Deities, Dhyan Chohans, Buddhas, Christs and Masters, and many others who are to us not even names, and to see that through them the light and the life are flowing down to the lower planes.

Little by little, as we become more accustomed to this marvellous reality, we begin to perceive that we are one with them, though far below the summit of their splendour, that we are part of the One that dwells somehow in them all, and also in every point of space between, and that we ourselves are also a focus, and through us at our much lower level the light and life are flowing to those who are still further away (not from it, for all are part of it and there is nothing else anywhere) but from the realization of it, the comprehension and experience of it.

Madame Blavatsky often spoke of that consciousness as having its centre everywhere and its circumference nowhere, a profoundly suggestive sentence, attributed variously to Pascal, Cardinal de Cusa and the *Zohar*, but belonging by right to the Books of Hermes. Far indeed from annihilation is such consciousness; the Initiate reaching it has not in the least lost the sense that he is himself; his memory is perfectly continuous; he is the same man, yet all this as well, and now indeed he can say " I am I " knowing what " I " really means.

Wonderfully well was this expressed by Sir Edwin Arnold in *The Light of Asia* :

> ∴ . . . . Seeking nothing, he gains all;
>   Foregoing self, the Universe grows " I ";
> If any teach Nirvana is to cease,
>   Say unto such they lie.
>
> If any teach Nirvana is to live,
>   Say unto such they err; not knowing this,
> Nor what light shines beyond their broken lamps,
>   Nor lifeless, timeless bliss.

Not lifeless in the sense of being dead, for he is the very exemplification and expression of the most vivid life imaginable; lifeless because he is far beyond both death and life alike, quit of the *samsāra* for ever. Hell has been defined as time without God, and heaven as God without time ; surely this latter description is still more applicable to Nirvana.

Any description of Nirvana which we may attempt must sound strange. No words that we can use can give even the least idea of such an experience as that, for all with which our minds are acquainted has long ago disappeared before that level is attained. There is, of course, even at that level, a sheath of some sort for the Spirit, impossible to describe, for in one sense it seems as though it were an atom, and yet in another it seems to be the whole plane. The man feels as if he were everywhere, but could focus anywhere within himself, and wherever for a moment the outpouring of force diminishes, that is for him a body.

The ineffable splendour of Nirvana necessarily surpasses all physical comprehension, and consequently even the most poetical attempts to depict it are foredoomed to failure. Nevertheless each man who writes of it approaches it from a different angle, and each may contribute some point which the others have missed. I have already tried to give my own impressions ; let me now quote for you those of my lifelong friend and brother, George Sydney Arundale, who in his book *Nirvana* has made a very remarkable and most valiant effort to convey that which cannot be conveyed. We all fail, of course ; yet I cannot but feel that he comes nearer to the achievement of success than I have done. He writes :

My first remembrance is of seeing the Master K. H. looking as I had never seen him before. Radiant he is always, supremely radiant, but now he was more than radiant, and I cannot find a word down here to describe him in the glory in which I perceived him with the first flash of Nirvanic consciousness. Majestic and radiant are poor words—" blinding" perhaps expresses it better, for just for a moment I was overwhelmed. I almost wanted to veil my face from sight of him, and yet I could not keep my eyes from him, so unfathomably splendid did he appear—only less glorious than the King, as I afterwards realized, though at the time no greater glory could I conceive.

I summon up my courage. I feel as if he were saying to me : " Welcome to a new kingdom which you must learn to conquer." In his power my consciousness unfolds, and I step as it were across a threshold into Nirvana. Words and phrases, however beautiful, however majestic, almost desecrate as they strive to describe conditions there. Even the faint touch of first experience of this lofty level dwarfs into insignificance all other experiences of all other planes, save only the entry into the Presence of the One Initiator. I remember my first glimpse of the Buddhic plane on the occasion of admission to the ranks of the Great White Brotherhood ; I recall to this day my marvelling at the vision of the Master in his Buddhic vehicle, and well do I remember, in the days that followed, the wondrous sense of unity with all things, with the trees and flowers, feeling with them all, growing with them and in them, suffering and rejoicing in and with them. I remember, too, the casting off of the friend of ages—the causal body ; and I remember a vivid rendering contrast between the moment before and the moment after the glimpse into the new kingdom.

But today the Master seems to me as One whom I have never known before, robed in the glories of a Kingdom I am entering as a little child. The new consciousness enfolds me, and in a moment my world is full of new, strange, glorious values. All is different, supremely different, though the same. A new Divinity is open to my eyes, and unfolds to my gaze a new meaning, a new purpose. It is the Buddhic unity transcended, glorified—a more marvellous unity ; in some wonderful way it is merged in a state vaster and more tremendous. There is something even more true than unity, something more real. It seems impossible, and yet it is so.

What is the nature of that of which even Buddhic glory is but a limitation ? I must use words, and words seem a terrible anti-climax. I can only say it is the Glory of a Light Transcendent, a world of Light which is the image of God's own Eternity. I am face to face with an unspotted mirror of his Power and with an image of his Goodness. And the mirror, the image , is an endless ocean of Light, of which I become (though in one sense I already have been) a part, by an apotheosis of at-one-ments on plane after plane below. Brotherhood in the outer world ; Unity in the Buddhic world ; Light Transcedent in Nirvana.

This Light Transcendent is nearer to the Real even than the Buddhic Unity which hitherto had seemed the most stupendous fact in all the world. Light the beginning ; Light the path ; Light the future ; God said : " Let there be Light," and there was and is Light indescribable. Beautiful as is the light in the world, it is but the faint and feeble image of the Light Triumphant—the adjective somehow seems appropriate—of these regions of the Real. It is the Sun-Light of the Sun ere it descends into the forms in which we know it. It is Light purified of form. It is Light which is the Life of form. It is an ever-present " intimation of immortality," a future within the Now, and yet Eternal. It is an—I do not say " the "—apotheosis and essence of the light we know. All the glory of the most wonderful dawn (and one feels nothing can be more wonderful than a perfect Eastern dawn) is brought to glorious fruition and splendid perfection in the noon-day which is Nirvana.

God is Light ; Light is God ; Man is Light ; all is Light—a new meaning to the ancient Egyptian exhortions : " Look for the Light ! Follow the Light ! Perceive and learn to be at one with the Light of God in all things." I look upon the world. I see the world in terms of Light. God-Light in manifestation in man-light, in rock-light, in tree-light, in creature-light. All is light—a blinding glory at the centre, translated into colour as it radiates towards its circumference. The blinding glory everywhere—the God-Light—the blazing seed of futurity in each individual thing in every kingdom. And the light-seed breaks up its white-ness (the word seems wrong, but " lightningness " is awkward) into colours of the spectrum.

In each kingdom of Nature, seven great pathways of colour, potential in each pathway in the beginning, unfolding into glorious fruition at the close. I see the diamond, the ruby, the emerald, the sapphire—kings of the mineral kingdom—superb in the perfection of their colours. Yet at the bottom these glories exist, imprisoned, slowly being released through the evolutionary process, until they stand free and splendid as the kingdom's jewels. In every kingdom it is the same. The free once more imprisoned that a mightier and more splendid freedom still may be achieved.

Bathed in the lightning-standing-still which is Nirvana, I perceive the imprisoned lightnings in all things. I perceive the Light which is dull—the savage ; the Light which is bright—the man evolved ; the Light which is glory—the Superman, the Master. I see colour everywhere in process of transmutation, of glorification, of transcendence. There is no blackness anywhere in the sense of a negation of Light. God said : " Let there be Light." And there was and is light everywhere. " His Light shineth even in our darkness."

What is Niryana ? The Light Divine. I am touching, perhaps only for a moment, its lowest reaches, its densest layers. I cannot conceive down here even this Glory, but it leaves in me as I return to earth a new perception of Reality. I have taken a step nearer to the Real. There is a greater comradeship in the world than I had thought—a deeper identity, a more glorious origin, a more glorious way, and a more glorious goal. Round everywhere and at all times are God's Sunshine Messengers. Every colour speaks his Word and his Voice. Every form breathes his purpose. I, dust in the Sunshine, yet am part of it, and looking upward to the Sun I see the sign of my own Divinity, and the embodied promise of my ultimate achievement. As is our Lord the Sun so shall we all be, for He has willed it so.

Light is language, thought, vesture and vehicle. A flash of light conveys for us down here a whole philosophy.

Light is the Will of the Sun, the Wisdom of the Sun, the Love of the Sun. It is written in books that Nirvana is bliss. Even from the outermost region, at the frontiers, I know Nirvana to be *infinitely* more. Just one glimpse and all things seem to be made new, within me and without me. I remain, yet am wholly changed, and everything round me seems to be undergoing a process of re-valuation. Even now, everything means far more than before. Every object, in every kingdom, seems in one way far more a shadow of Reality than a reality, for I perceive how feeble and inadequate must be all reflections of the Light. I did not know before that they were so feeble. And yet, equally true is it that every object is far more real, far less of a shadow of Reality, than I had thought. I see the prison-opportunity of form, and I perceive the shadows. I see the unfolding splendour of the Light-Eternal, and I perceive the Real. All other worlds are shadow-worlds compared with this Nirvanic world. And yet they are more real worlds because of this Nirvanic world, for I now perceive the seal of God's purpose set upon all things, and I must reverence all things in far deeper measure than before.

Philosophers talk of pure Being. I seem to be able to sense what pure Being must be, not because I have contacted it, but because I have contacted that which is less short of pure Being than all other consciousness states I have so far experienced.

How true it is that language in this case conceals thought and meaning ! I need Nirvanic language to convey the sense of Nirvanic things. As Myers has said so beautifully :

> O, could I tell, ye surely would believe it !
> O, could I only say what I have seen !
> How should I tell or how can ye receive it,
> How, till He bringeth you where I have been ?

It is only fair to the distinguished author to say that the quotation given above is but a series of disconnected extracts.

The Buddhist monk Ananda M. in his book *The Wisdom of the Aryas* writes of Nirvana as follows :

The literal meaning of the word is simply " *blown out* "—extinguished as is the flame of a lamp when it has been blown out ; but you who have so far followed what has been said concerning it will understand how great has been the error of those who have expounded it as simply tantamount to sheer annihilation. Annihilation it is indeed in one sense—the annihilation of Desire, of Passion, of Self-delusion. But when we come to try to expound its meaning in terms other than negative, we are met with an insurmountable difficulty ; that, namely, all our positive definitions must necessarily be in terms of the life we know, in terms of human thought ; and here we speak of That which is *beyond* all Life, the very Goal towards which all Life is tending. . . .

To the instructed Buddhist, Nirvana stands for the Ultimate, the Beyond, the Goal of Life—a state so utterly different from this conditioned ever-changing being of the self-dream that we know as to lie not only quite beyond all naming and describing, but far past even Thought itself. And yet—and herein lies the wonder and the greatness of this Wisdom of the Aryas, won by the Greatest of the Aryans for the enfranchisement of man from all his self-wrought bondages—this Glory utterly beyond all grasp of thought, this Peace that is the very purpose of all strife-involving being lies nearer to us than our nearest consciousness ; even as, to him who rightly understands, it is dearer than the dearest hope that we can frame. Past all the glory of the moon and sun, still infinitely far above the starry heights of conscious being sublimated to its ultimate ; beyond the infinite abysses of that all-embracing Æther wherein these universes have their bourneless home ;—illimitably far remote above the utmost altitudes where Thought, with vainly-beating wings, falls like some lost bird that had aspired till the thin air no longer could support it ;—*still* it dwells higher than the very thought we now are thinking, higher than the consciousness that, for the transitory moment, is all that truly can be termed ourselves. . . .

Selfless to live and selfless die—seeking for no reward, but only service of the greater life ; hoping for no high heaven, for no aeonian bliss, but only to grow selfless every day—such is the lesson that pervades alike the Master's life, the Master's Teaching ; thereby may Peace come to all life at last !

Dr. Besant, referring to this subject in a recent lecture, said :

There is, in the Buddhist philosophy, a wonderful sentence of the Lord Gautama Buddha, where he is striving to indicate in human language something that would be intelligible about the condition of Nirvana. You find it in the Chinese translation of the *Dhammapada*, and the Chinese edition has been translated into English in Trübner's *Oriental Series*. He puts it there that, unless there were Nirvana, there could be nothing; and he uses various phrases in order to indicate what he means, taking the uncreated and then connecting with it the created; taking the Real and then connecting with it the unreal. He sums it up by saying that Nirvana *is*; and that if it were not, naught else could be. That is an attempt (if one may call it so with all reverence) to say what cannot be said. It implies that unless there existed the Uncreate, the invisible and the Real, we could not have a universe at all. You have there, then, the indication that Nirvana is a plenum, not a void. That idea should be fundamentally fixed in your mind, in your study of every great system of philosophy. So often the expressions used may seem to indicate a void. Hence the western idea of annihilation. If you think of it as fullness, you will realize that the consciousness expands more and more, without losing utterly the sense of identity; if you could think of a centre of a circle without a circumference, you would glimpse the truth.

The man who has once realized that marvellous unity can never forget it, can never be quite as he was before; for however deeply he may veil himself in lower vehicles in order to help and save others, however closely he may be bound to the cross of matter, " cribbed, cabined and confined ", he can never forget that his eyes have seen the King in his Beauty, that he has beheld the land which is very far off—very far off, yet very near, within us all the time if we could only see it, because to reach Nirvana we need not go away to some far-distant heaven, but only open our consciousness to its glory. As the Lord Buddha said long ago : " Do not complain and cry and pray, but open your eyes and see ; for the light is all about you, and it is so wonderful, so beautiful, so far beyond anything of which men have ever dreamt, for which they have ever prayed, and it is for ever and for ever."

" The land that is very far off " is a quotation from the Prophet Isaiah, but strangely enough it is a mistranslation. Isaiah did not speak of the land which is very far off, but of the land of far distances, which is a very different idea and one of great beauty. It suggests that the Prophet had had some experience of these higher planes, and was comparing in his thought the splendour of the star-strewn fields of heaven with the cramped catacombs through which we crawl on earth ; for that is what this life is as compared with that higher one, a blind crawling through dark and devious ways as compared with a splendid purposeful life, an utter realization of the Divine Will ensouling and working through the wills of those who dwell therein.

THE WORK OF THE ARHAT

A mighty work the Arhat has before him to climb to the topmost heights of that utmost of human planes of existence, and while he is doing it he must cast off the remaining five of the ten great fetters, which are :

6. *Ruparaga*—desire for beauty of form or for physical existence in a form, even including that in the heaven-world.

7. *Aruparaga*—desire for formless life.

8. *Mana*—pride.

9. *Uddhaccha*—agitation or irritability, the possibility of being disturbed by anything.

10. *Avijja*—ignorance.

The sixth and seventh fetters include not only the idea of *rāga*, or attraction, but also that of *dvesha* or repulsion, and the casting off of these fetters implies a quality of character such that nothing in the lower planes of form, or the higher and formless planes, can hold him by its attraction even for a moment, or can repel him by its disagreeableness if he have work therein. As the eighth fetter, *Māna*, is filed away he forgets the greatness of his own achievements, and pride becomes impossible for him, since now he stands always in the light, and measures himself against no lower thing. Then comes the perfect serenity which naught can disturb, leaving him free to acquire all knowledge, to become practically omniscient as regards our planetary chain.

THE FIFTH INITIATION

Now does the candidate approach the fifth Initiation, that of the Adept ; " he hath wrought the purpose through of that which made him man ", so now he takes the final step that makes him

Superman—*Asekha*, as the Buddhists call him, because he has no more to learn, and has exhausted the possibilities of the human kingdom of nature; *Jīvanmukta*, as the Hindus speak of him, a liberated life, a free being, free not because of any separate independence but because his will is one with the universal Will, that of the One without a second. He stands ever in the light of Nirvana, even in his waking consciousness, should he choose to remain on earth in a physical body, and when out of that body he rises still higher into the Monadic plane, beyond not merely our words but our thought. Hear again the Lord Buddha:

> . . . Measure not with words
> The Immeasurable; nor sink the string of thought
> Into the Fathomless. Who asks doth err;
> Who answers, errs. Say naught!

In Christian symbolism the Ascension and the Descent of the Holy Ghost stand for the attainment of Adeptship, for the Adept does ascend clear above humanity, beyond this earth, although if he so chooses, as did the Christ, he may return to teach and help. As he ascends he becomes one with the Holy Spirit, and invariably the first thing he does with his new power is to pour it down upon his disciples, even as the Christ poured down tongues of fire upon the heads of his followers at the Feast of Pentecost. A glance at any of the diagrams showing the principles in man, which have been published in earlier books, will show the relation between the manifestations of the Logos in the Prakritic Cosmic plane and in the soul of man; we shall see that the triple ātmā, the threefold Spirit of man, lies in the lower part of the nirvanic or spiritual plane, and that the lowest manifestation of the Third Person, God, the Holy Spirit, is in the higher part of the same plane. The Adept becomes one with him at that level, and that is the real explanation of the Christian feast of Whitsunday, the festival of the Holy Spirit. It is on account of unity with him that the *Asekha* can take pupils; the Arhat, though he has very much to teach, still works under an Adept, acts for him and carries out his orders on the physical plane, but does not take pupils for himself, because he has not yet that special link with the Holy Spirit.

BEYOND ADEPTSHIP

Above the Initiation of the Adept lies that of the Chohan, and further on still others, of which I will speak in the Chapter on the Occult Hierarchy. The ladder of being extends up into clouds of light, into which few of us as yet can penetrate, and when we ask those who stand higher than we and know infinitely more than we do, all they can say is that it extends beyond their sight also. They know very many more steps of it than we do, but it goes still further, onward and upward to unimaginable heights of glory, and no one knows its end.

Although what I have just said is absolutely accurate—that none of us can see the end of that ladder, and that the work of those in the higher ranks of the Hierarchy is almost incomprehensible, still I wish to make it perfectly clear that their existence and work is as real and definite as anything in the world—nay, more so, and that there is not the slightest vagueness about our vision of those Great Ones. Though I know but little about the higher part of his work, for many years past I have seen the Bodhisattva constantly, almost daily, engaged in that work, and I have very many times seen the Lord of the World in his wonderful and incomprehensible existence ; so that they are to me people just as real as any whom I know, and I am as certain as I can possibly be of their existence and of something of the part that they play in the world.

Of the tremendous truth of what I *can* say about them I am utterly certain, and yet I cannot explain them, nor understand more than a fragment of what they are doing. I have seen Dhyan Chohans and Planetary Spirits and Ambassadors from other solar systems, and I know absolutely of the existence and transcendent glory of those people, but what their tremendous life-work may be I do not know at all. I have myself seen the Manifestation of the Logos of the Solar System, seen him as he is among his Peers, and yet millions of times more than the unspeakable grandeur that I have seen in him must be that which they see when they look at him. As Arjuna in the *Bhagavad Gītā* is said to have seen the Divine Form, so have I seen, without the shadow of a doubt. And I want to put my testimony on record that these things are so. I dare say that I lay myself open to a certain amount of scorn for writing this ; people will ask : " Who are you, to say these things ? " But I have seen, and it would be cowardly to refuse to bear witness.

I have repeatedly declared, both in speech and in writing, that I wish no one to base his belief in Theosophy upon any assertion of mine. I think that each man should study the system for himself and come to his own conclusions, the fundamental reason for his accept- ance of any doctrine being either that he knows it from his own experience or that he finds it the most reasonable hypothesis at present before him. But that in no way alters the fact that I have evidence to give to those who care to listen to it—evidence which I have placed before them in this and other books. We who write upon Theosophy in this twentieth century can fully reaffirm St. John's plain statement of nearly two thousand years ago :

That which was from the beginning, which we have heard, which we have seen with our eyes, which we have looked upon, and our hands have handled . . . that which we have seen and heard declare we unto you.[1]

We who have seen bear witness ; whether the world accepts our testimony makes little difference to us.

Whoso has felt the Spirit of the Highest,
Cannot confound nor doubt Him nor deny :
Yea, with one voice, O world, though thou deniest,
Stand thou on that side, for on this am I.[2]

THE SEVEN PATHS

Immediately beyond the Asekha Initiation this higher path opens up in seven great ways among which the Adept must take his choice, and on this subject I cannot do better than quote what was said in *Man : Whence, How and Whither* :

When the human kingdom is traversed, and man stands on the threshold of his superhuman life, a liberated Spirit, seven paths open before him for his choosing : he may enter into the blissful omniscience and omnipotence of Nirvana,

[1] I John, i, 3.
[2] *St. Paul*, by Professor Myers.

with activities far beyond our knowledge, to become, perchance, in some future world an Avatāra, or divine Incarnation; this is sometimes called "taking the Dharmakāya vesture". He may enter on "the Spiritual Period"—a phrase covering unknown meanings, among them probably that of "taking the Sambhogakāya vesture". He may become part of that treasure-house of spiritual forces on which the Agents of the Logos draw for their work, "taking the Nirmānakāya vesture". He may remain a member of the Occult Hierarchy which rules and guards the world in which he has reached perfection. He may pass on to the next Chain, to aid in building up its forms. He may enter the splendid Angel— or Deva—Evolution. He may give himself to the immediate service of the Logos, to be used by him in any part of the Solar System, his servant and messenger, who lives but to carry out his will and do his work over the whole of the system which he rules. As a General has his staff, the members of which carry his messages to any part of the field, so are these the staff of him who commands all, "Ministers of his that do his pleasure". This seems to be considered a very hard Path, perhaps the greatest sacrifice open to the Adept, and is therefore regarded as carrying with it great distinction. A member of the General Staff has no physical body, but makes one for himself by *kriyāshakti*—the "power to make"—of the matter of the globe to which he is sent. The Staff contains Beings at very different levels, from that of Arhatship upwards.

The man who takes the Dharmakāya robe retires into the Monad, and drops even his nirvanic atom; the Sambhogakāya retains his nirvanic atom and shows himself as the Triple Spirit, and the Nirmānakāya retains his causal body and also the permanent atoms which he has carried all through his evolution, so that at any moment he can materialize round them mental, astral and physical bodies, if he so desires. He definitely keeps his link with the world from which he has come, in order that he may supply the reservoir from which spiritual power is poured down upon that world. The Nirmānakāyas are spoken of in *The Voice of the Silence* as forming a Guardian Wall which preserves the world from further and far greater misery and sorrow. For those who do not understand the inner meaning, that seems to imply that the misery and sorrow come to the world from outside, and that these Great Ones ward it off, but that is not so at all, for all the trouble in the world comes from those who suffer it. Each man is his own lawgiver, each decrees his own doom or reward; but the duty of the Nirmānakāya is to supply a great store of spiritual force for the helping of men. All the time they generate this force, taking no part for themselves, but putting it all at the service of the Brotherhood for their use in lifting the heavy burden of the world.

It will thus be seen that of those who attain Adeptship comparatively few remain on our earth as members of the Occult Hierarchy, but these and their work are of vital importance, so we will devote to that subject the remaining chapters of this book.

PART IV

THE HIERARCHY

CHAPTER XI

THE WORK OF THE MASTERS

A SUMMARY

I HAVE just explained that of the human beings who attain Adeptship, but a few remain on our earth as members of the Occult Hierarchy, to promote the evolution of life upon it in accordance with God's plan. At present there are some fifty or sixty of these Supermen so engaged, and of their general work Dr. Besant has written as follows in her book on *The Masters*:

They aid, in countless ways, the progress of humanity. From the highest sphere they shed down light and life on all the world, that may be taken up and assimilated, as freely as the sunshine, by all who are receptive enough to take it in. As the physical world lives by the life of God, focused by the sun, so does the spiritual world live by that same life, focused by the Occult Hierarchy. Next, the Masters specially connected with religions use these religions as reservoirs into which they pour spiritual energy, to be distributed to the faithful in each religion through the duly appointed "means of grace". Next comes the great intellectual work, wherein the Masters send out thought-forms of high intellectual power to be caught up by men of genius, assimilated by them and given out to the world; on this level also they send out their wishes to their disciples, notifying them of the tasks to which they should set their hands. Then comes the work in the lower mental world, the generation of the thought-forms which influence the concrete mind and guide it along useful lines of activity in this world, and the teaching of those who are living in the heavenly world. Then the large activities of the inter-mediate world, the helping of the so-called dead, the general direction and super-vision of the teaching of the younger pupils, and the sending of aid in numberless cases of need. In the physical world the watching of the tendencies of events, the correction and neutralizing, as far as law permits, of evil currents, the constant balancing of the forces that work for and against evolution, the strengthening of the good, the weakening of the evil. In conjunction with the Angels of the Nations also they work, guiding the spiritual forces as the others guide the material.

THE PARISHES

We may consider more fully some of the lines of work, here indicated in small compass with the sweep of vision for which Dr. Besant is world-renowned. Though the number of Adepts is small, they have arranged that in all the world no life shall be disregarded or neglected; so they have divided the earth into special areas in somewhat the same way as in older countries the Church has divided the whole land into parishes, so that wherever a man may live he is within one of these geographical divisions and has a definite Church organization to administer to his spiritual and sometimes to his bodily needs. The parishes of the Adepts, however, are not country districts or parts of towns, but huge countries and even continents.

As the world is at present divided, one great Adept may be said to be in charge of Europe, and another looks after India; and in the same way the whole world is parcelled out. The parishes do not follow our political or geographical boundaries, but within his territory the Adept has all the different grades and forms of evolution to regard—not only our own, but also the great kingdom of the Angels, of the various classes of nature-spirits, the animals, vegetables and minerals beneath us, the kingdoms of the elemental essence, and many others of which so far nothing has been heard by mankind; so there is a vast amount of work to be accomplished. In addition to the guardianship of the Adepts, each race or country has also the assistance of a Spirit of the Race, a Deva or guardian Angel who watches over it and helps to guide its growth, and corresponds in many ways to the ancient conception of a tribal Deity, though he stands at a considerably higher level. Such, for example, was Pallas Athene.

There are many different sets of influences at work in the service of the Logos for the evolution of man, and naturally they all operate in the same direction, and in co-operation with one another.

We must never make the mistake of attributing to these great agencies the disasters which sometimes overtake countries, as in the case of the French Revolution and the upheavals in Russia. Those are due entirely to the savage passions of the people, which

have run riot and caused destruction instead of construction, and
they illustrate the danger to which the work of the Adepts and the
Spirit of the Race is exposed, when they make experiments along
democratic lines. There is terrible evil involved in tyranny, and
sometimes great suffering also, but at least there is some sort of
control ; and the great problem in getting rid of the tyranny is how
to do it without losing social stability and self-control. When that
goes, many persons fail to keep the human end uppermost in their
own personalities, passion rises, crowds run riot, and the people
become liable to obsession by great waves of undesirable influence.
The national Angel tries to guide the feelings of the people ; he is
interested in them in great masses, and he would when necessary
urge them to great patriotism and heroic deeds, just as a general
might encourage his men to advance on the field of battle ; but he is
never reckless of their lives or careless of their suffering, any more
than a wise general would be.

DISTRIBUTION OF FORCE

A large part of the Adepts' work, as we have seen in an earlier
chapter, lies at levels far beyond the physical, as they are engaged in
pouring out their own power, and also the force from the great store
filled by the Nirmanakaya. It is the karma of the world that it shall
have a certain amount of this uplifting force at its service, and even
ordinary men who turn their wills into line with the Divine Will (by
directing their thought and feeling to the service of humanity) add
little to the reservoir, and are thus privileged to share in the great
sacrifice. On account of this, humanity is evolving as a unit, and
the miracle of brotherhood enables every one to make much more
progress than would be even remotely possible were he standing
entirely by himself. All this is part of the scheme of the Logos, who
apparently has calculated upon our taking part in his plan. When
he devised it he thought : "When my people shall rise to a certain
level, they will begin to co-operate intelligently with me ; therefore I
will arrange so that when they come to that point they will be able
to draw upon my power." Thus he is counting upon everyone.

The Brotherhood is one with all humanity on higher levels, and through its agency the distribution of the supply of force from the great reservoir takes place for men. The Adepts are raying upon all egos without exception in the higher mental plane, and thus giving the greatest possible assistance to the unfoldment of the indwelling life. That life is like a seed which cannot die and must grow, because the principle of evolution, the Logos himself, is at the heart of its very being; in man the plant has already risen through the soil and is seeking the upper air, and the rapidity of its development is now very largely due to the sunlight of the spiritual force that comes through the channel of the Hierarchy. This is one of the many ways in which the more advanced help the less advanced, as they share more and more the divine nature, in accordance with the divine plan.

Each of the Adepts who have undertaken this special work is raying out upon enormous numbers of people, running often into many millions simultaneously; and yet, such is the wonderful quality of this power which he pours forth, that it adapts itself to each one of these millions as though he were the only object of its influence, and it appears as though what for us would be full attention were being given to that one.

It is difficult to explain on the physical plane how this may be —but it arises from the fact that the Master's nirvanic consciousness is a kind of point which yet includes the entire plane. He can bring that point down through several planes and spread it out like a kind of vast bubble. On the outside of that huge sphere are all the causal bodies which he is trying to affect, and he, filling the sphere, appears all in all to each individual. In this way he fills with his life the ideals of millions of people, and is for them respectively the ideal Christ, the ideal Rāma, the ideal Krishna, an Angel or perhaps a spirit-guide.

This is quite a different kind of work from the superintendence of one of the great parishes, and in it the Master pays attention chiefly to people of one type, those who are developing along his own line of evolution, though naturally most of them are quite unconscious of his action. He has also many special cases to deal with, and for this purpose sometimes delegates part of this work to Devas, leaving them considerable liberty within certain well-defined limits. The Devas in their turn employ nature-spirits and make a variety of thought-forms, and there is thus a large field of activity connected with their work.

THE USE OF DEVOTION

In *The Science of the Sacraments* I have explained how the Great Ones take advantage of the ceremonies of all religions to pour out their power over the world on the lower planes, and thus to stimulate in as many men as possible the spiritual growth of which each is capable. But it is not only in connection with religious ceremonial that this is done, for the Brotherhood makes use of every opportunity that offers. If there be a gathering of people who are all under the influence of devotion, all bent for the time being upon nobler and higher thought, such a gathering offers to the Adepts an unusual opportunity, of which they will straightway make use, since it forms a focus which they can employ as a channel for spiritual influence. When people are scattered and living in their homes, they are like a number of separated lines down each of which but a little force can flow, but when they come together at a meeting, it is as though these were combined to make a kind of pipe through which a much greater flood of blessing may be poured than the sum of what could descend through the separate lines.

I have seen a million pilgrims together in the holy city of Benares, many of them no doubt ignorant and superstitious, but for the time full of devotion and utterly one-pointed. The mass of devotional feeling generated by such a crowd is almost incalculable, and the Adepts never miss the opportunity of utilizing it for good. It is, of course, unquestionable that a similar number of equally enthusiastic but intelligent people would supply vastly more force—and also force capable of playing upon a higher plane altogether; but we must not for a moment make the mistake of ignoring the value of the vast amount of energy produced by ignorant and even fanatical people. The members of the Brotherhood have a wonderful faculty of separating the evil from the good, or rather of drawing out the last ounce of force which can be used for good, even from the midst of a great deal that is evil.

It is common to find the most intense devotion allied with bitter sectarian feeling ; in such a case the Adept will extract and make use of every particle of the devotional feeling, simply ignoring and leaving behind the savage hatred which to us seems to be a part of it. Therefore people with most undesirable characteristics often produce a certain amount of good karma, though it is undeniable that it would be far greater if it were dissociated from the other unfortunate qualities.

Such a city as Benares is always a tremendous centre of force, even quite apart from the annual pilgrimages. It is a city of shrines and relics, and these also can be utilized as channels by the Adepts ; and the same is true of such things the world over. In some place, for example, there may be a relic of a great saint belonging to any one of the religions of the world. If the relic is genuine, a certain amount of strong magnetism does radiate from it, on account of its connection with a worthy man, and it may therefore be used, by sending through it a stream of force, to bless those who reverence it. In many cases, however, the relic is not genuine ; but that, which to us would seem a most important fact, in reality matters less than one might suppose.

If for a long time people have made a great centre of devotional feeling around it, on that account alone the Brotherhood can use it as effectively as a genuine relic, and the fact that the people are deluded in their belief does not affect its usefulness, since their devotion is genuine, and that is the important thing. If this were more fully understood, it would probably check many thoughtless people who are inclined to ridicule the superstitions of the Catholic peasants in Italy, Sicily or Spain, or to look down upon Indian coolies because they pay homage at some shrine which is obviously not what it is supposed to be. There is no doubt that truth is better than error, yet we must remember that it is not well to tear away from the ignorant the objects of their devotion until they are able to rise to higher things ; by such iconoclasm the world is the poorer, for by it not only is devotion destroyed, but useful channels of the Masters' force may be closed.

Besides, it is obviously impossible for an ignorant peasant to judge as to the genuineness of a relic, and it would be grossly unfair that the effect of his devotion, poured out with good intention and in all innocence of heart, should be made to depend upon a fact as to which he can have no knowledge. In the great world of realities things are never so badly managed as that ; the true devotion will find full and hearty response whether the object round which it is centred is or is not all that the devotee thinks it to be. The devotion is the real thing—the only thing that matters, and it must and does receive the real return which it deserves. The supposed relic is merely a point upon which it is focused, and an imaginary point will do for this as well as any other.

WORK BY THE PUPILS

I have already mentioned that the pupils of the Masters are also apprentices, that at their lower level they serve as transmitters of force, and also do a great variety of work in every branch of civilization and human culture, all of which is part of the Adept's work in the world. A vast amount of this is done by others who have received inspiration or suggestion from these pupils, or through the various societies and agencies that they have set going or influenced. Without these influences humanity would be poor indeed, though for the most part it knows little of the source of its true wealth. The Adepts themselves cannot turn aside from their exalted work to do these lower and easier tasks, because if they did the whole machinery of evolution would suffer.

Men sometimes ask why these Great Ones have not written books, for example. They forget that the Adepts are carrying on the evolution of the world ; they can hardly drop that in order to give people information with regard to some part of it. It is true that if one of the Great Ones had the time to write a book, if his energy could not be better employed, that book would be far superior to

any that we have. But if it were the plan of things that all work
should be done by those who can already do it perfectly there would
be no field for the exercise of our faculties, and it would be difficult
to see any utility in our existence in this world.

A department of activity which has recently been organized on
a large scale by pupils of the Masters is that of practical service on
the astral plane, about which I have written in the book *Invisible
Helpers*. The greater part of that work is among the newly-dead,
who often find themselves there confused, bewildered, and even
suffering, especially when they have been frightened during life by
the hideous stories of dreadful torture after death, which form part of
the stock-in-trade of some perverted religious sects. Though it is
many years ago, it was still within the life of the Theosophical
Society that the organized band of invisible helpers was founded and
set to work. It was originally composed of people still living, who
had decided to use their time during the sleep of the body in this
definite way ; but they soon drew to themselves a great many already
dead, who had not thought of this work before.

Until that time new-comers to the astral world were mostly
left to themselves, unless it occurred to their relations to meet them
and introduce them to the new life. For example, a mother who
died would still watch over her children, and if any of the children
died shortly after the mother she would give them what help and
information she could ; and generally the good-natured people among
the dead would pass on to others what knowledge they possessed
when they saw the need of help. In older civilizations, when
large families and joint families were the rule, perhaps comparatively few people found themselves without a friend in need
on the other side of death. Readers of Oriental literature will
remember how much is said in Hindu religious books about the
importance of the family ties and duties as extending to the invisible
regions beyond the veil of death. Still, the condition there was somewhat like that of a country without hospitals, or schools, or bureaux
of public information, where many must suffer, and in times of special
calamity and war that was often most serious.

THE CENTENNIAL EFFORT

An excellent picture of the way in which the Adepts work for the betterment of civilization is given in Dr. Besant's *London Lectures of* 1907, in which she tells us something of the steps that were taken by the Brotherhood to lift Europe out of the terrible darkness of the Middle Ages. She explains that in the thirteenth century a mighty Personage, then living in Tibet, promulgated his order to the Brotherhood that in the last quarter of every century an effort should be made to enlighten Europe. Looking through history carefully, we can see that from that time onward, a new ray of light was sent forth towards the end of each century from the Lodge.

The latest of these efforts was the founding of the Theosophical Society in 1875. After careful consideration the Masters Morya and Kuthumi undertook the responsibility of that step, and chose that noble worker Madame Blavatsky to help them on the physical plane. Most students of Theosophical literature know how she was prepared for what she had to do ; how in due course the Brotherhood sent her to America to search for Colonel Olcott, the comrade who would supply what was lacking in herself—the power of organization and of speaking to men and gathering them round him and shaping them into a movement in the outer world—and how the Society was founded in New York, and later had its Headquarters removed to India.

As I write,[1] the Society has completed its fiftieth year of service to humanity, and it is impossible to estimate the vast amount of good it has done in every department of human life. Its influence cannot in the least be measured by the number of its members or branches, although that is by no means insignificant, since it extends to every civilized part of the globe. But in each field of human endeavour it has sounded its characteristic note, the reverberations of which multiply around us in the words and work of statesmen and scientists, literary men and artists, and many others, of whom, great numbers perhaps have never even heard the word Theosophy. It

[1] in 1925.

has drawn attention to the realities of the invisible world and the power of mind. It has voiced the claims in outward life of the organization for mutual support of widely different individuals, each of whom shall be strong in his special type, and all of whom shall be bound together by the indissoluble bond of respect for the man who is different from oneself. It has brought together East and West as never before; it has demanded fair play in the comparison of religions, and revealed with unmistakable clearness their essential unity of teaching and their common source. And it has brought thousands to the feet of the Masters to serve them with all their power and with all their hearts for the good of mankind for all time to come.

THE RACES

In its work for the world the Brotherhood deals not only with the present, but looks far into the future, and prepares for the evolution of new races and nations in which the qualities of humanity shall be developed in harmonious sequence. As we shall see in Chapter XIII, the progress of mankind takes place in no haphazard manner, but the formation of the races with their special characteristics, physical, emotional and mental (serving as classes in the great world-school, for the development of special qualities) is as precise and definite as the curriculum and time-table of any modern college.

The great Aryan race which, though not yet at its prime, dominates the world today with its supreme gift of intellect, has followed after the Atlantean race, the people of which still form the majority of mankind and occupy a great portion of the land surface of our globe.

THE SIXTH SUB-RACE

The moulding of the form of body, emotions and mind of the sixth sub-race of our Aryan root race, has already begun to appear in America and Australia and perhaps in other parts of the world.

The great modelling power of the Manu's mind and will is at work on the inner planes, modifying even the physical type of the children of the new age, wherever they may be susceptible to it, and some of the junior members of the Brotherhood, working in the outer world, have their instructions to provide for these when possible the education and training that befits the new race. This work is small as yet, but it is destined to swell into voluminous proportions, until within a few short centuries the sixth sub-race will stand out distinct and admirable in its young manhood in the new world, while the old world continues to develop the fifth sub-race to its maturity and perfection. And perchance later still the sixth sub-race, radiant and glorious in its manhood, will shed its blessing upon the fifth, so that for the first time a race shall have a serene and dignified decline into fruitful and venerable age. That may be the reward of its present and coming service to the infant race, and of its fight, full of sacrifice but triumphant, against the powers of darkness, opening up possibilities for man such as the race has never known before.

We must try to understand what is meant by belonging to the new sixth sub-race. Our ideas are liable to be too inelastic. When the sixth sub-race is fully established, it will show certain definite characteristics—physical, astral and mental—which are not to be seen in the *average* man of the fifth sub-race. Remember, it has to be built gradually out of the fifth sub-race, and these new characteristics must be developed one by one in each of the egos concerned. The process of preparation is a long one, and may well extend over several lives. So when we look round and examine people (and especially *young* people) from this point of view, we must not expect to be able to say off-hand that one belongs to the new sub-race, and another does not.

A more accurate statement would be something like this : " A seems to possess about twenty-five per cent of the new sub-race ; B has perhaps as much as fifty per cent ; C has a large proportion— perhaps seventy-five per cent ; in D, I cannot see anything lacking ; as far as I can tell, he is a fully developed example ". And you must understand that the average boy or girl whom you think hopeful is probably an A, for B's are as yet very rare in the world, and C's and D's practically non-existent. Remember also that developments are very unequal; a boy may have made a considerable amount of astral or mental progress before it shows much in his physical body; and on the other hand, through good heredity, he may have a physical body capable of expressing greater advancement on the higher planes than he has yet attained. Very few can expect to show all the signs yet; they may be well satisfied if they show one or two.

Even at its culmination it will not be uniform; for example, it is in the main a dolichocephalous race, but it will always have brachycephalous sub-divisions; it will contain fair-haired and dark-haired people, people with blue eyes and people with brown. Naturally the astral and mental traits are the more important, but in most cases it is only by the physical appearance that one can make an estimate. The keynote is unselfishness, and the dominant is eager enthusiasm for service; and these must be accompanied by active kindliness and large-hearted tolerance. He who forgets his own pleasure, and thinks only how he can help others, has already gone far on the path. Discrimination and common sense are also marked characteristics.

If we wish to know for what physical tokens we may look, perhaps the most marked of all are delicate, well-shaped hands and feet, thin fingers and oval nails, especially thinness in fingers and thumb when seen edgewise. The texture of the skin is also important. It is always clear, and never coarse. Of faces there are three types —the markedly oval with high forehead, the slightly less oval with broad forehead, and the practically brachycephalous (this last being rare; the definition of a brachycephalous skull is that its breath is four-fifths of its length). There is about the person who is approaching the sixth sub-race a distinguishing *expression* which one who looks for it will soon begin to recognize.

We frequently hear from independent observers and students of their recognition of a new type seen especially in California, Australia and New Zealand. For example, in 1923 an address was delivered by Captain Pape to the British Association, dealing with

what he called the Austral-American Race, and his remarks included
the following description of its peculiarities :

> The head tends to be dome-shaped, especially over the frontal region :
> there is a departure from what is known as the " low-set ear " ; hair and skin are
> fine ; eyes luminous, intelligent, but not full ; bridge of the nose early developed ;
> lips sensitive and mobile ; eyebrows prominent ; frontal brain development large ;
> type of face somewhat triangular, but not sharp ; general physiology harmonious,
> proportionate, healthy, not at all the " all brain and no body " type. The psy-
> chology of the new-race child manifests as rapid response to sympathy, pity
> in suffering, power to comprehend principles easily, quick intuitions, thoroughness,
> sensitiveness, quick sense of justice, absence of parrot-like intelligence, eagerness to
> help others. They also show a dislike of coarse food, and often have not a large
> appetite along any lines. In other respects they are normal children but specially
> need sympathy and understanding teachers.

In the previous year there was a long article in *The Los Angeles
Sunday Times* devoted to the subject of the new-race appearing in
California and New Zealand. After referring to some of the mental
and physical characteristics ascribed to the children of the new-race,
it remarked particularly upon their qualities of exceptional poise and
intuition.

THE SIXTH ROOT RACE

Another great event is the foundation of the sixth root race,
which is to take place physically in California about seven hundred
years from now. A community will be established there with the
Manu of that race, he who is now our Master Morya, at the Head
of it, and beside him his co-worker throughout the ages, the Master
Kuthumi, who is to be the Bodhisattva of the sixth root race. We
have written of that community in *Man : Whence, How and Whither.*
Although it lies some hundreds of years ahead, which after all is but a
brief time in the life of a man, as all of us will realize when we
look back upon it, preparations are already afoot for that also,
and the Theosophical Society is playing no inconsiderable part
in those.

Every branch of the Society is or ought to be encouraging each
one of its members in his efforts to apply in the outer world the
Theosophical knowledge that he has gained ; he must of course do that

according to his temperament and ability, and his opportunities as he mixes with men ; but all that helps the present race. Within the Theosophical Lodge, where so many different types of men forgather and must help one another, if the Lodge be true to its ideals, a breadth of character should be developed in the members, for they receive in this respect an education in the spirit of brotherhood which can scarcely be had elsewhere in the world. Most societies are organized for the attainment of one goal or one purpose, but in the Theosophical Society we know that although one model of perfection appeals most strongly to one man and another to another, the brotherhood of man will not be achieved by the triumph of any one ideal, be it love, or truth, or beauty alone, but by the twisting of all these strands into one mighty rope which will bind man for ever to the Divine. As was said in the *Hitopadesha* long ago :

> Small things wax exceeding mighty,
>   Being cunningly combined ;
> Furious elephants are fastened
>   With a rope of grass-blades twined.

Such is the spirit of brotherhood gradually acquired by the true Theosophist, holding to his fellow by inner impulse, not by outward compulsion.

CHAPTER XII

THE CHOHANS AND THE RAYS

THE CHOHANS

IN the last chapter I have tried to describe some of the numerous avenues of work of the great Masters, but there are of course many others, about some of which we know practically nothing ; yet what we do know indicates that the work is vast and varied, and that the Adepts deal with it in different ways, according to their own temperaments and preferences. There is a sevenfold division running through all things, as I must explain more fully presently, and this appears also in the Great White Brotherhood. In the Hierarchy the seven Rays are clearly distinguished. The first or ruling Ray is governed by the Lord of the World ; at the head of the Second Ray stands the Lord Buddha, and under these come respectively the Manu and the Bodhisattva of the root race which is predominant in the world at any given time. Parallel in rank with these is the Mahāchohan, who supervises all the other five Rays, each of which nevertheless has also its own Head. In my next chapter I will explain what I can about the loftier ranks of the Hierarchy, attempting in this to render some account of the work of the Heads of Rays Three to Seven, and of the Masters Morya and Kuthumi, who stand at their level on the First and Second Rays.

The title Chohan is given to those Adepts who have taken the sixth Initiation, but the same word is employed also for the Heads of Rays Three to Seven, who hold very definite and exalted offices in the Hierarchy. We are given to understand that the meaning of the word Chohan is simply " Lord ", and that it is used both generally and specifically, in much the same way as the word Lord is employed in England. We speak of a man as a lord because he possesses that title, but that is quite different from what we mean when we speak, for example, of the Lord Chancellor or the Lord-Lieutenant of the country. The term appears again in the name Dhyan Chohan, which occurs frequently in *The Secret Doctrine* and elsewhere, and then it refers to Beings of very high station, altogether outside the Occult Hierarchy of our planet.

THE MASTER DJWAL KUL'S TABLE

It is necessary at this point, if we are to understand at all this part of the work of the Masters, to digress a little and say something of what is meant by the Seven Rays. This is a matter of considerable difficulty. Long ago we received some information, very incomplete certainly, but still very valuable, about these Rays. I remember well the occasion on which it was given to us. Mr. Cooper-Oakley and I and a Hindu brother were sitting talking on the roof at Adyar in the very early days, when there was only the one headquarters house and twenty-nine acres of half-jungle behind it; and there came to us suddenly the Master Djwal Kul, who was at that time the chief pupil of the Master Kuthumi. He gave us a great deal of teaching in those days, and was always very kind and patient, and while he sat and talked to us that day this question of the Rays came up. Mr. Cooper-Oakley in his characteristic way said: " Oh, please, Master, will you tell us all about the Rays ? "

There was a twinkle in our Teacher's eye as he said: " Well, I cannot tell you *all* about them until you have reached a very high Initiation. Will you have what I *can* tell you, which will be partial and inevitably misleading, or will you wait until you can be told the whole thing ? " Not unnaturally we thought that half a loaf was better than no bread, so we said we would take what we could get. We noted down the very interesting information that he gave, but much of it was incomprehensible to us, as he had foretold. He said: " I cannot tell you any more than that, for I am bound by certain pledges; but if your intuition can make out more I will tell you whether you are right." Even that little fragmentary information was of very great value to us.

The following is the table of Rays and their characteristics which he then gave to us :

RAY	CHARACTERISTIC OF RAY	CHARACTERISTIC MAGIC	LAST RELIGION
I	Fohat, Shechinah	...	Brahmanical
II	Wisdom	Raja Yoga (Human Mind)	Buddhism
III	Akasha	Astrology (Natural Magnetic forces)	Chaldean
IV	Birth of Horus	Hatha Yoga (Physical Development)	Egyptian
V	Fire	Alchemy (Material Substances)	Zoroastrian
VI	Incarnation of Deity	Bhakti (Devotion)	Christianity, etc. (Kabala, etc.)
VII	...	Ceremonial Magic	Elemental Worship

DIAGRAM 3

It was explained that the religion written opposite each Ray is not to be taken as necessarily a perfect exposition of it, but is simply that which now remains on earth as a relic of the last occasion on which that Ray exercised dominant influence on the world. The Magic of the First Ray and the characteristics of the Seventh were not given ; we may imagine the first to be *kriyāshakti* and the second to be co-operation with the Deva kingdom. The meaning of the Birth of Horus could not be explained, but one of the characteristics of the Fourth Ray was stated to be the use of the forces of action and interaction—the male and female forces of nature, as it were. Whenever phallicism occurs in the various religions, it is always due to a materialization and misconception of some of the secrets connected with this Ray. The true development of the Seventh Ray would be communication with and instruction from the higher Devas.

After what I have said above it should be clear that the information that has as yet reached us about the Rays is fragmentary. It is not only not a full account of the subject, but it is not even a perfect outline, for we were plainly told that there were huge gaps in the description given to us, which could not possibly be filled up till much later. So far as we know, very little has hitherto been written on this subject and that little so guardedly expressed as not to be at all readily intelligible, and occult teachers are markedly reticent when questioned about it.[1]

THE SEVENFOLD DIVISION

The essential thing to understand is that there is a certain sevenfold division of everything that exists in the manifested world, whether of life or matter. All life which exists in our chain of worlds passes through and belongs to one or other of Seven Rays, each having seven sub-divisions. In the universe there are forty-nine such Rays, making, in sets of seven, the seven great Cosmic Rays, flowing from or through the seven Great Logoi. In our chain of worlds, however, and perhaps in our solar system, only one of these great Cosmic Rays is operating, and its sub-divisions are our seven Rays. It must not of course be supposed that our solar system is the only manifestation of that particular Logos, since each of the Seven Great Logoi may have millions of systems dependent on it. As I have explained in *The Inner Life* :

The whole of our solar system is a manifestation of its Logos, and every particle in it is definitely part of his vehicles. All the physical matter of the solar

---

[1] While the first edition of this book was passing through the press an important work on the subject appeared—*The Seven Rays*, by Professor Ernest Wood. The material which it gives is illuminative, and is presented from quite a new angle.

system taken as a totality constitutes his physical body; all the astral matter within it constitutes his astral body; all the mental matter, his mental body, and so on. Entirely above and beyond his system he has a far wider and greater existence of his own, but that does not in the least affect the truth of the statement which we have just made.

This Solar Logos contains within himself seven Planetary Logoi, who are as it were centres of force within him, channels through which his force pours out. Yet at the same time there is a sense in which they may be said to constitute him. The matter which we have just described as composing his vehicles also composes theirs, for there is no particle of matter anywhere in the system which is not part of one or other of them. All this is true of every plane; but let us for a moment take the astral plane as an example, because its matter is fluid enough to answer the purposes of our inquiry, and at the same time it is near enough to the physical to be not entirely beyond the limits of our physical comprehension.

Every particle of the astral matter of the system is part of the astral body of the Solar Logos, but it is also part of the astral body of one or other of the seven Planetary Logoi. Remember that this includes the astral matter of which your astral body and mine are composed. We have no particle which is exclusively our own. In every astral body there are particles belonging to each one of the seven Planetary Logoi, but the proportions vary infinitely. The bodies of those Monads which originally came forth through a Planetary Logos will continue all through their evolution to have *more* of the particles of that Planetary Logos than of any other, and in this way people may be distinguished as primarily belonging to one or other of the seven Great Powers.

THE SEVEN SPIRITS

In Christian terms these seven great Beings are found in the vision of St. John the Evangelist, who said: " And there were seven lamps of fire burning before the throne, which are the Seven Spirits of God ".[1] Those are the Mystical Seven, the great planetary Logoi, who are life-centres in the very Logos himself. Those are the true Heads of our Rays—the Heads for the whole solar system, not for our world only. Out through one or other of that mighty Seven everyone of us must have come, some through one, some through another.

They are the Seven Sublime Lords of *The Secret Doctrine*, the Primordial Seven, the Creative Powers, the Incorporeal Intelligences, the Dhyan Chohans, the Angels of the Presence. But remember that

[1] Rev. iv: 5.

this last title is used in two quite different senses, which must not be confused. At every Celebration of the Holy Eucharist among our Christian brethren there appears an " Angel of the Presence ", who is in truth a thought-form of the Lord Christ, a vehicle of his consciousness, and so is rightly called a manifestation of his Presence ; but these Seven Great Ones receive the title for a very different reason —because they stand ever in the very presence of the Logos himself, representing there the Rays of which they are the heads—representing *us* therefore, since in every one of us is part of the Divine Life of every one of them.

For though each of us belongs fundamentally to *one* Ray—the channel through which he, as a Monad, flowed forth from the Eternal into Time—yet has he within himself something of *all* the Rays ; there is in him no ounce of force, no grain of matter, which is not actually *part* of one or other of these wondrous Beings ; he is literally compacted of their very substance—not of one, but of all, though always one predominates. Therefore, no slightest movement of any of these great Star Angels can occur without affecting to some extent every one of us, because we are bone of their bone, flesh of their flesh, Spirit of their Spirit ; and this great fact is the real basis of the often misunderstood science of Astrology.

We all stand always in the presence of the Solar Logos, for in his system there is no place where he is not, and all that is, is part of him. But in a very special sense these Seven Spirits are part of him, manifestations of him, almost qualities of his—centres in him through which his Power flows out. We may see a hint of this in the names assigned to them by the Jews. The first of them is always Michael, " your Prince ", as he is called ; and this name means " The Strength of God ", or, as it is sometimes interpreted, " he who is like God in strength ". *El*, in Hebrew, means God ; we find it in Beth-El, which is " The House of God " ; and Elohim is the word used for " God " in the very first verse of the Bible. This word *El* occurs as a termination in the name of each of the Seven Spirits. Gabriel means " The Omniscience of God ", and He is sometimes called God's Hero. He is connected with the planet Mercury, as Michael is with

Mars. Raphael signifies " The Healing Power of God ", and he is associated with the Sun, which is the great health-giver for us on the physical plane. Uriel is " The Light or Fire of God " ; Zadkiel is " The Benevolence of God ", and is connected with the planet Jupiter. The other Archangels are usually given as Chamuel and Jophiel, but I do not at present recollect their meanings or their planets.

St. Denys speaks of these Seven Spirits as the Builders, and also calls them the Co-operators of God. St. Augustine says that they have possession of the Divine Thought, or the Prototype, and St. Thomas Aquinas wrote that God is the primary and these Angels are the secondary cause of all visible effects. Everything is done by the Logos, but through the mediation of these Planetary Spirits. Science will tell you that the planets are fortuitous aggregations of matter, condensations from the mass of the nebula, and so no doubt they are ; but why at those particular points ? Because behind each there is a living Intelligence to choose the points so that they will balance one another. Truly whatsoever exists is the outcome of natural forces working under cosmic laws ; but do not forget that behind every force is always its administrator, an Intelligence directing and managing. In thus describing them I have used the Christian terminology, but the same Beings can be found under different names in every great Religion.

THE SEVEN TYPES OF BEINGS

When, then, that primordial matter or spirit, which in the future was to become ourselves, first emerged from undifferentiated infinity, it issued through seven channels, as water might flow from a cistern through seven pipes, each of which, containing its peculiar colouring matter, would so tinge the water that passed through it that it would forever after be distinguishable from the water of the other pipes. Through all the successive kingdoms, the elemental, the mineral, the vegetable, the animal, the Rays are always distinct one from another, as they are also distinct in man, though in the lower kingdoms the influence of the Ray naturally acts in a somewhat different manner. Since in them there is no individualization, it is obvious that the whole of one species of animals, for example, must be on the same Ray ; so that the different kinds of animals in the world might be arranged in seven parallel columns according to the Rays to which they belong, and since an animal can individualize only through association with man, at the head of each of these Rays stands some class of domestic animal through which alone individualization on that particular Ray takes place. The elephant, dog, cat, horse and monkey are examples of such classes, so it is clear that the impulse of the Universal Life which is now animating, let us say, a dog, can never animate a horse or a cat, but will continue to manifest through the same species until individualization takes place.

Researches have not yet been made as to the particular animals and vegetables which stand on each Ray, but I had reason a few years ago to investigate the precious stones, and found that each Ray had its own representatives, through which the force of the Ray works more readily than through any other. I print here the table that appears in *The Science of the Sacraments*, in which is shown the jewel at the head of each Ray, and others which stand on the same Ray and therefore hold the same kind of force, though less strongly.

RAY	JEWEL AT THE HEAD OF RAY	SUBSTITUTES
1.	Diamond ...	Rock Crystal.
2.	Sapphire ...	Lapis Lazuli. Turquoise, Sodalite.
3.	Emerald ...	Aquamarine. Jade. Melachite.
4.	Jasper ...	Chalcedony. Agate. Serpentine.
5.	Topaz ...	Citrine. Steatite.
6.	Ruby ...	Tourmaline. Garnet. Cornelian, Carbuncle.
7.	Amethyst ...	Porphyry. Violane.

DIAGRAM 4

From all that I have said above it follows that these seven types are visible among men, and that every one of us must belong to one or other of the Rays. Fundamental differences of this sort in the human race have always been recognized; a century ago men were described as of the lymphatic or the sanguine temperament, the vital or the phlegmatic, and astrologers classify us under the names of the planets, as Jupiter men, Mars men, Venus or Saturn men, and so on. I take it that these are only different methods of stating the basic differences of disposition due to the channel through which we happen to have come forth, or rather, through which it was ordained that we should come forth.

It is, however, by no means an easy matter to discover to what Ray an ordinary man belongs, for he has become very much involved in matter and has generated a great variety of karma, some portion of which may be of a kind that dominates and obscures his essential type, even perhaps through the whole of an incarnation; but the man who is approaching the Path ought to be showing in himself a definite driving impulse or leading power, which has the character of the Ray to which he belongs, and tends to lead him into the kind of work or service which distinguishes that Ray; and it will also bring him to the feet of one of the Masters upon it, so that he becomes enrolled, as it were, in the college of which the Chohan of the Ray may be regarded as the Principal.

MAGIC AND HEALING POWERS

It may help a little towards the comprehension of these differences of type if I give one or two examples of the methods likely to be employed, judging from the table that I have printed above, by persons on the different Rays, when they want to use magic to produce a given result. The First Ray man would attain his object by sheer force of resistless will, without condescending to employ anything in the nature of means at all; he of the Second Ray would also work by force of will, but with the full comprehension of the various possible methods, and the conscious direction of his will into the channel of the

most suitable one ; to the Third Ray man it would come most naturally to use the forces of the mental plane, noticing very carefully the
exact time when the influences were most favourable to his success ;
the Fourth Ray man would employ for the same purpose the finer
physical forces of the ether, while his Fifth Ray brother would be
more likely to set in motion the currents of what used to be called
the astral light ; the devotee of the Sixth Ray would achieve his
result by the strength of his earnest faith in his particular Deity and
in the efficacy of prayer to him, while the Seventh Ray man would
use elaborate ceremonial magic, and probably invoke the assistance
of non-human spirits if possible.

Again, in attempting the cure of disease, the First Ray would
simply draw health and strength from the great fountain of Universal
Life ; the Second would thoroughly comprehend the nature of the
malady and know precisely how to exercise his will-power upon it to
the best advantage ; the Third would invoke the Great Planetary
Spirits, and choose a moment when astrological influences were
beneficent for the application of his remedies ; the Fourth would trust
chiefly to physical means such as massage ; the Fifth would employ
drugs ; the Sixth faith-healing ; and the Seventh mantras or magical
invocations. In all the above cases the operator is of course free to
use any of the different powers mentioned, but would probably find
the most effective instrument in his hands to be that which is typical
of his own Ray.

THE CHOHANS OF THE RAYS

In the members of the Adept Brotherhood the distinctions of
Rays are much more clearly marked than in others, and are visible in
the aura ; the Ray to which an Adept belongs decidedly affects not
only his appearance, but also the work that he has to do. We may
perhaps best see what are the distinctive characters of the Rays by
observing the work of the five Chohans of Rays Three to Seven, and
of the two Chohans who stand at their level on the First and Second
Rays, and carry on work of the same grade in the service of the

Greater Ones who are their directing Heads. In the Seven Heads of the Rays in the Hierarchy we have a reflection of the Seven Spirits before the Throne.

It must be understood that we can here mention but the merest outline of the qualities that are grouped under each of the Rays, and but a fragment of the work that the Adepts on those Rays are doing ; and care must be taken also to realize that full possession of the qualities of one Ray in no case implies a lack of those of the other Rays. If we speak of one of the Adepts as pre-eminent in strength, for example, it is also true that he has achieved nothing less than human perfection in devotion and love and every other quality as well.

Of the Master Morya, who is the representative of the First Ray at the level of the Chohan Initiation, I have already written to some extent. He stands with all the unshakable and serene strength of his Ray, playing a great part in that work of guiding men and forming nations, of which I must speak more fully in the next chapter. On that Ray too, there is the Master whom we have called Jupiter, acting as Guardian of India for the Hierarchy, Guardian of that nation which throughout the long life-time of the fifth race cherishes the seeds of all its possibilities, and sends them out in due course to each sub-race, that there they may grow and ripen and fructify. He also penetrates deeply into the abstruser sciences of which chemistry and astronomy are the outer shells, and his work in this respect is an example of the variety of activity that may exist within the limits of one Ray.

The Master Kuthumi, who was formerly the great teacher Pythagoras, is also a Chohan, and he represents the Second Ray at the same level. This is the Ray of Wisdom, which gives great Teachers to the world, and the work that lies upon it can best be described in connection with that of the Bodhisattva and the Buddha in my next chapter. I have already spoken of the marvellous love and wisdom that radiate from the Master whom I have the inexpressible delight and honour to serve and follow, and all that I have said about the teaching and training of pupils expresses especially his method. Other teachers on other Rays bring their pupils to the same point and develop in them exactly the same noble qualities, and always by the most irreproachable means, yet there are distinct differences in their methods; indeed, there are varieties in the way in which the same Master deals with different pupils.

At the Head of the Third Ray stands the great Master called the Venetian Chohan. In the men of that Ray engaged in the service of man there appears very strongly the characteristic of adaptability that belongs to the Ray, and its influence tends to make them fit themselves to people, so as to help them the better, and thus become, as St. Paul said, " all things to all men ". Those who are advanced on this Ray have great tact, and a rare faculty for doing the right thing at the right moment. Astrology is connected with this Ray, because, so far as an outsider may understand, the science of it is to know exactly when is the best time to do anything, to set any given forces in motion, and to know also when the present time is *not* a fitting one to do a certain thing, and in that way save ourselves a great deal of trouble and make ourselves more useful.

The Fourth Ray is under the care of the Master Serapis. In the earlier days of the Theosophical Society we used to hear a good deal about him, because of the fact that he at one period took charge of the training of Colonel Olcott, when his own Master, the Master Morya, was otherwise engaged for a time. Such interchange of pupils among the Masters, for special and temporary purposes, is not infrequent. The particular line of this Chohan is harmony and beauty, and people who belong to his type are always unhappy until they can introduce harmony into their environment, for it is along that line that they do most of their work. Art counts for much on this Ray, and many artists belong to it.

At the Head of the Fifth Ray stands the Master Hilarion, with his splendid quality of scientific accuracy. He was once Iamblichus, of the Neoplatonic School, and he gave to us, through M. C., *Light on the Path* and *The Idyll of the White Lotus*, he being, as Dr. Besant puts it, a " skilled craftsman in poetic English prose and in melodious utterance ". His influence is upon most of the great scientists of the world, and people well advanced along his Ray are notable for their ability to make accurate observations, and be absolutely dependable where scientific investigation is concerned. The Master's science extends, of course, far beyond what is commonly called by that name, and he knows and works with many of the forces which nature introduces into the life of man.

Nature is responsive to the moods of mankind and intensifies them in various ways. If a man is happy and joyous, other creatures enjoy his presence ; the nature-spirits go forth to meet him, and his own happiness is thus increased. This sort of reaction takes place everywhere. In the north of Europe, for example, the nature-spirits are somewhat wistful, and have moods of mournful introspection, and such as these find a ready home in Scotland, Ireland, Wales, Brittany and similar places ; they respond less readily to joy, and the people there are also colder and more difficult to rouse. In those countries nature is less joyous ; they are all lands of much rain and dull skies, grey and green, where life and poetry take a wistful turn.

The contrast is tremendous between those and Greece or Sicily, where everything is radiant, golden and blue and red, and all the people are joyous and happy on the surface. The creatures of nature actually bathe in a person's happiness, and most of all they are drawn to anyone who is full of joyous love, and they are happy in his aura and regard him with high favour. Today much of this side of life is ignored, though our knowledge of the physical plane is wide and detailed. We know, for example, that water$=H_2O$; the ancient Hindus and the ancient Greeks may or may not have been aware of that, but at any rate they recognized the presence of the different types of nature-spirits connected with the water, and utilized their services as definitely as we today use the power of electricity and the expansion of steam to drive many forms of machinery.

The Master Jesus, who became an Adept in his incarnation as Apollonius of Tyana, and was afterwards the great South Indian religious reformer, Shri Rāmānujāchārya, rules the Sixth Ray, that of *bhakti* or devotion. This is the Ray of the devotional saints and mystics of every religion, and the Chohan Jesus has charge of such people, under whatever form they may worship the Divine Being. Nineteen hundred years ago Apollonius of Tyana was sent out by the Brother-hood upon a mission, one feature of which was that he was to found, in various countries, certain magnetic centres. Objects of the nature of talismans were given to him, which he was to bury at these chosen spots, in order that the forces which they radiated might prepare these places to be the centres of great events in the future. Some of these centres have already been utilized, but some have not.

The Head of the Seventh Ray is the Master the Comte de St. Germain, known to history in the eighteenth century, whom we sometimes call the Master Rakoczy, as he is the last survivor of that royal house. He was Francis Bacon, Lord Verulam, in the seven-teenth century, Robertus the monk in the sixteenth, Hunyadi Janos in the fifteenth, Christian Rosenkreuz in the fourteenth, and Roger Bacon in the thirteenth; He is the Hungarian Adept of *The Occult World*. Further back in time He was the great Neoplatonist Proclus, and before that St. Alban. He works to a large extent through ceremonial magic, and employs the services of great Angels, who obey him implicitly and rejoice to do his will. Though he speaks all European and many Oriental languages, much of his working is in Latin, the language which is the especial vehicle of his thought, and the splendour and rhythm of it is unsurpassed by anything that we know down here. In his various rituals he wears wonderful and many-coloured robes and jewels. He has a suit of golden chain-mail, which once belonged to a Roman Emperor; over it is thrown a magnificent cloak of crimson, with on its clasp a seven-pointed star in diamond and amethyst, and sometimes he wears a glorious robe of violet. Though he is thus engaged with ceremonial, and still works some of the rituals of the Ancient Mysteries, even the names of which have long been forgotten in the outer world, he is also much concerned with the political situation in Europe and the growth of modern physical science.

THE QUALITIES TO BE DEVELOPED

The following is a summary of the characteristics of these Chohans and their Rays as I have given them in *The Science of the*

Sacraments, with the thought to be held in mind by those who wish to serve along their respective lines :

1. Strength.

   " I will be strong, brave, persevering in his service."

2. Wisdom.

   " I will attain that intuitional wisdom which can be developed only through perfect love."

3. Adaptability or Tact.

   " I will try to gain the power of saying and doing just the right thing at the right moment—of meeting each man on his own ground, in order to help him more efficiently."

4. Beauty and Harmony.

   " So far as I can, I will bring beauty and harmony into my life and surroundings, that they may be more worthy of him ; I will learn to see beauty in all Nature, so that I may serve him better."

5. Science (detailed knowledge).

   " I will gain knowledge and accuracy, that I may devote them to his work."

6. Devotion.

   " I will unfold within myself the mighty power of devotion, that through it I may bring others to him."

7. Ordered Service.

   " I will so order and arrange my service of God along the lines which he has prescribed, that I may be able fully to take advantage of the loving help which his holy Angels are always waiting to render."[1]

All these different qualities will have to be developed in each one of us in due time, but we shall possess them all perfectly only when we ourselves have reached perfection and become Supermen. At the present time one of the ways in which our imperfection shows itself in our lives is in the fact that we have some one characteristic developed in excess of the others. There are some, for example, who have scientific accuracy and discrimination well unfolded within them, but because as yet they have not cultivated affection and devotion their nature is cold and hard ; they often appear unsympathetic and are liable to misjudge their fellow-men, and in matters of judgement or in the consideration of an intellectual problem their attitude is often intensely critical. Their decision would always tend

[1] *Op. cit.*, p. 92.

to be against rather than in favour of any person who happened to cross their path, whereas the devotional or affectionate type of people would make far more allowance for the other man's point of view, and would on the whole be more likely to judge favourably, and even if their judgement were wrong, as they might easily be swayed by their feelings, it would err on the side of mercy. Both these are deflections from strictly accurate judgment, and in ourselves it will be necessary in the course of time to balance these qualities perfectly, for the Superman is the perfectly balanced man. As it says in the *Bhagvad Gītā*, "Equilibrium is called Yoga"

CYCLIC CHANGES

In the seven Planetary Logoi certain cyclic changes periodically occur, which correspond perhaps to in-breathing and out-breathing or to the beating of the heart down here on the physical plane. However that may be, there seems to be an infinite number of possible permutations and combinations of them ; and since our astral bodies are built of the very matter of their astral bodies, it is obvious that no one of these Planetary Logoi can change astrally in any way without thereby affecting the astral body of every man in the world, though of course more especially those in whom there is a preponderance of matter expressing him. If it be remembered that we take the astral plane merely as an example, and that exactly the same thing is true on all the other planes, we shall then begin to have some idea of the importance to us of the emotions and thoughts of these Planetary Spirits.

Whatever these may be, they are visible in the long history of human races as regular cyclic changes in the temperament of the people and the consequent character of their civilization. Putting aside the thought of world-periods and considering only the period of a single root race, we find that in it the Seven Rays are preponderant in turn (perhaps more than once) but in the period of that dominance of each Ray there will be seven sub-cycles of influence, according to a rather curious rule which requires some explanation.

Let us take, for example, that period in the history of a race when the Fifth Ray is dominant. During the whole of that epoch the central idea of that Ray (and probably a religion founded upon it) will be prominent in the minds of men ; but that time of predominance will be subdivided into seven periods, in the first of which this idea, though still the principal one, will be coloured by the idea of the First Ray, and the methods of the First Ray will be to some extent combined with its own. In the second of its subdivisions its idea and methods will be similarly coloured by those of the Second Ray, and so on, so that in its fifth subdivision it will naturally be at its purest and strongest. It would seem as if these divisions and subdivisions ought to correspond with the sub-races and branch races respectively, but it has not so far been possible for us to see that they do so.

THE REIGN OF DEVOTION

In discussing a subject so complex and so obscure as this with a knowledge of it so slight as is ours at present, it is perhaps hardly safe to adduce instances ; yet since we are told that the Sixth or devotional Ray has been recently dominant, we may fancy that we can trace the influence of its first sub-cycle in the stories of the wonderful powers exhibited by the earlier saints ; of its second in the Gnostic sects whose central idea was the necessity of the true wisdom, the Gnosis ; of the third in the Astrologers ; of the fourth in the strangely distorted efforts to develop will-power by the endurance of painful or loathsome conditions, as did St. Simeon Stylites or the Flagellants ; of the fifth in the Alchemists and Rosicrucians of the Middle Ages ; while its sixth division of the purest devotion might be imaged in the ecstasies of the contemplative monastic orders, and the seventh cycle would produce the invocations and exact adherence to external forms of the Roman Church.

The advent of modern spiritualism and the devotion to elemental worship which is so often a characteristic of its degraded forms, may be regarded as a premonition of the influence of the coming Seventh Ray, the more so as this movement was originated by a secret society which has existed in the world since the last period of the Seventh Ray predominance in Atlantis.

How real and decided a dominance is exerted by a Ray in the course of its cycle of influence is very evident to those who have read anything of Church history. They realize how much of utterly blind devotion there was all through the Middle Ages, how people who were very ignorant about religion nevertheless spoke in its name, and tried to force the ideas bred of their ignorance on other people who in many cases knew much more. Those who wielded the power—the dogmatic Christians—were precisely the people who knew least about the real meaning of the dogmas they taught. There were those who could have told them a great deal more, and could have explained the meaning of many points in Christian doctrine; but the majority would not hear, and they cast out these more learned men as heretics.

Throughout this dark period the people who really knew something, such as the alchemists (not that all alchemists knew very much, but certainly some of them knew more than the Christians), were to be found among such secret orders as the Templars and the Rosicrucians, and some of the truth was hidden in Freemasonry. All these people were persecuted by the ignorant Christians in those days, in the name of devotion to God. A great many of the mediæval saints were very full of a devotion that was often beautiful, and even spiritual; but it was generally so narrow in form that it usually allowed them, in spite of their spirituality, to hold uncharitable views about others who differed from them, and even to persecute them openly. There were a few who held really spiritual ideals, but they were regarded with suspicion. Such were the Quietists : Ruysbroek, Margaret and Christina Ebner, Molinos and Jacob Boehme. In almost all cases the more ignorant people rode down those who knew; they always did it in the name of devotion, and we must not forget that their devotion was very real and very intense.

It was not only in Christianity that the reign of devotion showed itself. It reflected itself powerfully into the religions left behind by the earlier Rays. Hinduism might be thought distinctly cold by devotional people. The religion of Shiva, God the Father, the First Person of the Blessed Trinity, spread almost entirely over India; and even to this day three-fourths of the Hindus are worshippers of that aspect of the Divine. Before these people is set up the ideal of duty—dharma—which is unquestionably the strong point of that religion. They held that men were born in the different castes according to their deserts; that wheresoever a man was born, it was his duty to carry on the dharma of his caste, and to rise out of it he must be so exceptional that for a long time such a thing was almost unknown. They worshipped law and order, and did not approve of discontent as applied to environment, but taught that the way to God was to use to the utmost the conditions in which a man found himself. If he did that, those conditions would improve from birth to birth. Nevertheless, they always said that the door to God was open to a man from any caste if he lived rightly, not seeking to better his opportunities by strife, but by doing his dharma to the uttermost in the state of life to which God had called him.

To the very devotional mind that would seem cold and scientific, and perhaps it was; but when the devotional Ray began to influence the world there came a great change, and the worship of the Second Person of the Trinity, Vishnu, incarnating as Shri Krishna, came prominently forward. Then devotion surged forth without restraint; so extreme it was that it became in many ways a mere orgy of emotion; and it is probable that there is greater devotion at the moment among the followers of Vishnu in India than can be found even among Christians, whose religion is confessedly devotional. The emotion is so great that its demonstration is often uncomfortable for us of the colder races to watch. I have seen hard men of business throw themselves into an ecstasy of devotion, which led them to burst into tears and apparently to break up and change entirely, merely at the mention of the Child Shri Krishna. All that has ever been felt for the Child Jesus among Western nations, is felt for the Child Krishna amongst the Hindus.

This was the effect of devotion on a religion which in itself was not devotional in character. Buddhism also can hardly be called a devotional faith. The Buddhist religion was a gift of Hinduism to the great Fourth Race, and devotional cycle for that race does not necessarily coincide with ours. That religion does not hold the necessity for prayers ; it tells its people, in so far as it recognizes the existence of God, that he knows his own business very much better than they can hope to know it ; that it is quite useless for them to pray to him, or to try to influence him, for he is already doing better than any man can think. The Buddhists in Burma would say : " The boundless Light exists, but that is not for us. We shall reach that one day ; meantime our business is to follow the teaching of our Lord, and see to it that we do those things which he would have us do ".

It is not that they disbelieve in a God, but that they set God so far—so infinitely far—above us all ; they are so sure about him, that they take it all for granted. The missionaries say that they are atheistical. I have lived among them and know them more intimately than does the average missionary, and my impression is that they are not in the least atheistical in spirit, but their reverence would be too great for them to put themselves on such familiar terms with God, or, like many in the West, to talk with intimacy of him, as if they knew precisely what he is going to do and all about his work. That would strike the Oriental as a very irreverent attitude.

Buddhism itself has been touched by this fire of devotion, and in Burma they worship the Lord Buddha almost as a God. I noticed this when I had to write a catechism for Buddhist children. Colonel Olcott wrote the first catechism of Buddhism, intending it for the use of children, but he made his answers difficult even for grown-up people to understand. We found it necessary to write an introduction to it for children, and to reserve his catechism, which was a splendid work, for older students. He asked in that catechism : " Was Buddha a God ? " and the answer was : " No, not a God, but a man like ourselves, only far more advanced than we ". That was accepted fully in Ceylon and Siam, but when we came to Burma they objected to the negative answer, saying : " He is greater than any God of whom we know anything ". The Sanskrit word for God is " deva " and the Hindus never use " God " in our sense of the word, unless they

are speaking of Ishvara, or else of the Trinity, Shiva, Vishnu and
Brahmā.

When the missionaries talk about the Hindus as having thirty-
three million (or three hundred and thirty million) gods, the word
which they translate as god is " deva ", and that includes a great many
beings—angels, nature-spirits and so on—but the Indians no more
worship them than we should.   They know that they exist and they
catalogue them, that is all.   In Burma we found that devotion had
thus appeared in Buddhism, but in Ceylon, where the people are
mostly descendants of Hindu immigrants, they will tell you, if you
ask them why they make offerings to the Lord Buddha, that it is out
of gratitude for what he has done for them.   When we asked if they
thought that he knew of it and was pleased, they said : " Oh no ! he
has passed far away into Paranirvāna ; we do not expect him to
know anything about it, but to him we owe this knowledge of the
Law which he has taught us, and for that we perpetuate his Name,
and make our offerings out of gratitude ".

So this wave of devotion has influenced the world powerfully
since the coming of the Child Krishna two thousand four hundred
years ago, but now the special intensity of that sixth phase has gone,
and is rapidly giving place to the influence of the incoming Ray, the
Seventh.   There is still ignorant devotion among the peasantry in
many Aryan countries, but the more educated people are not now
readily moved to devotion unless they have at the same time some
understanding of its object.   There was a phase which had its own
value, in the fourth sub-race particularly, when the people were
prepared to be devoted to almost anything that would draw out their
emotion, and from that, with the stronger development of the lower
mind in the fifth sub-race, there was a reaction into agnosticism.
That now in its turn has proved unsatisfactory, so that that wave has
practically passed over, and men are now ready at least to inquire
and examine instead of frantically denying everything.

There is a double change now taking place, for in addition to
the modification of Ray influence, there is also the beginning of the
sixth sub-race, which brings in intuition and wisdom, blending all

that is best in the intelligence of the fifth sub-race and the emotion of the fourth.

THE ADVENT OF CEREMONIAL

The Ray that is now coming into force is very largely one of ceremonial. There was plenty of that in the Middle Ages, but it was chiefly due to the influence of the seventh sub-ray of the Sixth Ray, whereas ours is due rather to the first sub-ray of the Seventh ; so it will not be regarded principally from the point of view of its devotional effect, but rather from that of its usefulness in connection with the great Deva evolution. It will be most beneficial when the people make it their business to understand, as much as may be, what is going on.

In modern religion, ceremonial is year by year playing a more prominent part. In the middle of the last century in England the churches and cathedrals had but little life in them. The average country church was then scarcely different from a dissenting chapel ; there were no vestments, no painted windows nor decorations of any kind, and everything was as dull and unornamental as could be. No attention was paid to making things beautiful and reverent and worthy of God and his service ; thought was given to preaching more than to anything else, and even that was done mainly from a practical point of view. If we were to go into the same churches in England today, we should find hardly a parish in that condition. The old carelessness has been replaced by reverence ; the churches have in many cases been beautifully decorated, and in many of them, and of the cathedrals, the ceremonies are performed with accuracy and reverence. The whole conception of church work has changed.

The influence of the change of Ray is beginning to manifest in other ways as well. There is now rising a special form of Freemasonry, called Co-Masonry, which differs from other forms of the same Craft in that the necessity of our time is met by accepting women as well as men, for it is the tendency of our present age that women shall take their place beside men and equal to them in every

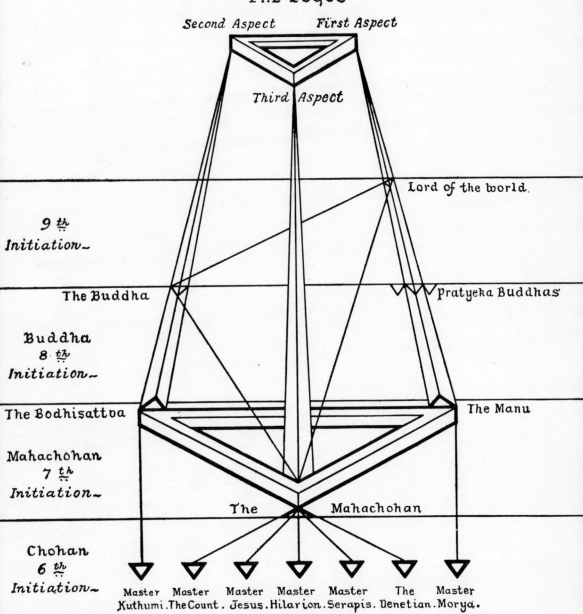

THE LOGOS

Second Aspect   First Aspect

Third Aspect

Lord of the world.

9th Initiation—

The Buddha   Pratyeka Buddhas

Buddha 8th Initiation—

The Bodhisattva   The Manu

Mahachohan 7th Initiation—

The   Mahachohan

Chohan 6th Initiation—

Master Master Master Master Master The Master
Kuthumi. The Count. Jesus. Hilarion. Serapis. Venetian. Morya.

Asekha 5th Initiation—

DIAGRAM 5

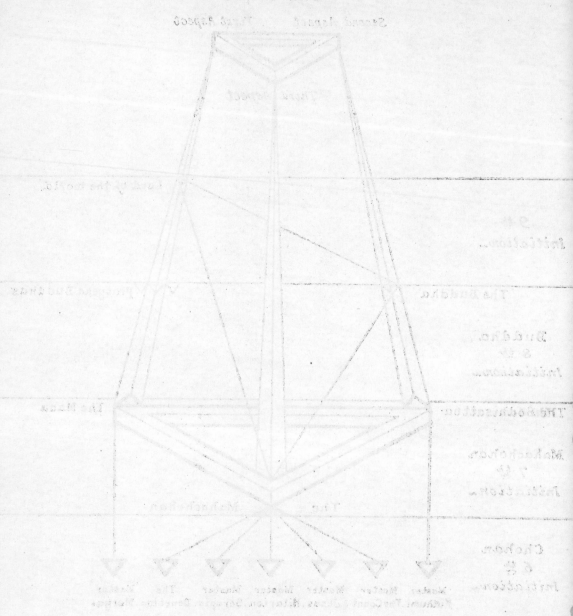

respect. Those who initiated the movement were not thinking about the influence of the Ray; nevertheless, it has been formed and directed by the ceremonial tendency of the age. I remember that for a long time in the reign of Queen Victoria there was but little ceremonial to be seen in the streets of London, but it was revived towards the end of her rule, and Edward VII restored it to its original splendour. Many people will now begin to feel the influence of the new Ray, and will desire to see and perhaps take part in ceremonial as they have not done before.

CHAPTER XIII

THE TRINITY AND THE TRIANGLES

THE DIVINE TRINITY

WE know that the Logos of our solar system—and that is what most men mean when they speak of God—is a Trinity ; he has, or rather is, Three Persons; he functions through Three Aspects.   These are called by many different names in the different religions, but they are not always viewed in the same way ; for this mighty scheme of a Trinity has so many aspects that no one religion has ever succeeded in symbolizing the whole truth.   In some faiths we have a Trinity of Father, Mother, Son, which is at least comprehensible to us when we think of methods of generation and interaction.   Of this type we find Osiris, Isis and Horus in the Egyptian teaching, and in Scandinavian mythology Odin, Freya and Thor.   The Assyrians and Phœnicians believed in a Trinity the Persons of which were Anu, Ea and Bel.   The Druids called them Taulac, Fan and Mollac.   In Northern Buddhism we hear of Amitabha, Avalokiteshvara and Manjushri.   In the Kabala of the Jews the Three are Kether, Binah and Chokma, and in the Zoroastrian religion Ahuramazda, Asha and Vohumano, or sometimes Ahuramazda, Mithra and Ahriman.   Everywhere the principle of the Trinity is acknowledged, though the manifestations are different.

In the great Hindu system there is the Trinity of Shiva, Vishnu and Brahma.   The Mother element is not shown in this Trinity, but it is indirectly recognized in that each of these Three is said to have a Shakti or power, which is sometimes in the symbolism named his consort.   This is evidently a manifestation of his power in matter, perhaps a somewhat lower manifestation than that of which we must think when we mention the Trinity itself. In the Christian system we have the Trinity of Father, Son and Holy Ghost; and it is interesting in this connection to note that in some of the old books the Holy Ghost is definitely mentioned as being feminine. Apart from this, the instinctive need of man to recognize the divine Motherhood has in Christianity found expression in the cult of the Blessed Virgin, who, though not a Person of the Holy Trinity, is nevertheless the Universal Mother, the Queen of the Angels, the Star of the Sea.

Students should understand that a great department of Motherhood exists, and has an important place in the Inner Government of the world. Just as the Manu is the head of a great department which looks after the physical development of races and sub-races, just as the Bodhisattva is the head of another which attends to religion and education, so is the great official who is called the Jagat-Ambā or World-Mother the head of a department of Motherhood. Just as the Lord Vaivasvata is at present filling the office of the Manu, and the Lord Maitreya that of the World-Teacher, so is the great Angel who was once the mother of the body of Jesus filling the post of World-Mother.

It is the work of this department to look especially after the mothers of the world, and the duty of its officials is to look after every woman in the time of her suffering, and give her such help and strength as her karma allows. As we have said, the World-Mother has at her command vast hosts of angelic beings, and at the birth of every child one of these is always present as her representative. To every celebration of the Holy Eucharist comes an Angel of the Presence, who is in effect a thought-form of the Christ himself—the form through which he endorses and ratifies the Priest's act of consecration; and so it is absolutely true that, though the Christ is one and indivisible, he is nevertheless simultaneously present upon many thousands of altars. In something the same way, though of course at a far lower level, the World-Mother herself is present in and through her representative at the bedside of every mother. Many women have seen her under such conditions, and many who have not been privileged to see have yet felt the help and the strength which she outpours.

It is the earnest desire of the World-Mother that every woman in her time of trial should have the best possible surroundings—that she should be enfolded in deep and true affection, that she should be filled with the holiest and noblest thoughts, so that none but the highest influences may be brought to bear upon the child who is to be born, so that he may have a really favourable start in life. Nothing but the purest and best magnetism should await him, and it is imperatively necessary that the most scrupulous physical cleanliness should be observed in all particulars. Only by the strictest attention to the rules of hygiene can such favourable conditions be obtained as will permit of the birth of a noble and healthy body, fit for the habitation of an exalted ego.

It would indeed be well that women in all countries should band themselves together in an endeavour to spread abroad among their sisters accurate information on this most important subject ; every woman should fully realize the magnificent opportunities which the feminine incarnation gives her ; every woman should be taught the absolute necessity for proper conditions before, during and after her pregnancy. Not only the most perfect cleanliness and the most careful attention should surround the baby body, but also it should be encompassed by perfect astral and mental conditions, by love and trust, by happiness and holiness. In this way the work of the World-Mother would be immensely facilitated and the future of the race would be assured.

It has often been asked whether there are any adepts living in feminine bodies. The existence of the World-Mother is an answer to that question. Because of her wonderful quality of intense purity and because of her development in other ways, she was chosen to be the mother of the body of the disciple Jesus long ago in Palestine ; and because of the wonderful patience and nobility of soul with which she bore all the terrible suffering which came to her as the consequence of that position, she attained in that same life the level of Adeptship. Having reached that, and finding the seven paths open before her, she chose to enter the glorious Deva evolution and was received into it with great honour and distinction.

That is the truth which lies behind the Roman Catholic doctrine of her Assumption; not that she was carried up into heaven among the Angels in her physical body, but that when she left that body she took her place among the Angels, and being presently appointed to the office of World-Mother she became very truly a queen among them, as the Church so poetically says. A great Deva needs no physical body; but while she holds her present office she will always appear to us in feminine form, as will those Adepts who have chosen to help her in her work.

All through the centuries thousands upon thousands both of men and of women have poured heartfelt devotion at her feet, and it is very certain that no jot or tittle of that devotion has been mis-directed or wasted; for she, whose love for mankind has evoked it, has always used its force to the uttermost in the onerous task which she has undertaken. However little men have known it, they have poured such a splendid wealth of love at her feet not because she was once the mother of Jesus, but because she is now the Mother of all living.

We must not think of this knowledge about the World-Mother as exclusively the possession of Christianity; she is clearly recognized in India as the Jagat-Ambā, and in China as Kwan-Yin, the Mother of Mercy and Knowledge. She is essentially the representative, the very type and essence of love, devotion and purity; the heavenly wisdom indeed, but most of all *Consolatrix Afflictorum*, the Consoler, Comforter, Helper of all who are in trouble, sorrow, need, sickness or any other adversity.

The Shakti or feminine element in each Person of the Blessed Trinity is also recognized in certain quarters in the well-known emblem of the Triple Tau, as shown in diagram 6.

There is also a similar Trinity in the case of higher and greater Logoi; and far behind and beyond all that we can know or imagine there is the Absolute, of which the presentation is also a Trinity. At the other end of the scale we find a Trinity in man, his Spirit, his

DIAGRAM 6

Intuition and his Intelligence ; which represent the threefold qualities of will, wisdom and activity. This Trinity in man is an image of that other and greater Trinity ; yet it is also much more than an image. It is not only symbolical of the Three Persons of the Logos, but in some way impossible to understand in physical consciousness, it is also an actual expression and manifestation of those Three Persons at this lower level.

THE TRIANGLE OF AGENTS

As the Logos is a Trinity, so the Occult Government of the world is in three great departments, ruled by three mighty Officials, who are not merely reflections of the Three Aspects of the Logos, but are in a very real way actual manifestations of them. They are the Lord of the World, the Lord Buddha and the Mahāchohan, who have reached grades of Initiation which give them waking conscious-ness on the planes of nature beyond the field of evolution of humanity, where dwells the manifested Logos.[1] The Lord of the World is one with the First Aspect on the highest of our seven planes, and wields the divine Will on earth ; the Buddha is united with the Second Aspect which dwells on the Anupadaka plane, and sends the divine Wisdom down to mankind ; the Mahāchohan is utterly one with the Third Aspect, which resides in the Nirvanic plane and exercises the divine Activity—representing the Holy Ghost. He is verily the Arm of the Lord stretched out into the world to do his work. The follow-ing table will make this clear.

[1] See *A Study in Consciousness*, by Annie Besant, pp. 3-5.

The first and second members of this great Triangle are different from the third, being engaged in work of a character that does not descend to the physical plane, but only to the level of the buddhic body in the case of the Lord Buddha, and the atmic plane in that of

LOGOS	DIVINE POWERS	PLANES OF NATURE	TRIANGLE OF AGENTS	RAY
1st Aspect	Will	Adi or Originating	The Lord of the World	1
2nd Aspect	Wisdom	Anupadaka or Monadic	The Lord Buddha	2
3rd Aspect	Activity	Atmic or Spiritual	The Maha-chohan	3—7

DIAGRAM 7

the great Agent of the First Aspect. Yet without their higher work none of that at lower levels would be possible, so they provide for the transmission of their influence even to the lowest plane through their representatives, the Manu Vaivasvata and the Lord Maitreya respectively.

These two great Adepts stand parallel with the Mahāchohan on their respective Rays, both having taken the Initiation that bears that name; and thus another Triangle is formed, to administer the powers of the Logos down to the physical plane. We may express the two Triangles in one diagram (No. 8).

For the entire period of a root race the Manu works out the details of its evolution, and the Bodhisattva, as World-Teacher, Minister of Education and Religion, helps its members to develop whatever of spirituality is possible for them at that stage, while the Mahāchohan directs the minds of men so that the different forms of culture and civilization shall be unfolded according to the cyclic plan. Head and Heart are these, and the Hand with five Fingers, all active in the world, moulding the race into one organic being, a Heavenly Man.

This last term is no mere simile, but describes a literal fact, for at the close of each root race effort those who have attained Adeptship within it form a mighty organism which is in a very real sense *one*, a Heavenly Man, in whom, as in an earthly man, are seven great centres, each of which is a mighty Adept. The Manu and the Bodhisattva

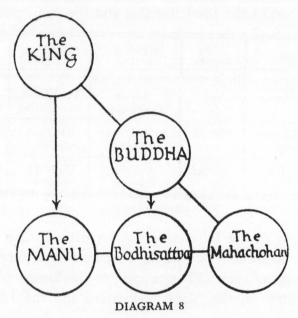

DIAGRAM 8

will occupy in this great Being the place of the brain and heart centres, and in them and as part of them, gloriously one with them, shall we their servants be ; and the splendid totality will go on in its further evolution to become a Minister of some future Solar Deity. Yet so transcending all comprehension is the wonder of it all that this union with others does not mar the freedom of any Adept in the Heavenly Man, nor preclude his acting quite outside its scope.

Until recently it was not the rule that the office of Mahā-chohan should be occupied by a permanent Adept of that grade. It was usual that each of the five Chohans, in rotation, should be appointed to leadership over all five Rays, though before occupying that position he was required to take the Mahāchohan Initiation. At present, however, we find a Chohan in charge of each of the five Rays, and also a Mahāchohan separate from all of them —a departure from what we understand to be the ordinary method.

LIMITS OF THE RAYS

On these five Rays, Three to Seven, the highest Initiation that can be taken on our globe is that of the Mahāchohan, but it is possible to go further on the First and Second Rays, as is indicated in the following table of Initiations, in which it will be seen that the Buddha Initiation is possible on the Second and First Rays, and that the Adept may go still further on the First.

INITIATIONS POSSIBLE ON THE RAYS		
FIRST RAY	SECOND RAY	RAYS THREE TO SEVEN
Initiation 9		
LORD OF THE WORLD		
Initiation 8		
THE PRATYEKA BUDDHA	THE BUDDHA	
Initiation 7		
THE MANU	THE BODHISATTVA	THE MAHACHOHAN
Initiations 1 to 6		

DIAGRAM 9

Lest it should seem as though in this fact there lay something in the nature of an injustice, it must be made clear that Nirvana is attainable as soon on one Ray as on another : any man on reaching the Asekha level is at once free to enter this condition of bliss for a period that to us would seem eternity; but he enters its first stage only, which, exalted infinitely beyond our comprehension as it is, is yet far below the higher stages available to the Chohan and Mahā-chohan respectively, while even these, in turn, pale before the glory of those divisions of the Nirvanic state which those Adepts reach who make the tremendous effort necessary to take during earth-life the still higher Initiations of the First and Second Ray. Further progress is also possible on the five Rays to those who take up other lines of work outside our Hierarchy.

CHANGE OF RAY

The possibility of changing one's Ray by the firm determination to do so leaves all paths alike open to the occult student. It is known that both the Masters with whom the Theosophical Society has been most closely connected have chosen to make this effort, and those of us who wish to retain our affiliation to them as individuals are therefore, consciously or unconsciously, in course of making it also. The method by which the transfer is effected is simple enough in theory, though often very difficult to carry out in practice. If a student on the Sixth or devotional Ray wishes to transfer himself to the Second Ray, that of wisdom, he must first endeavour to bring himself under the influence of the second sub-division of his own Sixth Ray. Then he will try steadily to intensify the influence of that sub-ray in his life, until finally it becomes dominant. Thus instead of being on the second sub-division of the Sixth Ray he will find himself on the sixth sub-division of the Second Ray ; in a word, he has tempered his devotion by increasing knowledge till it has become devotion to the Divine Wisdom. From that he can if he wishes, by sufficiently strenuous and long-continued effort, further transfer himself to some other sub-division of the Second Ray.

Evidently here we have a departure from the ordinary rules of procedure, for a Monad who came forth through one Planetary Spirit will return through another. Such changes are comparatively rare, and tend to balance one another satisfactorily at the end. The transfers are usually to the First and Second Rays, and there are relatively few persons on those two at the lower levels of evolution.

PERFECT UNITY

The marvellous unity of the members of these Triangles with the Logos may be well illustrated by the case of the Bodhisattva. We have seen that the union of pupil with Master is closer than any tie imaginable on earth; closer still, because at a higher level, was that between the Master Kuthumi and his Teacher the Master Dhruva, who was in his turn a pupil of the Lord Maitreya, during the time when the latter look pupils. Thereby the Master Kuthumi became also one with the Lord Maitreya, and as at their level unity is still more perfect, the Master Kuthumi is one with the Bodhisattva in a very wonderful way.

The Adepts seem so far above us that we can hardly distinguish any difference in glory between the lower and the higher levels. They all look like stars above us, and yet they speak of themselves as dust under the feet of the Lord Maitreya. There must be an enormous difference there, even though we cannot see it. We look up to these stupendous heights and all appears a blinding glory, in which we cannot presume to distinguish one as greater than another, except that we can see by the size of the aura that there are differences. But at least we can comprehend that the unity of the Master Kuthumi with the Lord Maitreya must be a far greater and more real union than anything imaginable at lower levels.

Still more is the Bodhisattva one with that Second Person of the Logos whom he represents. He has taken the office of representing him here on earth, and that is the meaning of the hypostatic union between Christ as God and Christ as man. For he, the Bodhisattva, whom in the West we call the Lord Christ, is the Intuitional Wisdom, the Representative and Expression of the Second Person of the Blessed Trinity. Herein is the mystery which underlies the two natures of the Christ, " who, although he be God and Man, yet he is not two, but one Christ—One, not by conversion of the Godhead into flesh, but by taking of the manhood into God ".

The Second Person of the Ever-blessed Trinity existed ages before the Lord Maitreya came into evolution ; and the first descent of that Second Person into incarnation was when as the Second Outpouring he took the vehicles of his manifestation out of the virgin matter of his new solar system, already impregnated and vivified by God the Holy Spirit. When that had been done we had for the first time Christ unmanifested as opposed to Christ manifested, and even

18

at that time it must have been true that Christ as God was in one sense greater than Christ as man. As the Bodhisattvas, who are to represent this Second Person on different planets of his system, one by one attain the Headship of their Ray, they in turn become so thoroughly one with him that they deserve the title of Christ as Man ; and so at the moment of the consummation of such Initiation the hypostatic union takes place for each of them.

This Second Aspect of the Logos pours himself down into matter, is incarnated, and becomes man ; and is therefore " equal to the Father as touching his Godhead, and inferior to the Father as touching his manhood ", as is said in the Athanasian Creed. Our Lord the Bodhisattva has been a man like ourselves, and is such a man still, though a perfected man ; yet that Manhood has so been taken into the Godhead that he is in truth a very Christ, a Representation of the Second Aspect of the Trinity ; for in Him and through him it is possible for us to reach to that Divine Power. That is why the Christ is spoken of as the Mediator between God and man ; it is not that he is making a bargain on our behalf, or buying us off from some horrible punishment, as many orthodox Christians believe, but that he is in truth a Mediator, One who stands between the Logos and man, whom man can see, and through whom the power of the Deity pours forth to humankind. Therefore is he the Head of all religions through which these blessings come.

CHAPTER XIV

THE WISDOM IN THE TRIANGLES

THE BUDDHA

THE Buddha of the present time is the Lord Gautama, who took his last birth in India about two thousand five hundred years ago, and in that incarnation finished his series of lives as Bodhisattva, and succeeded the previous Buddha Kasyapa as Head of the Second Ray in the Occult Hierarchy of our globe. His life as Siddartha Gautama has been wonderfully told in Sir Edwin Arnold's *The Light of Asia*, one of the most beautiful and inspiring poems in our language.

Seven Buddhas appear in succession during a world-period, one for each root race, and each in turn takes charge of the special work of the Second Ray for the whole world, devoting himself to that part of it which lies in the higher worlds, while he entrusts to his assistant and representative, the Bodhisattva, the office of World-Teacher for the lower planes. For one who attains this position Oriental writers think no praise too high, no devotion too deep, and just as we regard those Masters to whom we look up as all but divine in goodness and wisdom, so to an even greater degree do they regard the Buddha. Our present Buddha was the first of our humanity to attain that stupendous height, the previous Buddhas having been the product of other evolutions, and a very special effort was needed on his part to prepare himself for this lofty post, an effort so stupendous that it is spoken of constantly by the Buddhists as the *Mahābhinishkramana*, the Great Sacrifice.

Many thousands of years ago there arose the need for one of the Adepts to become the World-Teacher of the fourth root race ; for the time had come when humanity should be able to supply its own Buddhas. Up to the middle of the fourth round of the fourth incarnation of our Chain, which was exactly the central point of the scheme of evolution to which we belong, the great Officers who were required —the Manus and the World-Teachers and others—were supplied to our humanity by more advanced humanities of other Chains, which had made more progress or perhaps were older than we; and we ourselves, having been thus assisted, shall in our turn have later on the privilege to make provision for other and more backward schemes of evolution.

In such ways the real brotherhood of all that lives is demonstrated; and we see that it is not merely a brotherhood of humanity, or even of the life in this chain of worlds, but that all the chains in the solar system mutually interact and help one another. I have no direct evidence that solar systems give assistance to each other in such ways, but I should imagine it by analogy to be almost certain that even that is done. At least I have myself seen Visitors from other systems, as I have said before, and have noticed that they are not merely travelling for pleasure, but are certainly in our system for some good purpose. What their purpose is I do not know; but of course it is not my business.

Now at this time in the remote past to which we have referred, humanity should have begun to provide its own Teachers; but we are told that no one had quite reached the level required for the incurring of so tremendous a responsibility. The first-fruits of humanity at this period were two Brothers who stood equal in occult development; one being he whom we now call the Lord Gautama Buddha, and the other our present World-Teacher, the Lord Maitreya. In what way they fell short of the required qualifications we do not know; but, out of his great love for humanity, the Lord Gautama instantly offered to make himself ready to undertake whatever additional effort might be necessary to attain the required development. We learn from tradition that life after life he practised special virtues, each life showing out some great quality achieved.

That great sacrifice of the Buddha is spoken of in all the sacred books of the Buddhists; but they have not understood the nature of the sacrifice, for many believe it to have been the descent of the Lord Buddha from Nirvanic levels after his Illumination to teach his Law. It is true that he did so descend, but that would not be anything in the nature of a sacrifice; it would only be an ordinary, but not very pleasant piece of work. The great sacrifice that he made was this spending of thousands of years in order to qualify himself to be the first of mankind who should help his brother-men by teaching to them the Wisdom which is life eternal.

That work was done, and nobly done. We know something of the various incarnations that he took after that, as Bodhisattva of his time, though there may be many more of which we know nothing. He appeared as Vyasa; he came to ancient Egypt as Hermes, the Thrice-Greatest, who was called the Father of All Wisdom; he was the first of the twenty-nine Zoroasters, the Teachers of the Religion of the Fire; still later he walked amongst the Greeks as Orpheus, and taught them by means of music and of song; and finally he took his last birth in the north of India, and wandered up and down the Ganges valley for five and forty years, preaching his Law, and drawing round himself all those who in previous lives had been his pupils.

In some way which we cannot hope yet to understand, because of the great strain of those many ages of effort, there were certain points in the work of the Lord Buddha which it may be that he had not time to perfect utterly. It is impossible at such a level for there to be anything in the nature of a failure or a fault, but perhaps the strain of the past was too great even for such power as his. We cannot know; but the fact remains that there were certain minor matters to which at the time he could not perfectly attend, and therefore the after-life of the Lord Gautama was not quite the same as that of his Predecessors. It is usual, as I have said, for a Bodhisattva when he has lived his final life and become Buddha—when he has entered into glory, bearing his sheaves with him, as it is put in the Christian Scriptures—to hand over his external work entirely to his successor, and devote himself to his labours for humanity at higher levels. Whatever may be these manifold activities of a Dhyani Buddha, they do not bring him again into birth on earth; but because of the peculiar circumstances surrounding the life of the Lord Gautama two differences were made, two supplementary acts were performed.

THE SUPPLEMENTARY ACTS

The first was the sending by the Lord of the World, the Great King, the One Initiator, of one of his three Pupils, who are all Lords of the Flame from Venus, to take earthly incarnation almost immediately after the attainment of Buddhahood by the Lord Gautama, in order that by a very short life spent in travelling over India he might establish therein certain centres of religion called *mathas*. His name in that incarnation was Shankaracharya—not he who wrote the commentaries, but the great Founder of his line, who lived more than two thousand years ago.

Shri Shankaracharya founded a certain School of Hindu philosophy, revived Hinduism to a large extent, putting new life into its forms, and gathering together many of the teachings of the Buddha. Hinduism today, though in many ways it may fall short of its high ideal, is a very much more living faith than in the old days before the coming of the Buddha, when it had degenerated into a system of formalism. Shri Shankaracharya was also largely responsible for the disappearance of animal sacrifices; although such sacrifices are still offered in India, they are but few, and those are on a very small scale. Besides his teaching on the physical plane, Shri Shankaracharya accomplished certain occult work in connection with the higher planes of nature which was of considerable importance to the later life of India.

The second supplementary act to which I have referred above was undertaken by the Lord Gautama himself. Instead of devoting himself wholly to other and higher work, he has remained sufficiently in touch with his world to be reached by the invocation of his successor when necessary, so that his advice and help can still be obtained in any great emergency. He also undertook to return to the world once in each year, on the anniversary of his death, and shed upon it a flood of blessing.

The Lord Buddha has his own special type of force, which he outpours when he gives his blessing to the world, and this benediction is a unique and very marvellous thing ; for by his authority and position a Buddha has access to planes of nature which are altogether beyond our reach, hence he can transmute and draw down to our level the forces peculiar to those planes. Without this mediation of the Buddha these forces would be of no use to us here in physical life ; their vibrations are so tremendous, so incredibly rapid, that they would pass through us unsensed at any level we can reach, and we should never even know of their existence. But as it is, the force of the blessing is scattered all over the world ; and it instantly finds for itself channels through which it can pour (just as water instantly finds an open pipe), thereby strengthening all good work and bringing peace to the hearts of those who are able to receive it.

THE WESAK FESTIVAL

The occasion selected for this wonderful outpouring is the full moon day of the Indian month of Vaisakh (called in Ceylon Wesak), and usually corresponding to the English May, the anniversary of all the momentous occurrences of his last earthly life—his birth, his attainment of Buddhahood, and his departure from the physical body.

In connection with this visit of his, and quite apart from its tremendous esoteric significance, an exoteric ceremony is performed on the physical plane at which the Lord actually shows himself in the presence of a crowd of ordinary pilgrims. Whether he shows himself *to* the pilgrims I am not certain ; they all prostrate themselves at the moment when he appears, but that may be only in imitation of the prostration of the Adepts and their pupils, who *do* see the Lord Gautama. It seems probable that some at least of the pilgrims have seen him for themselves, for the existence of the ceremony is widely known among the Buddhists of central Asia, and it is spoken of as the appearance of the Shadow or Reflection of the Buddha, the description given of it in such traditional accounts being as a rule fairly accurate. So far as we can see there appears to be no reason why any person whatever who happens to be in the neighbourhood at the time may not be present at the ceremony; no apparent effort is made to restrict the number of spectators; though it is true that one hears stories of parties of pilgrims who have wandered for years without being able to find the spot.

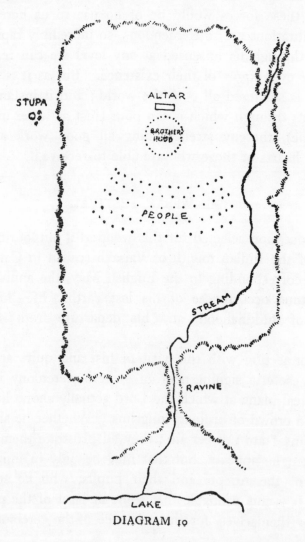

DIAGRAM 10

All members of the Great White Brotherhood, except the King himself and his three disciples, usually attend this ceremony; and there is no reason why any of our earnest Theosophical members should not be present at it in their astral bodies. Those to whom the secret has been confided usually try so to arrange matters as to put their physical bodies to sleep an hour or so before the exact moment of full moon, and to be undisturbed until about an hour after it.

THE VALLEY

The place selected is a small plateau surrounded by low hills, which lies on the northern side of the Himalayas, not far from the frontier of Nepal, and perhaps about four hundred miles west of the city of Lhasa. This little plain (see Diagram 10) is roughly oblong in shape, its length being perhaps a mile and a half and its breadth rather less. The ground slopes slightly downwards from south to north, and is mostly bare and stony, though in some places covered with coarse wiry grass and rough scrubby vegetation. A stream runs down part of the west side of the plateau, crosses its north-west corner, and escapes about the middle of the north side through a pine-clothed ravine, eventually reaching a lake which is visible at a distance of some miles. The surrounding country seems wild and uninhabited, and there are no buildings in sight except a single ruined stupa with two or three huts beside it, on the slope of one of the hills on the eastern side of the plain. About the centre of the southern half of the plain lies a huge block of greyish-white stone, veined with some glittering substance—an altar-like block, perhaps twelve feet in length by six feet wide, and standing about three feet out of the ground.

For some days before the appointed time an ever-increasing cluster of tents of strange and uncouth appearance (most of them black) may be seen along the banks of the stream, and down the side of the neighbouring hills; and this otherwise desolate spot is enlivened by the camp-fires of a considerable multitude. Large numbers of men come in from the wandering tribes of central Asia, and some even from the far north. On the day before the full moon all these pilgrims take a special ceremonial bath, and wash all their clothes in preparation for the ceremony.

Some hours before the time of the full moon these people gather in the lower or northern part of the plain and seat themselves in a quiet and orderly manner on the ground, always taking care to leave a considerable space before the great altar-stone. Generally some of the lamas are present, and they usually take this opportunity to deliver addresses to the people. About an hour before the moment when the moon is full the astral visitors begin to arrive, among them the members of the Brotherhood. Some of these generally materialize themselves so as to be seen by the pilgrims, and are received with genuflections and prostrations. Often our Masters and some even greater than they condescend on this occasion to converse in a friendly manner with their pupils and with others who are present. While this is going on those who are appointed to do so prepare the great altar-stone for the ceremony by covering it with the most beautiful flowers and placing at each corner of it great garlands of the sacred lotus. In the centre is placed a magnificently chased golden bowl full of water, and immediately in front of that a space is left among the flowers.

THE CEREMONY

About half an hour before the moment of full moon, at a signal given by the Mahāchohan, the members of the Brotherhood draw together in the open space in the centre of the plain to the north of the great altar of stone, and arrange themselves three deep in a large circle, all facing inwards, the outermost circle being composed of the younger members of the Brotherhood, and the greater Officials occupying certain points in the innermost circle.

Some verses from the Buddhist scriptures are then chanted in the Pali language, and as the voices die into silence, the Lord Maitreya materializes in the centre of the circle, holding in his hands the Rod of Power. This wonderful symbol is in some way a physical centre or fulcrum for the forces poured forth by the Planetary Logos, and was magnetized by him millions of years ago, when first he set the human life-wave in motion round our chain of globes. We are told that it is the physical sign of the concentration of the attention of the Logos, and that it is carried from planet to planet as that attention shifts—that where it is, that is for moment the central theatre of evolution, and that when it leaves this planet for the next, our earth will sink into comparative inertia. Whether it is carried also to the non-physical planets we do not know, nor do we under- stand exactly the way in which it is used, nor the part which it plays in the economy of the world. It is kept usually in the custody of the Lord of the World at Shamballa, and so far as we know this Wesak Festival is the only occasion on which it ever leaves his care. It is a round bar of the lost metal orichalcum, perhaps two feet in length and about two inches in diameter, having at each end a huge diamond shaped into a ball with a cone projecting from it. It has the strange appearance of being always surrounded by fire—of having an aura of brilliant yet transparent flame. It is noteworthy that no one but the Lord Maitreya touches it during any part of the ceremony.

On his materialization in the centre of the circle all the Adepts and Initiates bow gravely towards him, and another verse is chanted. After this, still intoning verses, the inner rings divide into eight parts, so as to

DIAGRAM 11

form a cross within the outer circle, the Lord Maitreya still remaining at the centre. At the next movement of this stately ritual, the cross becomes a triangle, the Lord Maitreya moving forward so as to stand at its apex, and therefore close to the altar-stone. Upon that altar, in the open space left in front of the golden bowl, the Lord Maitreya reverently lays the Rod of Power, while behind him the circle changes into a rather involved curved figure, so that all are facing the altar. At the next change the curved figure becomes a reversed triangle, so that we have a representation of the well-known sign of the Theosophical Society, though without its encircling snake. This figure in turn resolves itself into the five-pointed star, the Lord Maitreya being still at the southern point nearest the altar-stone, and the other great Officials or Chohans at the five points where the lines intersect. A diagram of the symbolic figures is herewith appended, as some of them are not easy to describe.

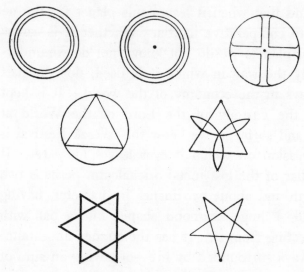

DIAGRAM 12

When this seventh and final stage is reached the chanting ceases, and after a few moments of solemn silence the Lord Maitreya, again taking the Rod of Power into his hands and raising it above his head, utters in a few sonorous words of Pali :

" All is ready ; Master, come ! "

Then as he again lays down the fiery rod, at the exact moment of the full moon, the Lord Buddha appears as a gigantic figure floating in the air just above the southern hills. The members of the Brotherhood bow with joined hands, and the multitude behind them fall on their faces and remain prostrate, while the others sing the three verses which were taught by the Lord Buddha himself during his earth life to the schoolboy Chatta :

The Lord Buddha, the Sage of the Sakyas, is among mankind the best of Teachers. He has done that which was to be done, and has crossed to the other shore (Nirvana). He is filled with strength and energy ; him, the the Blessed One, I take for my guide.

The truth is non-material; it brings freedom from passion, desire and sorrow; it is free from all strain; it is sweet, plain and logical; this truth I take as my guide.

Whatever is given to the eight kinds of the Noble Ones, who in pairs form the four grades, who know the truth, verily brings great reward; this Brotherhood of the Noble Ones I take as my guide.

THE GREATEST BLESSING

Then the people rise and stand gazing at the presence of the Lord while the Brotherhood chants for the benefit of the people the noble words of the *Mahāmangala Sutta*, which has been translated thus by Professor Rhys Davids [1]:

When yearning for good, many devas and men
Have held divers things to be blessings;
Do thou then inform us, O Master,
    What is the greatest blessing?

Not to serve the foolish,
But to serve the wise;
To honour those worthy of honour;
    This is the greatest blessing.

To dwell in a pleasant land,
To have done good deeds in a former birth,
To have a soul filled with right desires;
    This is the greatest blessing.

Much insight and much education,
Self-control and a well-trained mind,
Pleasant words that are well spoken;
    This is the greatest blessing.

To support father and mother,
To cherish wife and child,
To follow a peaceful calling;
    This is the greatest blessing.

To bestow alms and live righteously,
To give help to one's kindred,
To do deeds which cannot be blamed;
    This is the greatest blessing.

[1] Certain slight modifications have been introduced from other sources, when they seemed decided improvements.

To abhor and cease from sin,
To abstain from strong drink,
Not to be weary in well-doing ;
    This is the greatest blessing.

Reverence and lowliness,
Contentment and gratitude,
The hearing of the Law at due seasons ;
    This is the greatest blessing.

To be long-suffering and meek,
To associate with the tranquil,
Religious talk at due seasons ;
    This is the greatest blessing.

Self-restraint and purity,
The knowledge of the Four Great Truths,
The realization of Nirvana ;
    This is the greatest blessing.

Beneath the stroke of life's changes
The soul that stands unshaken,
Passionless, unsorrowing, secure ;
    This is the greatest blessing.

Invincible on every side
Is he who acteth thus ;
On every side he walks in safety ;
    And his is the greatest blessing.

The figure which floats above the hills is of enormous size, but exactly reproduces the form and features of the body in which the Lord last lived on earth. He appears seated cross-legged, with the hands together, dressed in the yellow robe of the Buddhist monk, but wearing it so as to leave the right arm bare. No description can give an idea of the face—a face truly God-like, for it combines calmness and power, wisdom and love in an expression containing all that our minds can imagine of the Divine. We may say that the complexion is clear yellowish-white, and the features clearly cut ; that the forehead is broad and noble ; the eyes large, luminous and of a deep dark blue ; the nose slightly acquiline ; the lips red and firmly set ; but all this puts before us merely the outer mask and gives but a little grasp of the living whole. The hair is black—almost blue-black —and wavy ; curiously, it is neither worn long according to Indian custom, not shaved off altogether in the manner of Oriental monks, but is cut off just before it reaches the shoulders, parted in the centre and swept back from the forehead. The story is told that when the Prince Siddartha left home to seek the truth, he seized his long hair and cut it off close above his head with a sweep of his sword, and that ever afterwards he kept it at the same length.

One of the most striking features of this wondrous apparition is the splendid aura which surrounds the figure. It falls into concentric spheres, as do the auras of all highly advanced men; its general plan is the same as that of the Arhat depicted in Plate XXVI in *Man Visible and Invisible*, but the arrangement of its colours is unique. The figure is englobed in light which is somehow at the same time dazzling and yet transparent—so bright that the eye can hardly rest upon it, and yet through it the face and the colour of the robe stand out with perfect clearness. Outside of that comes a ring of glorious ultramarine; then in succession glowing golden yellow, the richest crimson, pure silvery white and a magnificent scarlet— all these being of course really spheres, though showing as bands when seen against the sky. Shooting out at right angles, outside all these, are rays of all these hues intermingled, and interspersed with flashes of green and violet, as will be observed when we refer to our frontispiece.

These colours, in exactly this order, are described in ancient Buddhist scriptures as constituting the aura of the Lord; and when in 1885 it was thought desirable that a special flag should be found for the Buddhists of Ceylon, our President-Founder, Colonel Olcott, in consultation with our Sinhalese brothers at Colombo, evolved the idea of utilizing for that purpose that same significant grouping of colours. The Colonel tells us[1] that he learnt some years later from the Tibetan ambassador to the Viceroy of India, whom he met at Darjeeling, that the colours are the same as those in the flag of the Dalai Lama. The idea of this symbolical standard seems to have been widely accepted; I have myself seen it in Buddhist temples at places as far apart as Rangoon and Sacramento in California.

[1] *Old Diary Leaves*, Vol. III, p. 352.

It is of course impossible to obtain in a printed illustration any approach to the brilliancy and purity of the colours as seen in the sky ; all we can do is to offer a suggestion to help the imagination of the reader.

In earlier books we have described scarlet in man's aura as expressing anger only ; so it does in the ordinary lower astral ; but quite apart from this, we find that at higher levels a far more magnificent and luminous scarlet, the very essence of living flame, betokens the presence of dauntless courage and high determination. It is of course as denoting the possession of these qualities in a superlative degree that it appears in the aura of the Lord Buddha. We might conjecture that the somewhat unusual prominence of this brilliant scarlet band may be significant of the special manifestation of those qualities in that age-long work of self-development to which I have referred on page 262.

The Lord Maitreya, who takes so prominent a part in this ceremony, will in due course of time succeed to the office now held by the Lord Gautama. It will perhaps be of interest to compare his aura with that which we have just described. The easiest way to imagine it is to look at the illustration of the aura of an Arhat on Plate XXVI of *Man Visible and Invisible* and then modify it in imagination as here indicated. It has a general resemblance to that, but besides being so much larger the colours are somewhat differently arranged.

The heart of it is blinding white light, just as in the case of the Arhat ; then, eliminating the yellow from that part, let the rose-coloured oval retain its present position, but extend inwards up to the edge of the white. Outside that rose-coloured oval put a band of yellow instead of the blue ; outside the green comes a belt of blue ; outside of that the violet, as in the book, but outside of the violet again a broad band of the most glorious pale rose, into which the violet imperceptibly melts. Outside of all comes the radiation of mixed colours, just as in the book. The rays of white light flash through it in the same way, yet even they seem faintly tinged with the ever-present pale rose. The whole aura gives the impression of being suffused with the most delicate yet glowing rose, much as is Plate XI in *Man Visible and Invisible*.

A point which seems worthy of notice is that in this aura the colours come exactly in the same order as in the solar spectrum, though orange and indigo are omitted. First the rose (which is a form of red), then the yellow, shading into green, blue, violet in succession. And then it goes on into the ultra-violet, melting into rose—the spectrum beginning again in a higher octave, just as the lowest astral follows upon the highest physical.

Of course that is a very poor description, but it seems the best that we can do. It must be understood that it exists in many more dimensions than we can anyhow represent. In order to say this much about it I have tried to do something nearly equivalent to taking a three-dimensional section of it. But it is wise for us to remember that it is by no means impossible that another section might be taken in a slightly different manner, which would yield somewhat dissimilar results, and yet be quite as true. It is hopeless to try to explain on the physical plane the realities of the higher worlds.

When the *Mahāmangala Sutta* is finished, the Lord Maitreya takes the golden bowl of water from the altar-stone, and holds it above his head for a few moments, while the multitude behind, who have also provided themselves with vessels filled with water, follow his example. As he replaces it on the altar-stone another verse is chanted :

He is the Lord, the Saint who is perfect in knowledge, who possesses the eight kinds of knowledge and has accomplished the fifteen holy practices, who has come the good journey which led to the Buddhahood, who knows the three worlds, the unrivalled, the Teacher of gods and men, the Blessed One, the Lord Buddha.

As this ends, a smile of ineffable love beams forth from the face of the Lord as he raises his right hand in the attitude of benediction, while a great shower of flowers falls among the people. Again the members of the Brotherhood bow, again the crowd prostrates itself, and the figure slowly fades out of the sky, while the multitude relieves

19

itself in shouts of joy and praise. The members of the Brotherhood come up to the Lord Maitreya in the order of their admission, and each sips the water in the golden bowl, and the people also sip theirs, taking the remainder home in their quaint leather bottles as holy water to drive away all evil influences from their houses, or perhaps to cure the sick. Then the vast company breaks up with mutual congratulations, and the people bear away to their far-distant homes an ineffaceable memory of the wonderful ceremony in which they have taken part.

THE PREDECESSORS OF THE BUDDHA

An interesting glimpse of the predecessors of the Buddha is to be found in the Vision of St. John the Divine: " And round about the throne were four and twenty seats ; and upon the seats I saw four and twenty elders sitting, clothed in white raiment ; and they had on their heads crowns of gold."

He who is privileged to see this—and remember, it will come to everyone someday—does so from the special point of view of his own beliefs. Therefore St. John saw what he expected to see, the twenty-four elders of the Jewish tradition. That number, twenty-four, marks the date at which this vision was first seen, or rather the date at which the Jewish idea of that glory was formulated. If we now could raise ourselves into the Spirit, and could see that ineffable glory, we should see twenty-five, not twenty-four Elders, for there has been one Lord Buddha who has attained since this vision was crystallized in the Jewish scheme of higher thought. For those elders are the great Teachers who have taught the worlds in this our Round. There are seven Buddhas to each world ; that makes twenty-one for the three worlds which we have passed, and then the Lord Gautama was the fourth of the Buddhas of this world. Therefore, twenty-four were the elders in those old days, but they would be twenty-five if we could see them now.

The Christian Church has translated that somewhat differ-ently, taking those elders as its twelve apostles and the twelve Jewish

prophets.   If those twenty-four were the apostles and the prophets, the
seer must have seen himself among the rest, which would surely have
been mentioned.   Those elders had on their heads crowns of gold, it
is said, and a little later on we read that they cast their crowns before
him, as we sing in the glorious Trinity hymn.

I remember that as a child I marvelled much how that could be.
It seemed a strange thing that these men could constantly cast down
those crowns, and still have crowns to cast.   I could not understand it, and I wondered what scheme there was for the returning of
the crowns to their heads, so that they could cast them down again.
Such faintly ridiculous ideas are perhaps not unnatural in a child;
but they disappear when one understands.   If we have seen images
of the Lord Buddha we must have noticed that out of the crown of his
head there usually comes a little mound or cone.   It is as a crown,
golden in colour, which represents the outpouring spiritual force from
what is called the *sahasrāra* chakra, the centre at the top of the man's
head—the thousand-petalled lotus, as it is poetically called in
Oriental books.[1]

In the highly developed man that centre pours out splendour
and glory, which makes for him a veritable crown ; and the meaning
of the passage is that all that he has developed, all the splendid karma
that he makes, all the glorious spiritual force that he generates—all
that he casts perpetually at the feet of the Logos to be used in his
work.   So, over and over again, can he continue to cast down his
golden crown, because it perpetually re-forms as the force wells up
from within him.

THE BODHISATTVA MAITREYA

The Lord Maitreya, whose name means kindliness or compassion, took up the office of Bodhisattva when the Lord Gautama laid
it down, and since then he has made many efforts for the promotion
of Religion.   One of his first steps on assuming office was to take
advantage of the tremendous magnetism generated in the world by

[1] See *The Chakras*, by C. W. Leadbeater, The Theosophical Publishing House, Adyar,
Madras.

the presence of the Buddha, to arrange that great Teachers should simultaneously appear in many different parts of the earth ; so that within a comparatively short space of time we find not only the Buddha himself, Shri Shankaracharya and Mahavira in India, but also Mithra in Persia, Laotse and Confucius in China, and Pythagoras in ancient Greece.

Twice he has himself appeared—as Krishna in the Indian plains, and as Christ amid the hills of Palestine. In the incarnation as Krishna the great feature was always love ; the Child Krishna drew round him people who felt for him the deepest, the most intense affection. Again in his birth in Palestine, love was the central feature of his teaching. He said : " This new commandment I give unto you, that ye love one another as I have loved you." He asked that his disciples might all be one in him even as he was one with the Father. His closest disciple, St. John, insisted most strongly upon the same idea : " He that loveth not knoweth not God, for God is Love."

What is now called Christianity was undoubtedly a magnificent conception as he originally taught it, sadly as it has fallen away from that high level in the hands of ignorant exponents since. It must not be assumed, of course, that the teaching of brotherly and neighbourly love was new in the world. As St. Augustine said in his book *De Civitate Dei* :

> The identical thing that we now call the Christian religion existed among the ancients, and has not been lacking from the beginnings of the human race until the coming of Christ in the flesh, from which moment on the true religion, which already existed, began to be called Christian.

Readers of the *Bhagavad Gītā* will also remember the teaching of love and devotion with which it is filled. The Bodhisattva also occupied occasionally the body of Tsong-ka-pa, the great Tibetan religious reformer, and throughout the centuries he has sent forth a stream of his pupils, including Nāgārjuna, Āryāsanga, Rāmānujāchārya, Madhavāchārya, and many others, who founded new sects or threw new light upon the mysteries of religion, and among these was one of his pupils who was sent to found the Muhammadan faith,

The sending out of the teachers I have mentioned above is only part of his work, which is not confined to humanity, but includes the education of all creatures on earth, and among them the Deva evolution. He is thus the head of all the faiths at present existing, and of many others which have died out in the course of time, though he is of course responsible for them only in their original form, and not for the corruption which man has naturally and inevitably introduced into all of them as the ages have rolled by. He varies the type of religion to suit the period of the world's history at which it is put forth, and the people to whom it is given; but though the form may vary as evolution proceeds, the ethics are ever the same.

He will come to earth many times more during the progress of the root race, founding many such religions, and each time drawing round himself such men of that race as are prepared to follow him, from among whose number he chooses some whom he can draw into closer relation with himself, some who are pupils in the innermost sense. Then towards the end of the race, when it is already far past its prime, and a new race is beginning to dominate the world, he will arrange that all his special pupils, who have followed him in those previous incarnations, shall come to birth together about the time of his last life in the world.

In it he will attain the great Initiation of the Buddha, and thus gain perfect enlightenment; at that time these pupils of his, without physically knowing or remembering him, will all be strongly attracted towards him, and under his influence great numbers of them will enter the Path, and many will advance to the higher stages, having already in previous incarnations made considerable progress. We thought at first that the accounts given in the Buddhist books of the large numbers of men who instantly attained the Arhat level when the Lord Gautama became the Buddha were beyond the bounds of possibility; but we found on closer examination that there was truth underlying those accounts. It is possible that the numbers were exaggerated, but that very many pupils did suddenly attain these higher degrees of Initiation under the impetus given by the mighty magnetism and power of the Buddha is undoubtedly a fact.

THE ASALA FESTIVAL

Besides the great Wesak Festival, there is one other occasion in each year when the members of the Brotherhood all meet together officially. The meeting in this case is usually held in the private house of the Lord Maitreya, situated also in the Himalayas, but on the southern instead of the northern slopes. On this occasion no pilgrims on the physical plane are present, but all astral visitors who know of the celebration are welcome to attend it. It is held on the full moon day of the month of Āsāla, (in Sanskrit Ashādha), usually corresponding to the English July.

This is the anniversary of the delivery by the Lord Buddha of his first announcement of the great discovery—the sermon which he preached to his five disciples, commonly known as the *Dhammachak-kappavattana Sutta*, which has been poetically translated by Rhys Davids as " The Setting in Motion of the Royal Chariot Wheels of the Kingdom of Righteousness ". It is often more briefly described in Buddhist books as " The Turning of the Wheel of the Law ". It explains for the first time the Four Noble Truths and the Noble Eight-fold Path, expounding the great middle way of the Buddha—the life of perfect righteousness in the world, which lies midway between the extravagances of asceticism on the one hand and the carelessness of mere worldly life on the other.

In his love for his great predecessor the Lord Maitreya has ordained that, whenever the anniversary of that first preaching comes round, the same sermon shall be recited once more in the presence of the assembled Brotherhood ; and he usually adds to it a simple address of his own, expounding and applying it. The recitation of the sermon commences at the moment of full moon, and the reading and the address are usually over in about half an hour. The Lord Maitreya generally takes his place upon the marble seat which is set at the edge of a raised terrace in the lovely garden just in front of his house. The greatest of the Officials sit close about him, while the rest of the Brotherhood is grouped in the garden a few feet below. On this occasion, as on the other, there is often an opportunity for pleasant converse, and kindly greetings and benedictions are distributed by the Masters among their pupils and those who aspire to be their pupils.

It may be useful to give some account of the ceremony, and of what is usually said at these Festivals, though it is, of course, utterly impossible to reproduce the wonder and the beauty and the eloquence of the words of the Lord Maitreya on such occasions. The account which follows does not attempt to report any single discourse; it is a combination of, I fear, very imperfectly remembered fragments, some of which have already appeared elsewhere; but it will give to those who have not previously heard of it some idea of the line generally taken.

That great sermon of the Buddha is wonderfully simple, and its points are repeated. There was no shorthand in those days, so that it might be taken down and read by everyone afterwards; his disciples had to remember his words by the impression made on them at the time. So he made them simple, and he repeated them again and again like a refrain, so that the people might be sure of them. One may readily see in reading it that it is constructed for this special purpose—that it may be easily remembered. Its points are arranged categorically, so that when it has once been heard each point reminds one of the next, as though it were a kind of mnemonic, and to the Buddhist each of these separate and easily remembered words suggests a whole body of related ideas, so that the sermon, short and simple as it is, contains an explanation and a rule of life.

One might well think that all that can be said about the sermon has been said already many times over; yet the Lord, with his wonderful eloquence and the way in which he puts it, makes it every year seem something new, and each person feels its message as though it were specially addressed to himself. On that occasion, as in the original preaching, the Pentecostal miracle repeats itself. The Lord speaks in the original sonorous Pali, but every one present hears him " in his own tongue wherein he was born," as is said in the Acts of the Apostles.

THE FOUR NOBLE TRUTHS

The sermon begins with a proclamation that the Middle Path is the safest, and indeed the only true Path. To plunge on the one hand into the sensual excesses and pleasures of the ordinary worldly life is mean and degrading, and leads a man nowhither. On the other hand, extravagant asceticism is also evil and useless. There may be a few to whom the high ascetic and solitary life appeals, and they may be capable of leading it rightly, though even then it must not be carried to excess; but for all ordinary people the Middle Way of a good life lived in the world is in every way best and safest. The first step towards the leading of such a life is to understand its conditions; and the Lord Buddha lays these down for us in what he has called the Four Noble Truths. These are:

1. Sorrow or Suffering.
2. The Cause of Sorrow.
3. The Ceasing of Sorrow (or the Escape from Sorrow).
4. The Way which leads to the Escape from Sorrow.

1. The first Truth is an assertion that all manifested life is sorrow, unless man knows how to live it. In commenting upon this, the Bodhisattva said that there are two senses in which manifested life is sorrowful. One of these is to some extent inevitable, but the other is an entire mistake and is very easily to be avoided. To the Monad, who is the true Spirit of man, all manifested life is in one sense a sorrow, because it is a limitation; a limitation which we in our physical brain cannot in the least conceive, because we have no idea of the glorious freedom of the higher life. In exactly the same sense it has always been said that the Christ offers himself as a Sacrifice when he descends into matter. It is a sacrifice undoubtedly, because it is an inexpressibly great limitation, for it shuts off from him all the glorious powers which are his on his own level. The same is true of the Monad of man; he undoubtedly makes a great sacrifice when he brings himself into connection with lower matter, when he hovers over it through the long ages of its development up to the human level, when he puts down a tiny fragment of

himself (a finger-tip as it were) and thereby makes an ego, or individual soul.

Even though we may be only a tiny fragment—indeed, a fragment of a fragment—we are nevertheless a part of a magnificent reality. There is nothing to be proud of in being only a fragment, but there is a certainty that because we are therefore part of the higher, we can eventually rise into the higher and become one therewith. That is the end and aim of our evolution. And even when we attain that, remember that it is not for the sake of our delight in the advancement, but that we may be able to help in the scheme. All these sacrifices and limitations may rightly be described as involving suffering; but they are undertaken gladly as soon as the ego fully understands. An ego has not the perfection of the Monad, and so he does not fully understand at first; he has to learn like everybody else. That quite tremendous limitation at each further descent into matter is an unavoidable fact, and so there is that much of suffering inseparable from manifestation. We have to accept that limitation as a means to an end, as part of the Divine Scheme.

There is another sense in which life is often sorrow, but a kind of sorrow that can be entirely avoided. The man who lives the ordinary life of the world often finds himself in trouble of various kinds. It would not be true to say that he is always in sorrow, but he *is* often in anxiety, and he is always liable at any moment to fall into *great* sorrow or anxiety. The reason for this is that he is full of lower desires of various kinds, not at all necessarily wicked, but desires for lower things; and because of these desires he is tied down and confined. He is constantly striving to attain something which he has not, and he is full of anxiety as to whether he will attain it; and when he has attained it, he is anxious lest he should lose it. This is true not only of money but of position and power, of fame and of social advancement. All these cravings cause incessant trouble in many different ways. It is not only the individual anxiety of the man who has or has not some object of general desire; we have also to take into account all the envy and jealousy and ill-feeling caused in the hearts of others who are striving for the same object.

There are other objects of desire which seem higher than these and yet are not the highest. How often, for example, a young man desires affection from someone who cannot give it to him, who has it not to give ! From such a desire as that comes often a great deal of sadness, jealousy and much other ill-feeling. You will say that such a desire is natural ; undoubtedly it is, and affection which is returned is a great source of happiness. Yet if it cannot be returned, a man should have the strength to accept the situation, and not allow sorrow to be caused by the unsatisfied desire. When we say that a thing is natural, we mean that it is what we might expect from the average man. But the student of occultism must try to rise somewhat above the level of the average man—otherwise how can he help that man ? We must rise above that level in order that we may be able to reach down a helping hand. We must aim not at the natural (in the sense of the average), but at the supernatural.

One who is clairvoyant will readily subscribe to the truth of this great teaching of the Buddha, that on the whole life is sorrow ; for if he looks at the astral and mental bodies of those whom he meets he will see that they are filled with a vast number of small vortices all whirling vigorously, representing all sorts of odd little thoughts, little anxieties, little troubles about one thing or another. All these cause disturbance and suffering, and what is needed most of all for progress is serenity. The only way to gain peace is to get rid of them altogether, and that brings us to our Second Noble Truth, the *Cause of Sorrow*.

2. We have already seen that the Cause of Sorrow is always desire. If a man has no desires, if he is not striving for place or power or wealth, then he is equally tranquil whether the wealth or position comes or whether it goes. He remains unruffled and serene because he does not care. Being human, he will of course wish for this or that, but always mildly and gently, so that he does not allow himself to be disturbed. We know, for example, how often people are prostrated with sorrow when they lose those whom they love by

death. But if their affection be at the higher level, if they love their friend and not the body of their friend, there can be no sense of separation, and therefore no sorrow. If they are filled with desire for bodily contact with that friend on the physical plane, then at once that desire will cause sadness. But if they will put aside that desire and live in the communion of the higher life, the mourning passes away.

Sometimes people grieve when they find old age coming upon them, when they find their vehicles not so strong as they used to be. They desire the strength and the faculties that they once had. It is wise for them to repress that desire, to realize that their bodies have done good work, and if they can no longer do the same amount as of yore, they should do gently and peacefully what they can, but not worry themselves over the change. Presently they will have new bodies ; and the way to ensure a good vehicle is to make such use as one can of the old one, but in any case to be serene and calm and unruffled. The only way to do that is to forget self, to let all selfish desires cease, and to turn the thought outward to the helping of others as far as one's capabilities go.

3. *The Ceasing of Sorrow*. Already we see how grief ceases and how calm is to be attained ; it is by always keeping the thought on the highest things. We have still to live in this world, which has been poetically described as the sorrowful star—as indeed it is for so many, perhaps for most people, though it need not be ; yet we may live in it quite happily if we are not attached to it by desire. We are in it, but we must not be of it—at least not to such an extent as to let it cause worry and trouble and vexation. Undoubtedly our duty is to help others in their afflictions and troubles and worries ; but in order to do that effectively we must have none of our own ; we must let those ruffles which might cause them slip smoothly past us, leaving us calm and contented. If we take this lower life with philosophy we shall find that for us sadness almost entirely ceases.

There may be some who think such an attitude unattainable. It is not so, for if it were the Lord Buddha would never have pre-scribed it for us. We can all reach it, and we ought to do so, because only when we have attained it can we really and effectively help our brother man.

THE NOBLE EIGHTFOLD PATH

4. *The Way which leads to the Escape from Sorrow.* This is given to us in what is called the Noble Eightfold Path—another of the Lord Buddha's wonderful tabulations or categories. It is a very beautiful statement, because it can be taken at all levels. The man in the world, even the uneducated man, can take it in its lowest aspects and find a way to peace and comfort through it. And yet the highest philosopher may also take it and interpret it at his level and learn very much from it.

The first step in this Path is *Right Belief*. Some people object to the qualification, because they say that it demands from them something in the nature of blind faith. It is not at all that sort of belief which is required; it is rather a demand for a certain amount of knowledge as the ruling factors in life. It demands that we shall understand a little of the Divine Scheme as far as it applies to us, and if we cannot yet see that for ourselves, that we should accept it as it is always put before us. Certain broad facts are always put before men in some form or other. They are explained even to primitive tribes by their medicine-men, and to the rest of mankind by various religious teachers and in all kinds of scriptures. It is very true that scriptures and religions differ, but the points in which they all agree have to be accepted by a man before he can understand life sufficiently to live happily.

One of these facts is the eternal Law of Cause and Effect. If a man lives under the delusion that he can do anything that he likes, and that the effect of his actions will never recoil upon himself, he will most certainly find that some of these actions eventually involve him in unhappiness and suffering. If, again, he does not understand that the object of his life is progress, that God's Will for him is that he shall grow to be something better and nobler than he is now, then also he will bring unhappiness and suffering upon himself, because he will be likely to live for the lower side of life only, and that lower side of life never finally satisfies the inner man. And so it comes about that he must at least know something of these great laws of Nature, and if he cannot yet know them for himself it will be well for him to believe them. Later on, and at a higher level, before the second Initiation can be attained, we are told that we must kill out all doubt.

When the Lord Buddha was asked whether this meant that we must accept some form of belief blindly, he replied : " No, but you must know for yourself three great things—that only upon the Path of Holiness and good living can man finally attain perfection ; that in order to attain it he moves through many lives, gradually rising higher and higher ; and that there is a Law of Eternal Justice under which all these things work." At that stage the man must cast out all doubt, and must be thoroughly and inwardly convinced of these things ; but for the man of the world it is well that he should at least believe that much, because unless he has that as a guide in life he cannot get any further.

The second step of the Noble Eightfold Path is *Right Thought*. Now, Right Thought means two separate things. The first demands that we should think about right things and not about wrong things. We can have at the back of our minds always high and beautiful thoughts, or on the other hand those minds may be filled with thoughts of common everyday matters. Let there be no mistake here ; whatever work we are doing should be done thoroughly and earnestly, and with whatever concentration of thought upon it is necessary for that perfection. But most people, even when their work is done, or when there comes a pause in it, still have their thoughts running upon unimportant and comparatively ignoble things. Those who are devoted to the Master seek always to hold the thought of that Master in the back of their minds, so that when there is a moment's respite from worldly action, at once that thought of Him comes forward and occupies the mind. At once the pupil thinks : " What can I do to make my life like the Master's ? How can I so improve myself that I can show forth the beauty of the Lord to those around

me ? What can I do to carry on his work of helping other people ? "
One of the things we can all do is to send out helpful and sympathetic
thought.

Remember, also, that Right Thought must be definite and not
scattered ; thoughts resting for a moment on one thing and then
flying instantly to something else are useless, and will not help us at
all in learning to manage our thoughts. Right Thought must never
have the slightest touch of evil in it ; there must be nothing doubtful
about it. There are many people who would not deliberately think
of anything impure or horrible, and yet they will cherish thoughts
which are on the brink of that—not definitely evil, but certainly a
little doubtful. In Right Thought there must be nothing like that ;
wherever there is anything which seems in the least suspicious or
unkind, it must be shut out. We must be quite sure that all our
thoughts are thoroughly kind and good.

There is another meaning of Right Thought, and that is *correct*
thought—that we should think the truth only. So often we think
untruly and wrongly of persons just because of prejudice or ignorance.
We get an idea that a certain person is a bad person, and, therefore,
that all that he does must be evil. We attribute motives to him which
are often absolutely without foundation, and in doing so we are
thinking untruly of him, and therefore our thought is not Right
Thought. All men not yet Adepts have in them something of evil as
well as something of good ; but most unfortunately it is our custom
to fix all our attention on the evil, and to forget all about the good
—never to look for it at all. Therefore our thought about these
people is not Right Thought, not only because it is uncharitable, but
because it is untrue. We are looking only at one side of the person
and we ignore the other side. Furthermore, by fixing our attention
on the evil in the man instead of the good, we strengthen and
encourage that evil ; whereas by Right Thought we might give just
the same encouragement to the good side of that man's nature.

The next stage is *Right Speech* ; and here again we find just the
same two divisions. First we should speak always of good things. It is
not our business to speak of the evil deeds of others. In most cases **the**

stories about other people which reach us are not true, and so if we repeat them our words also are untrue, and we are doing harm to ourselves as well as to the person of whom we speak. And even if the story is true it is still wrong to repeat it, for we can do no good to the man by saying over and over again that he has done wrong; the kindest thing that we could do would be to say nothing about it. We should do that instinctively if the wrong thing were done by a husband, a son, a brother; we should certainly feel that it would be wrong to advertise the misdeed of one whom we loved to many people who would not otherwise hear of it. But if there is any truth at all in our profession of universal brotherhood we should realize that we have no right to circulate evil about *any* man, that we should speak with regard to others as we should wish them to speak with regard to us. Yet again we must remember that many people make their speech untrue because they allow themselves to fall into exaggeration and inaccuracy. They make little things into enormous stories; assuredly that is not Right Speech.

Again, speech must be kindly; and it must be direct and forceful, not silly. A large section of the world exists under the delusion that it must make conversation; that it is odd or rude not to be perpetually babbling. The idea seems to be that when one meets a friend one must keep talking all the time, or the friend will be hurt. Remember that when the Christ was on earth he made a very strict statement that for every idle word that a man should speak he would have to account hereafter. The idle word is so often a mischievous word; but quite apart from that, even innocent idle words involve waste of time; if we must talk, at least we might say something useful and helpful. Some people, with the idea of seeming smart, keep up a stream of constant half-joking or sneering talk. They must always be capping something that someone else has said. They must always be showing everything in a ridiculous or amusing aspect. Certainly all that comes under the heading of idle words, and there is no doubt that it is seriously necessary that we should exercise exceeding care in this matter of Right Speech.

The next step is *Right Action*. We see at once that these three steps necessarily follow one from another. If we think always of good things, we shall certainly not speak of evil things, because we speak what is in our mind ; and if our thought and speech are good, then the action which follows will also be good. Action must be prompt and yet well considered. We all know some people who, when any emergency arises, seem to become helpless ; they potter about and do not know what to do, and they get in the way of those who have their brains in better working order. Others plunge into some rash action without thinking at all. Learn to think quickly and act promptly, and yet always with consideration. Above all, always let action be unselfish ; let it never be actuated in the least by personal considerations. That is very hard for most people, and yet it is a power which must be acquired. We who try to live for the Master have many opportunities in our work to put that idea into practice. We must all think only what is best for the work and what we can do to help others, and we must entirely put aside any personal considerations. We must not think what part in the work we should like to bear, but we must try to do the best that we possibly can with the part that is assigned to us.

In these days few people live by themselves as monks or hermits used to do. We live among others, so that whatever we think or say or do will necessarily affect a great many people. We should always bear in mind that our thought, our speech and our action are not merely qualities, but powers—powers given to us to use, for the use of which we are directly responsible. All are meant to be used for service, and to use them otherwise is to fail in our duty.

We come now to the fifth step—*Right Means of Livelihood*—and this is a matter which may touch quite a large number of us. The right means of livelihood is that which causes no harm to any living thing. We see at once that would rule out such trades as those of a butcher or a fisherman ; but the command reaches much further than that. We should not obtain our livelihood by harming any creature, and therefore we see at once that the selling of alcohol is not a right means of livelihood. The seller of alcohol does not necessarily kill people, but he is unquestionably doing harm, and he is living on the harm he does to the people.

The idea goes yet further. Take the case of a merchant who in the course of his trade is dishonest. That is not a right means of livelihood, because his trading is not fair and he is cheating the people. If a merchant deals fairly, buying his articles wholesale and selling them retail at a reasonable profit, that is a right means of livelihood ; but the moment he begins to mislead people and sells a poor article for a good one, he is cheating them. A right means of livelihood may become a wrong means if it is treated in a wrong way. We must deal as honestly with people as we should wish them to deal with us. If a person is a trader in a certain class of goods, he has special knowledge of those goods. The customer trusts himself in the hands of the trader, because he himself has not that special knowledge. When you trust a doctor or a lawyer, you expect to be treated fairly. But it is exactly in the same way that the customer comes to the trader, and therefore the latter should be as honest with his customer as the lawyer or the doctor is with his client or his patient. When a man trusts you in that way, he puts you on your honour to do your best for him. You have a right to make a reasonable profit in the course of your bargain, but you must also look to your duty.

The sixth step is *Right Exertion* or *Right Endeavour*, and it is a very important one. We must not be content to be negatively good. What is desired of us is not merely absence of evil, but the positive doing of good. When the Lord Buddha made that wonderful short statement of his doctrine in a single verse, he began by saying : " Cease to do evil," but the next line runs : " Learn to do good." It is not enough to be passively good. There are so many well-meaning people who yet achieve nothing.

Every person has a certain amount of strength, not only physical, but mental. When we have a day's work before us, we know that we must reserve our strength for that, and therefore before we begin it we do not undertake something else which would so much exhaust us that the day's work could not be properly done. Similarly we

20

have a certain amount of strength of mind and of will, and we can perform only a certain amount of work on that level ; therefore we must take care how we spend that power. There are other powers too. Every person has a certain amount of influence among his friends and relations. That influence means power, and we are responsible for making good use of that power. All about us are children, relations, clerks, workmen, servants, and over all of these we have a certain amount of influence, at least by example ; we must be careful what we do and what we say, because others will copy us.

Right Exertion means putting our work into useful lines and not wasting it. There are many things that can be done, but some of them are immediate and more urgent than others. We must look about and see where our exertion would be most useful. It is not well that all should do the same thing ; it is wiser that the work should be divided among us so that it may be perfectly rounded off and not left in a one-sided condition. In all these matters we must use our reason and common sense.

Right Memory or *Right Remembrance* is the seventh step, and it means many things. The Right Memory of which the Lord Buddha spoke has often been taken by his followers to mean the memory of past incarnations, which he himself possessed most fully. In one of the Jātaka stories, a person spoke ill of him. He turned to his disciples and said : " I have insulted this man in a previous life, and therefore he speaks ill of me now ; I have no right to resent it." No doubt if we remembered everything that had happened to us before, we could arrange our present life better than we do. Most of us, however, have not the power of remembering our past lives ; but we must not therefore think that the teaching as to Right Memory does not apply to us.

First of all it means self-recollectedness. It means that we must remember all the time who we are, what our work is, what is our duty, and what we should be doing for the Master. Then again Right Memory means the exercise of a reasonable choice as to what we shall remember. To all of us in our lives there come pleasant things, and also things unpleasant. A wise person will take care to remember the good things, but he will let the evil die. Suppose someone comes and speaks rudely to us ; a foolish person will remember that for weeks, months and years, and will continue to say that such-and-such a person spoke unkindly to him. It will rankle in his mind. But what good will that do him ? Obviously, none at all ; it will only annoy him and keep alive in his mind an evil thought. That certainly is not Right Memory. We should immediately forget and forgive an evil thing done to us ; but we should always bear in mind the kindnesses which people have done us, because they will fill our minds with love and with gratitude. Again, we have all made many mistakes ; it is well that we should remember them in so far as not to repeat them ; but otherwise, to brood over them, to be always filling our minds with regret and with sorrow because of them, is not Right Memory.

The teaching given above as to right memory has been well illustrated in some verses by S.E.G., as follows :

Let us forget the things that vexed and tried us,
    The worrying things that caused our souls to fret ;
The hopes that, cherished long, were still denied us,
        Let us forget.

Let us forget the little slights that pained us,
    The greater wrongs that rankle sometimes yet ;
The pride with which some lofty one disdained us,
        Let us forget.

Let us forget our brother's fault and failing,
    The yielding to temptations that beset,
That he, perchance, though grief be unavailing,
        Cannot forget.

But blessings manifold, and past deserving,
    Kind words and helpful deeds, a countless throng ;
The fault o'ercome, the rectitude unswerving,
        Let us remember long.

The sacrifice of love, the generous giving
    When friends were few, the handclasp warm and strong ;
The fragrance of each life of holy living,
        Let us remember long.

Whatever things were good and true and gracious,
    Whate'er of right has triumphed over wrong,
What love of God or man has rendered precious,
        Let us remember long.

The last step is called *Right Meditation* or *Right Concentration*. This refers not only to the set meditation which we perform as part of our discipline, but it also means that all through our lives we should concentrate ourselves on the object of doing good and of being useful and helpful. In daily life we cannot be always meditating, because of the daily work that we must all do in the course of our ordinary lives; and yet I am not sure that a statement like that, made without reservation, is entirely true. We cannot always have our consciousness drawn away from the physical plane to higher levels; yet it is possible to live a life of meditation in this sense—that the higher things are always so strongly present in the background of our minds that, as I said when speaking about Right Thought, they may instantly come to the front when that mind is not otherwise occupied. Our life will then be really a life of perpetual meditation upon the highest and noblest objects, interrupted now and then by the necessity of putting our thoughts into practice in daily life.

Such a habit of thought will influence us in more ways than we see at the first glance. Like always attracts like; two people who adopt such a line of thought will presently be drawn together, will feel an attraction one for the other; and so it may well be that in time a nucleus of those who habitually hold the higher thought will be gathered together, their thoughts will react upon one another, and in that way each will greatly help the advancement of the rest. Again, wherever we go we are surrounded by invisible hosts, Angels, nature-spirits, and men who have laid aside their physical bodies. The condition of Right Concentration will attract to us all the best of those various orders or beings, so that wherever we go we shall be surrounded by good and holy influences.

This is the teaching of the Lord Buddha as he gave it in that first Sermon; it is upon this teaching that the world-wide Kingdom of Righteousness is founded, the Royal Chariot-Wheels of which he set in motion for the first time on that Āsāla festival so many centuries ago.

When in the far future the time shall come for the advent of another Buddha, and the present Bodhisattva takes that final incarnation in which the great step will be achieved, he will preach the Divine Law to the world in whatever form may seem to him most suited to the requirements of that era, and then will follow him in his high office the Master Kuthumi, who has transferred himself to the Second Ray to take the responsibility of becoming the Bodhisattva of the sixth root race.

---

[1] *Note.*—With regard to Right Speech, mentioned on p. 319, the student is recommended to read *Ecclesiasticus*, xix, 6-17.

CHAPTER XV

THE POWER IN THE TRIANGLES

THE LORD OF THE WORLD

OUR world is governed by a spiritual King—one of the Lords of the Flame who came long ago from Venus. He is called by the Hindus Sanat Kumara, the last word being a title, meaning Prince or Ruler. Other names given to him are the One Initiator, the One without a Second, the Eternal Youth of sixteen summers ; and often we speak of him as the Lord of the World. He is the Supreme Ruler ; in his hand and within his actual aura lies the whole of his planet. He represents the Logos, as far as this world is concerned, and directs the whole of its evolution—not that of humanity alone, but also the evolution of the Devas, the nature-spirits, and all other creatures connected with the earth. He is, of course, entirely distinct from the great entity called the Spirit of the Earth, who uses our world as a physical body.

In his mind he holds the whole plan of evolution at some high level of which we know nothing ; he is the Force which drives the whole world-machine, the embodiment of the Divine Will on this planet, and strength, courage, decision, perseverance and all similar characteristics, when they show themselves down here in the lives on men, are reflections from Him. His consciousness is of so extended a nature that it comprehends at once all the life on our globe. In his hands are the powers of cyclic destruction, for he wields Fohat in its higher forms and can deal directly with cosmic forces outside our chain. His work is probably usually connected with humanity *en masse* rather than with individuals, but when he

does influence any single person we are told that it is through the
atma, and not through the ego, that his influence is brought to bear.

At a certain point in the progress of an aspirant on the Path
he is formally presented to the Lord of the World, and those who
have thus met him face to face speak of him as in appearance a
handsome youth, dignified, benignant beyond all description, yet
with a mien of omniscient, inscrutable majesty, conveying such a
sense of resistless power that some have found themselves unable to
bear his gaze, and have veiled their faces in awe. Thus, for example,
did the great Founder of the Theosophical Society, Madame Blavatsky.
One who has had this experience can never forget it, nor can he ever
thereafter doubt that, however terrible the sin and sorrow on earth
may be, all things are somehow working together for the eventual good
of all, and humanity is being steadily guided towards its final goal.

During each world-period, we are told, there are three successive Lords of the World, and the present holder of the office is
already the third. He resides with his three Pupils in an oasis in
the Gobi desert called Shamballa, often spoken of as the Sacred
Island, in remembrance of the time when it was an island in the
Central Asian Sea. These four greatest of the Adepts are often
called " The Children of the Fire-Mist ", since They belong to an
evolution different from ours. Their bodies, though human in
appearance, differ widely from ours in constitution, being rather
garments assumed for convenience than bodies in the ordinary sense,
since they are artificial and their particles do not change as do those
of the human frame. They require no nourishment, and remain
unchanged through thousands of years.

The three Pupils, who stand at the level of the Buddha, and
are called Pratyeka or Paccheka Buddhas, assist the Lord in his
work, and are themselves destined to be our three Lords of the
World when humanity is occupying the planet Mercury.

Once in every seven years, the Lord of the World conducts at
Shamballa a great ceremony somewhat similar to the Wesak event, but
on a still grander scale and of a different type, when all the Adepts and
even some Initiates below that grade are invited, and have thus an

opportunity to come into touch with their great Leader. At other times he deals only with the Heads of the Official Hierarchy, except when for special reasons he summons others to his presence.

The exalted position of this our spiritual King has been described in *The Secret Doctrine*. It is there stated that as the ages pass the great steps which we now recognize as leading to perfection will remain unchanged as to their relative positions, though the system of things as a whole is moving upwards, and thus the actual attainments which in the remote future will mark a particular step will be far fuller than they are at present. The Perfected Men of the Seventh Round of our Chain will be, it is said, "but one remove from the Root-Base of their Hierarchy, the highest on Earth and our Terrestrial Chain." That is to say, the King stands even now one stage beyond the point to which only ages of evolution will bring the perfected men of our humanity—ages that must run into millions of years, taking us through two and a half rounds of varied experience. This wondrous Being came during the third-race period to take charge of the Earth evolution. That coming of the world's future King is thus described in *Man : Whence, How and Whither*:

The great Lemurian Polar Star was still perfect, and the huge Crescent still stretched along the equator, including Madagascar. The sea which occupied what is now the Gobi Desert still broke against the rocky barriers of the northern Himalayan slopes, and all was being prepared for the most dramatic moment in the history of the Earth—the Coming of the Lords of the Flame.

The Lords of the Moon and the Manu of the third root race had done all that was possible to bring men up to the point at which the germ of mind could be quickened, and the descent of the ego could be made. All the laggards had been pushed on ; there were no more in the animal ranks capable of rising into man. The door against further immigrants into the human kingdom from the animal was shut only when no more were in sight, nor would be capable of reaching it without a repetition of the tremendous impulse given only once in the evolution of a Scheme, at its midmost point.

A great astrological event, when a very special collocation of planets occurred and the magnetic condition of the Earth was the most favourable possible, was chosen as the time. It was about six and a half million years ago. Nothing more remained to be done, save what only they could do.

Then, with the mighty roar of swift descent from incalculable heights, surrounded by blazing masses of fire which filled the sky with shooting tongues of flame, flashed through the aerial spaces the chariot of the Sons of the Fire, the Lords of the Flame from Venus; it halted, hovering over the "White Island", which lay smiling in the bosom of the Gobi Sea; green was it, and radiant with masses of fragrant many-coloured blossoms, Earth offering her best and fairest to welcome her coming King. There he stood, "the Youth of sixteen summers", Sanat Kumara, the "Eternal Virgin-Youth", the new Ruler of Earth, come to his kingdom, his Pupils, the three Kumaras, with him, his Helpers around him; thirty mighty Beings were there, great beyond Earth's reckoning, though in graded order, clothed in the glorious bodies they had created by Kriyashakti, the first Occult Hierarchy, branches of the one spreading Banyan Tree, the nursery of future Adepts, the centre of all occult life. Their dwelling-place was and is the Imperishable Sacred Land, on which ever shines down the Blazing Star, the symbol of earth's Monarch, the changeless Pole round which the life of our Earth is ever spinning.[1]

Madame Blavatsky says in *The Secret Doctrine*:

The "Being" just referred to, who has to remain nameless, is the *Tree* from which, in subsequent ages, all the great *historically* known Sages and Hierophants, such as the Rishi Kapila, Hermes, Enoch, Orpheus, etc., have branched off. As objective *man*, He is the mysterious (to the profane—the ever invisible, yet ever present) Personage, about whom legends are rife in the Past, especially among the Occultists and the students of the Sacred Science. It is He who changes form, yet remains ever the same. And it is He, again, who holds spiritual sway over the *initiated* Adepts throughout the whole world. He is, as said, the "Nameless One" who has so many names, and yet whose names and whose very nature are unknown. He is the "Initiator", called the "Great Sacrifice". For, sitting at the Threshold of Light, He looks into it from within the Circle of Darkness, which He will not cross; nor will He quit his post till the last Day of this Life-Cycle. Why does the Solitary Watcher remain at His self-chosen post? Why does He sit by the Fountain of Primeval Wisdom, of which He drinks no longer, for He has naught to learn which He does not know—aye, neither on this Earth, nor in its Heaven? Because the lonely sore-footed Pilgrims, on their journey back to their Home, are never sure, to the last moment, of not losing their way, in this limitless desert of Illusion and Matter called Earth-Life. Because He would fain show the way to that region of freedom and light, from which He is a voluntary exile Himself, to every prisoner who has succeeded in liberating himself from the bonds of flesh and illusion. Because, in short, He has sacrificed Himself for the sake of Mankind, though but a few elect may profit by the Great Sacrifice.

It is under the direct, silent guidance of this Maha-Guru that all the other less divine Teachers and Instructors of Mankind became, from the first awakening of human consciousness, the guides of early Humanity. It is through these "Sons of God" that infant Humanity learned its first notions of all the arts and sciences, as well as of spiritual knowledge; and it is They who laid the first foundation-stone of those ancient civilizations that so sorely puzzle our modern generation of students and scholars.[2]

[1] *Op. cit.*, p. 101.
[2] *Op. cit.*, 4th ed., Vol. 1, p. 256.

THE HIGHEST INITIATIONS

It is on the First Ray that the greatest progress for man is possible within the Hierarchy of our Globe, for there are on it two Initiations beyond that of the Manu. The Paccheka Buddhas, who stand next above the Manu, have been strangely misunderstood by some writers, who have described them as selfish men who refused to teach what they had learnt, and passed away into Nirvana. It is true that these Buddhas do not teach, for they have the other work of their own Ray to do, and true also that a time comes when they will leave the world, but only to carry on their glorious work elsewhere.

The next step, the Initiation that none can give, but each must take for himself, puts the Adept on the level of the Lord of the World, an office which is held first for the shorter period of a First or Second Lord on one World, and when that has been achieved, for the longer responsibility of the Third upon some other.

The task of the Third Lord of the World is far greater than those of the First and Second Lords, because it is his duty to round off satisfactorily that period of evolution, and to deliver over the countless millions of evolving creatures into the hands of the Seed-Manu, who will be responsible for them during the inter-planetary Nirvana, and will hand them over in turn to the Root-Manu of the next globe. The Third Lord of the World, having fulfilled this duty, takes another Initiation entirely outside of our world and its Hierarchy, and attains the level of the Silent Watcher. In that capacity he remains on guard for the whole period of a Round, and it is only when the life-wave has again occupied our planet and is again ready to leave it that he abandons his strange self-imposed task, and hands it over to his Successor.

THE GOAL FOR ALL

Far above us as is all the splendour of these great heights at present, it is worth our while to lift our thought towards them and try to realize them a little. They show the goal before every one of us, and the clearer our sight of it the swifter and steadier will be our progress towards it, though we may not all hope to fulfil the ancient ideal in this, and fly as an arrow to the mark.

In the course of this great progress every man will some day reach full consciousness on the highest of our planes, the Divine plane, and be conscious simultaneously at all levels of this Prakritic Cosmic plane, so that having in himself the power of the highest, he shall yet be able to comprehend and function on the very lowest, and help where help is needed. That omnipotence and omnipresence surely await every one of us, and though this lower life may not be worth living for anything that we may gain from it for ourselves, yet it is magnificently worth enduring as a necessary stage for the true life that lies before us. " Eye hath not seen, nor ear heard, neither hath it entered into the heart of man to conceive the things which God hath prepared for them that love him," for the love of God, the wisdom of God, the power of God, and the glory of God pass all understanding, even as does his peace.

PEACE TO ALL BEINGS

INDEX

INDEX